ON THE BOWERY

BENEDICT GIAMO ON THE BOWERY

Confronting Homelessness in American Society

University of Iowa Press Iowa City

University of Iowa Press, Iowa City 52242
Printed in the United States of America
First edition, 1989

Design by Richard Hendel

Library of Congress
Cataloging-in-Publication Data

Giamo, Benedict.
  On the bowery: confronting homelessness in
American society/by Benedict Giamo.—1st ed.
     p.   cm.
  Bibliography: p.
  Includes index.
  ISBN 0-87745-243-1
  1. Homelessness—United States.   I. Title.
HV4505.G48   1989   89-32099
362.5'0973—dc20   CIP

To the Bowery men, who let me in,

to Iris, who led me out, and

to my two young sons, Crane and

Christopher, whose wondrous development

continues to mystify me.

CONTENTS

ACKNOWLEDGMENTS

Even though this quest was initiated as a venture into the great unknown, and even though the discoveries surfaced from a faith in the processes of descent and recovery, I could not have endured the solitude of the vision and its long pursuit without the generous guidance and sustenance offered by friends and colleagues. Without Peter Dowell's close reading of the manuscript and talent for reintroducing me to the deep structure of the text, I might not have found my way at all; for his keen understanding and insightful comments, I am profoundly grateful. Both Robert Paul and Robert Wheeler proved invaluable in helping to round out the interdisciplinary perspective of this study in the early stages of its broadened reformulation. I am highly appreciative of the time spent with Kenneth Burke during his winter visits to Emory University. Simply put, K.B. was more than a distinct influence; he inspired me to conduct this work with rigor, risk, and sheer enjoyment along with the intellectual predilection for "counter-gridlock." To Arthur Evans I would like to extend my gratitude for teaching me the importance of patience and promise. My indebtedness to Jeffrey Grunberg is long-standing and deep; for his vital partnership during the Bowery fieldwork and close friendship throughout the years I am extremely grateful. I would also like to thank Chaya Piotrkowski and Rayna Rapp for helping to launch this quest.

This study was originally designed as a dissertation and later altered into book form. Much of the writing of this project during the dissertation stage was supported in various and helpful ways. I would like to thank Helena Welch for her unquestioning support, which made it possible to get situated and continue the journey. To Ronald Welch for his generous financial support I owe more than I can give in return. I am grateful to the Graduate Institute of the Liberal Arts, Emory University, for assistance that helped me to begin the writing portion of the project. To the Scholarships Foundation, Inc., I am also grateful for the continued financial support provided. For her patient and skillful aid in typing the manuscript (in its dissertation and book-length forms), I would like to thank Beryl Glover. And, finally, to my parents, Nathan and Marie, I am thankful for simply reminding me just where I had begun.

PREFACE

If the social and cultural reality of the Bowery is best apprehended as a question to be answered, then it could be said that I went off in search of such a discovery. Initially, this quest took the form of an extended ethnographic encounter with the homeless men on the contemporary Bowery. (See the appendix for an account of the ethnographic method and process. The reader may benefit by reviewing this account after reading the preface.) In going out to meet the "other" within (in this case the "other" resided on native grounds), I was soon drawn downward into the deep structure of American society and culture. Perhaps that popular duet, down and out, is relevant here, for the journey down into the subculture of Bowery homelessness also entailed a journey out of social innocence. To go to the depths of the Bowery is to confront its grotesque reality, its radical departure from the accustomed realm of social structure, its vibrant humanistic energy, and its creative forms. The thematic patterns, social processes, existential categories, and structure of feeling and meaning which surfaced from my fieldwork on the Bowery both satisfied and disturbed my sense of discovery. I had collected a wealth of data from my encounters with the men and learned a great deal concerning their related processes of internal integration into the subculture and external adaptation to the larger society by which they were bound. Yet at this time my epistemological scouts, as I refer to the men, were also leading me to a nascent level of awareness which involved the dynamic relationship between competing cultural and subcultural systems of meaning, belief, and social action.

The contention between cultural and subcultural forms, between the ideological systems of structure and antistructure, became a generative source of expression for the men on the contemporary Bowery. As I bore witness to this, it was also significant for the development of my own thought, for, having moved from the field of social psychology to the ethnographically relevant disciplines of cultural and symbolic anthropology, I decided to broaden the scope of the project. This involved the inclusion of historical development and literary analysis. Once again, the Bowery men helped me to realize that a self-contained ethnographic account, though an essential experiential and empirical grounding for the study, could not fully apprehend the richly textured problem that emerged as the source of my continued inquiry:

the relation of mainstream or hegemonic culture to the marginalized subculture of the Bowery homeless.

This broadened focus was also accompanied by a struggle for representation. I soon realized that no one discipline treated separately could direct the free and unrestrained movement which the ramifications of this focus required. The result of such attempts to work entirely from within the successive singular forms, methods, and primary reality constructs of discrete academic disciplines amounted to a condition of sustained gridlock. In order to mobilize my quest further it became necessary to affirm the interdisciplinary scope of the project's development and acknowledge a method of inquiry that would formalize the progression of my evolving Bowery designs and the direction of my cross-disciplinary pursuits into a coherent pattern.

Therefore, in light of this, I attempted to create a unity of theme and purpose so as to achieve a synthesis of three primary modes of cultural analysis—historical, literary, and ethnographic—as they combined on a single subject—the dialectic between American culture and subculture. To realize this integrated understanding and place the movement of the dialectic within the shaping designs of American society, I employed concepts, frameworks, and analytical tools drawn from studies in symbolic action (and in the tradition of Kenneth Burke, Clifford Geertz, Victor Turner, and recent American studies scholarship). As such, the study incorporates a holistic perspective and is relational rather than specialized in intent. By removing the boundaries between traditionally conceived intellectual disciplines, I had hoped to find a common language in which otherwise discrete fields and subfields of knowledge could sensibly converse with one another on such a critical and persistent social problem.

Those readers who prefer that I advance knowledge consistent with the ideological requirements of the history department by mounting evidence and demonstrating the facts of social condition will no doubt be disappointed. The nature of my inquiry, though concerned with the illumination of social condition, is more forcefully directed at the discovery, identification, and discussion of the interplay between culture and subculture as represented in competing symbolic systems of apprehension and action. Therefore, my interest in historical fact is in the value it has as a precondition for revealing systems of meaning and ideology in contention.

As a project in culture studies, my method is more critical and interpretive in nature. It aims to substantiate the project's "findings" by examining specific rhetorical strategies. These strategies are seen as mediating schemes between agent and world, culture and subculture; they help to size up a situation and enable us to apprehend an expressed ideological and political purpose structured into a given response. In this sense, a rhetorical or narrative strategy given in response to the problem of urban poverty and Bowery homelessness performs on the public stage as the particular language of a social drama. As Kenneth Burke reminds us, language is "primarily a species of action, or expression of attitudes, rather than an instrument of definition." It has thus been my purpose to deal on this level of symbolic action and social attitude rather than on the level of historical definition and documentation.

My interest in symbolic action, however, does not lead to a "free-floating" cultural analysis and account. Just as ethnography has worked to ground my interpretations, so too has my incorporation of a distinct historical dimension. Culture and subculture are embedded within the same social context of American society and they have been mutually influenced by shared patterns of historical development. In keeping with this, and in order to broaden the critical argument and construct a social and cultural whole, I have found it necessary to relate the level of symbolic analysis, which inheres in cultural studies, with the level of historical processes and actualization. Since the relationship between culture and subculture grows out of the same encompassing historical situation, the basis for comparison between them is dynamic and thus makes for a more cohesive theoretical discussion and critical enterprise.

The Bowery exists, as it has for over the past three hundred years, as an identifiable fact of American geography. Its shifting contours down the ages—from large tracts of farmland (bouweries) to rural villages to urban slum and skid row—illustrate a rather pliant response to the pressures of American history. In its material and communal development, the Bowery tells a visible story of American society in transition. This context in which the Bowery originates, develops, and matures as a distinct social entity and symbolic construct frames our view of the Bowery, not only as a well-established sense of place—a street and section of New York City—but as an "embodiment" of urban poverty and homelessness as well. The gradual emergence of the Bowery as an embodiment of various immigrant subcultures and, in its evolution, as an embodiment of skid row homelessness is related to the shaping dynamic inherent in the late nineteenth-century thrust toward industrial capitalism.

So, rather than present the emergent dialectic between culture and subculture as residing in the void of an ahistorical perspective, I work here to make the necessary link between the dialectic and the paramount social and economic forces to which it is intricately related. By proceeding in this manner, I hope to have set the stage for the reader to see concrete referents and cultural responses in the context of the broad movements in social organization precipitated by a transformation in American society.

My reading of historical development highlights the influential social processes which issue from the progression of a dynamic inherent in the development of American society. This reading reveals that the Bowery's identity and value as a "detached milieu," a place physically, socially, and symbolically worlds apart from the dominant middle-class culture of urban society, are dependent upon the dynamics played out among the following: urban industrialization and its forms of economic and social segregation; class relations characterized by social distance amidst physical proximity (which produced an enticing sense of mystery); and the symbolic system of mystification, a rhetorical mode of apprehension which, although professing to expose urban poverty and homelessness, invariably resulted in obscuring both condition and process.

The emergence of the Bowery as a discrete urban entity in the late nineteenth century thus served as a precondition for the evocative presence of subculture and its symbolic interaction with the dominant urban culture. This interaction between culture and subculture, stimulated by the historical processes of industrial capitalism and by the opposition between poverty and affluence in the metropolis, found expression in the symbolic systems of mystification and critical realism. Both competing systems functioned to organize social perceptions on the nature of urban poverty and Bowery homelessness in such a way as to bring the contradictory precepts, viewpoints, ideological differences, and essential meanings into dynamic tension and continued movement. Though mystification, and the countering sign system of critical realism, comprise the bulk of the present study, the progression from segregation to distance to the evocation of mystery gives historic form and substance to the subsequent treatment of crucial social and symbolic processes.

In order to bring unity to the multitude of narrative strategies and expressive commentaries which comprise these social and symbolic processes considered in the study, I range my discussion along a continuum with mystification at one end and critical realism at the other. Since the continuum spans the study, it provides the major point of reference to compare and contrast various representations of Bowery life which cut across the three general modes of analysis. The dynamic between the two rhetorical forms of symbolic action parallels the dialectic between culture and subculture and highlights the opposition between social distance and social intercourse which underlies the continuum.

Whereas mystification maneuvers by way of idealized encounter and evasion, the demystifying strategies of critical realism operate by the rhythm of descent and discovery, bringing insights gained from the depths of Bowery subculture back to the surface of culture in order to challenge the settled ways of perceiving, framing, and conceptualizing both condition and process. Mystification is represented in the study by the sensationalistic genre, the urban picturesque school, and the realism of Jacob Riis's reportage and William Dean Howells's commentary and fiction. Playing off this symbolic system, critical realism contrasts these more distanced approaches and forms with the penetration of urban space and confrontation with the actualities of Bowery life. Stephen Crane's Bowery sketches and novellas and Theodore Dreiser's *Sister Carrie* are presented to investigate this more intimate interaction. The expressive commentaries of the contemporary Bowery men are also included in order to round out the discussion on the interplay between culture and subculture (mystification and critical realism). This is meant to demonstrate the vitality of the dialectic in our present era as a generative source of knowledge, activity, and completion emanating from within a unique subcultural perspective and program.

The progression from the symbolic system of mystification to that of critical realism necessarily involves the broad movement from cultural investigation to subcultural explication. By this, I mean the gradual movement by outsiders toward a more genuine discovery of the objective circumstances and subjective qualities of Bowery life. This entails a process of closer and closer approximation until the dialectic is inverted and subculture becomes the empowered point of reference for a fundamental critique on the values and patterns inherent in American culture.

The tension between culture and subculture, and between their competing systems of meaning, is also accompanied by the superimposed conflicts of affluence and poverty and structure and antistructure. Taken as a constitutive whole, culture, affluence, structure, and mystification align themselves thematically on one side of the dialectic, with subculture, poverty, antistructure, and critical realism on the other. On every level, the opposing constructs are interdependent despite their antipathy toward each other. This clustering is meant to enhance the complexity of the dialectic and heighten the inevitable collision between mainstream urban culture and Bowery subculture, thus moving the symbolic systems of mystification and critical realism to new levels and forms of apprehension and expression. It is in this relational sense that the dialectic can be seen as rooted in the fertile processes of historical development and social change.

Although my use of such constructs as culture and subculture, structure and antistructure, should be best understood in the context of the study, it might be helpful to provide an orientation to these critical categories of human condition and social processes. I view culture as both containing and transmitting the dominant ideological code of a given society in its process of historical development. As such, culture is intricately related to a given economic and political system of social control and works to formulate and articulate related systems of meaning and belief, patterns of social identification, normative frames of reference, clusters of value, and legitimate forms of social action. Since man, the symbol-using animal, can only know the world through his medium of language, symbolic action becomes the primary vehicle by which culture communicates these necessary mediations between self and world in order for a given society to assimilate and perpetuate knowledge and attitudes toward social life. Culture thus signifies the means by which we conceive of our presence in social life, interpret our condition, and evaluate the results.

As a shaping sphere of activity, culture is operative within the related realm of social structure. I take structure to be those finely organized and institutionalized networks of social existence which sanction a dominant system of order and formalize human relationships accordingly. Structure is thus necessarily materialistic, bureaucratically mechanized, and hierarchically differentiated. In its various economic, political, and legal forms, structure is the very concretized stuff out of which a dominant culture designs and manifests as well as contributes.

If culture and structure constitute the inheritance and development of a particular social system, then subculture and antistructure represent the anomalies. Although an outgrowth of the dominant culture and thus functioning along the same general principles and dynamics as given in the culture-making process, subculture defines a distinct yet discontinuous subgroup of people sufficiently differentiated from the common order. This degree of variation is dependent upon the extent and intensity of difference relative to a subculture's conditions of social life and to its shared assumptions of contradictory meaning and value.

In the case of Bowery homelessness, however, the radical estrangement of this subculture from the norm-governed ideology and political and economic framework of American society reconstitutes the notion of variance into the construct of extreme marginality. The Bowery is a *sub*culture which takes the prefix of that term literally to mean a human condition existing below and under the towering structure of society. This condition of structural inferiority obliterates this subculture's struggle with culture over the social commodities of power, wealth, status, and equality. The Bowery is thus steeped in a state of antistructure, the dissolution of social structure and its reformulation into the ecological base and subcultural network of skid row. Ironically, this strengthens the integrity of subculture and works to activate its remaining mission: the contravention of a dominant cultural system of order and control. The Bowery remains dramatically "alive," then, in its contention with culture over symbolic meaning and modes of social being. Shaped by the active presence of culture as well as by its own social processes and conditions, Bowery subculture works to engage culture and, by evoking competing forms of symbolic action, cohere the dialectic into dynamic relationship. It is by virtue of this dialogue that other mediating schemes rise as counter-statements to the familiar ideological code of culture so that that which was unseen and unrecognized can now be experienced and known. By challenging the established conceptions of culture, subculture reveals its struggle for inclusion in the symbolic stock of social understanding and change.

Because of my direct experience with the Bowery homeless, a subculture which has been historically operative since the late nineteenth century, I have come to view subculture, antistructure, poverty, and critical realism not as vacuous constructs or mere antireferential fetishisms but as dimensions of symbolic action embedded in both historical and contemporary experience. These constructs have been revealed in lives vanished and lingering and in words and motions related to expression of meaning, to articulation of feeling, to conflict, strategy, form, and function. In short, they are guiding concepts that have been lived, shaping both attitude and conduct. To be sure, the opposing categories seem more remote, otherworldly abstractions: culture, structure, affluence, and mystification. The Bowery does not fare well at making this dimension of discourse concrete. At best, these notions are vague remembrances, outlines of the generalized other, both reviled and necessary.

Since this study is grounded in an ethnographic encounter, I have included a discussion based on my fieldwork with the contemporary Bowery. This appears in the conclusion and serves as a complementary perspective to the historical moment of the late nineteenth century which comprises the major body of the text. In presenting this internal perspective, I have created a space for the otherwise silent Bowery men to speak out and have their say as principal actors on the evolving proscenium of historical actuality and transition. This discussion also serves as a point of demarcation between the contemporary situation of Bowery subculture and the altered, modern condition of homelessness.

As a theme and place, the Bowery has been rich in meaning, evocative in association, long in development, and central in the progression of a dialectic played out in the realm of social thought, popular culture, and aesthetic expression. Once again, the homeless men on the Bowery helped me to discover the persistent and overwhelming historical significance of their domain and embodiment for American society and culture. Whether they be the sensationalized Bowery, touristic treatments of the late nineteenth century, Jacob Riis's reportage and Dickensian portraits, Crane's Maggie, or Nicky Star's contemporary metaphoric extension on the meaning of the Bowery, such representations have been generated from the inherent conflict between culture and subculture. The nature of that conflict, its origins and development, and the interpretations which have framed or concealed it within American society are the interdisciplinary topics of this study. I hope we learn from such a treatment that the dialectic between culture and subculture is indeed generative and that the symbolic systems of mystification and critical realism are "alive" in both our historic and present periods; and I hope we acquire a certain perspective in the movement of thought, expression, and social action so that we might be better equipped to apprehend the continuity of the homeless problem and its current manifestation, so that word and deed might come together into a coherent whole.

Topic, approach, and significance are given in tribute to those men, living and otherwise, who have been so generative to the development of my own thinking and understanding. Living *in extremis*, they were living in the faded tradition of the Bowery. In a very real way they were living and dying in history, and they were among the last of their kind to do so. Though these men will not become "visible" until the conclusion, they have actually preceded this study by initiating this long, fruitful quest for origin and development. Thus, the chronological progression of the text is at odds with personal history, for "in my beginning is my end. . . . In my end is my beginning."

1 / BACKGROUND CIRCUMFERENCE

However hopeless it may seem, we have no other choice:
we must go back to the beginning; it must all be done over;
everything that is must be destroyed.
—*William Carlos Williams*
   In the American Grain

To be on the Bowery today, along that one-mile stretch from Chatham Square to Cooper Union, is to confront its dogged absence. The Bowery, as designation, asserts itself in terms of what it is not, for what has been actualized as an urban entity is at odds with its ghostly demarcation.

One returns to the original sense of the name, *Bouwerij* (the Dutch word for farm), by a process of erasure. The departure necessitates a reversal of presence and absence in which the formidable grid gives way to the unencumbered lay of the land. If the task of history is the studied resurrection of the past, then the Bowery, as an artery of American civilization, leads us back beyond its enclosed skid row, its immigrant slums, its rural settlements, even beyond its role as Post Road to Boston and bridle path to the country estate of Governor Petrus Stuyvesant. When it has fully run its course, the Bowery dissolves itself, along with the American experience, into a sinuous Indian trail on which the Weckquaeskecks fled through their silent nights.

Outside New Amsterdam, the first transformation of nature in its idyllic wholeness began with the clearing of land and the laying out of farms north of the small town. From 1626 on, the Dutch West India Company offered land grants to entice emigration from abroad. By its offer, the company did not intend to lure the commoner but, rather, the homeland's more prominent citizens whose wealth could establish them as the New World's landed gentry. Six bouweries were originally leased in large rectangular parcels with the hope of stimulating the growth of an agriculturally based colonial economy which would supplement the thriving fur trade at the lower tip of the island.

By the time Petrus Stuyvesant arrived in 1647, the last in a brief lineage of Dutch governors, the bouweries, which had been damaged during the Indian War of 1642–43, had been refurbished and advertised for sale. In 1651, Stuyvesant purchased the 120 acres of Bouwerie No. 1 for $5,000, a sum which attests to the high land values prevalent even at this early period. The size of the remaining five bouweries ranged from 50 to 97 acres; in addition, two other land grants of 25 and 76 acres were sold in the vicinity of the bouweries. In all, the transfer from leasing to ownership had placed a total of 588 acres of prime Manhattan land into the hands of eight individuals. This shift from public to private control of property was the first in a series of developments that would profoundly affect the direction and shape of the city's expansion. The immediate consequence of the transfer to ownership was the emergence of a more than provisional aristocracy on the American horizon. Yet it was an aristocracy uncharacteristic in its most essential ingredient; surrounded by wilderness instead of tradition, its members had exchanged preservation of nobility for speculation in profits.

This class of country gentlemen was perhaps best represented by the paternalistic style of Governor Stuyvesant, who promised to rule his subjects "as a father his children."[1] Stuyvesant's familial kingdom expressed itself most concretely in the manorial village (known as Bowery or Stuyvesant Village) that surrounded the governor's pre-eminent domain. The growth of the village was encouraged by Stuyvesant's estate and became a place of residence for his employees and slaves. This feudallike arrangement was further enhanced by the need for protection against sporadic Indian attacks. When the English wrenched control of the island from the Dutch in 1664, Stuyvesant found himself suddenly dethroned. His village, though sympathetic to the old master, took on a life and economy of its own. Its church, St. Mark's-in-the-Bouwerie, and its tavern, general store, blacksmith, wagon shop, and community center were on the whole quite amenable to the enterprising designs and customs of the new English burghers.

English rule stimulated development in New York and along its boweries commensurate with its commercial spirit. In 1673 Bowery Lane was converted into the first Post Road to Boston, thus opening up communication with the hinterland and port cities. Landowners during this time began to consolidate their holdings more for the purpose of investment and future sales than as an act of social distinction. Prior to the Revolution, several boweries had changed hands quite frequently and a pattern of parceling took effect which steadily atrophied the large tracts of farmland.

The Grim Plan of 1742 to 1744 captured the boweries just before the subdivisions began to erode the scale of their bucolic magnitude.

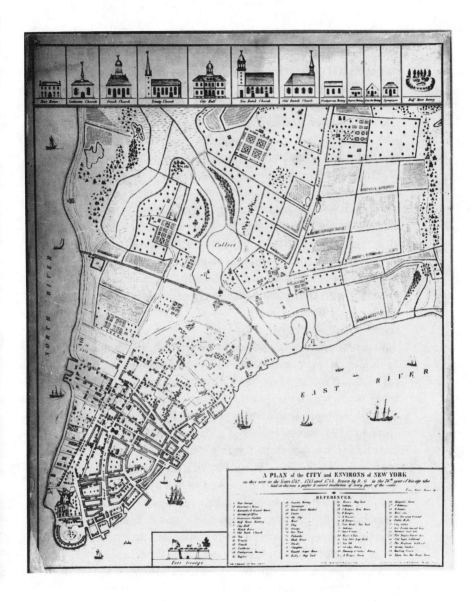

Plan of the city and environs of New York, 1742–1744, by David Grim. The New-York Historical Society, New York City. The Grim Plan captures the Bowery (upper right corner) in its early rural presence with large tracts of farmland both east and west of Bowery Road (Bowery Road runs north and south).

The only divisions given on the map are those between the large square or rectangular chunks of farmland. By 1750, however, streets had been laid off adjacent to Bowery Lane, fostering further fragmentation of neighboring farms. The Ratzer Map of 1767 shows both parallel and cross-streets laid out on the east and west sides along the southern end of Bowery Lane, cutting through the property of De Lancey and Bayard, respectively. These landowners began to maneuver with their holdings by taking advantage of the new development, which offered opportunities for the exchange of small packaged lots. In 1771, Bayard relinquished four hundred lots of his estate for a total value of 10,000 pounds. Many of Bayard's lots were of a standard dimension, 25' × 100', and they provided a high turnover for the buyer (one corner lot sold on the Bowery doubled its value in a matter of two years). The real estate ventures on the De Lancey estate, originally a consolidation of two boweries and a plantation, were also moving apace. Thirty-four houses were erected along his subdivisions, and on the Bowery Lane the lots were generating a more concentrated scale of building.[2]

This proclivity toward development effectively undermined the agricultural strategies of an aristocratic outpost along the boweries and paved the way for a transition to rural settlements and, eventually, urban planning. The fate of the Rutgers farm illustrates this progression and the rapid diminution of property. Purchased in 1728, the farm spanned ninety-seven acres and encompassed a bowerie and a plantation. Barley was grown to supply a number of breweries as well as a brew house on the site. When Hendrick Rutgers inherited the farm in 1753, he set off a portion of the land near Chatham Square in streets and lots and then retreated to a new residence near the East River. After his death, the property was divided further among his children, who experienced an increase in its value. Hendrick's son Henry then began a flurry of real estate activity by the long-term leasing of lots to tenants, who built their homes upon them. As many as four hundred deeds and leases were transacted during this period, and by 1800 the densely populated subdivisions ironically exerted their dominance in the form of containment. The private property of Henry Rutgers, having steadily receded, was now delimited to two meager city blocks.[3]

The commercial emphasis and capitalistic spirit which promoted expansion also brought about the disappearance of the boweries. This natural tendency toward exchange and development was rationalized and given legal sanction by the Gridiron (or Commissioners') Plan for

New York City in 1811.[4] The plan, based on Randel's map of 1807, was
in some ways a continuation of the process already begun along the
boweries and in other environs throughout the city. Yet it differed
significantly in the extent of its vision; that is, in its conception of the
land as a mechanism for a predictable circuitry of urban civilization.

The Commissioners' Plan imposed an intractable grid structure on
the city which reached as far north as 155th Street. The laying out of
blocks, streets, and lots conformed to a rectangular pattern which
relentlessly duplicated itself throughout the island. This monotonous
geometricity was justified by the commissioners on the grounds of
expediency and convenience. Economic motives usurped aesthetic
considerations in the interests of commerce and land value. The plan,
delineating lots to a dimension of 25' × 100', was land intensive in
scope and geared toward the pursuits of entrepreneurs. Owners,
speculators, real estate agents, buyers, builders, and landlords would
comprise the concatenation that would benefit from the economic
organization formulated by the grid. In its design and intention, the
Commissioners' Plan was aligned with the factory: both created conditions which stressed efficiency, mass markets, the speedy conversion
of materials, the facile exchange of commodities, and the private manipulation of capital.

There were some opponents to the Commissioners' Plan at the
time of its realization who objected to its stern utilitarian compulsion.
Criticism was waged on both aesthetic and financial grounds against
the leveling and filling which flattened the topography of the island.
But the implementation of the plan moved onward. In their attempt to
saddle and compartmentalize the terrain, the commissioners neglected natural contours and indigenous features of the landscape
(marshes, farms, salt meadows, ponds, hillsides, and woodlands). The
unsettling practice led one critic to this characterization of the operation: "The Corporation was resolved to spare nothing that bears the
resemblance of a rising ground. . . . These are men, as has been well
observed, who would have cut down the seven hills of Rome, on which
are erected her triumphant monuments of beauty and magnificence
and have thrown them into the Tyber or the Pomptine marshes."[5]

The Bowery, like all the surrounding villages, tracts, and estates of
the city, was molded by the manufactured scarcity of this urban machine. In its fulfillment, the Commissioners' Plan provided a crude
exaggeration of the methods employed by the Dutch West India Company: the transfer from public to private control of the land was completed with an entirely new conception of order in mind, one that

"marks the division between old and modern New York."[6] Looking ahead to the city's rapid development, the social and economic features of the plan (high land value and intensive building) would have important implications for the construction of residential, commercial, and industrial buildings. Not only would the plan lend itself to a bewildering physical agglomeration, but it would also, when fed by a concentrated urban populace, encourage the growth of tenements and slums. It seems as though the grid were laid in anticipation, an undergirding and determinant structure eager for the process of urbanization to commence. The industrial revolution would soon provide the necessary mobility for its habitation. Laissez-faire would continue to be its *raison d'être*, and social Darwinism, a later rationale, would embolden its reach.

At the beginning of the eighteenth century about four hundred people lived in the vicinity of Bowery Village. By mid-century, the population of the city and its environs had neared ten thousand. Though some of the city's numbers had advanced into the suburban districts, they did not appreciably alter its rustic quality. Bowery Lane was "then a fair country road, bordered with comfortable homes, blossoming orchards, vegetable and flower gardens, meadows dotted with cattle and horses, and an occasional tavern or windmill."[7] This arcadian vision belongs to old New York and can be glimpsed in the names of some of its Bowery taverns, such as Bull's Head, with its adjacent abattoir, the Dog and Duck, the Black Horse Inn, and, for a suggestion of royalty, Ye Sign of Ye King of Prussia, up Bowery Lane.

In 1790, the population of New York had reached 33,000, a figure that would double by the close of the century. The city had already begun to exert its magnetism, drawing immigrants from the interior as well as from abroad. During the first quarter of the nineteenth century, most of these newcomers descended from New England or other parts of New York State, followed in numbers by the Irish, who first began arriving in the 1790s. Scotch, German, and English immigration also swelled the population of the city, which had hit the half-million mark by 1850. While the diversity of the populace gave the burgeoning commercial city a distinctly cosmopolitan atmosphere, its growing density began to shape a more heterogeneous social structure into urban form.

As early as 1800, the Bowery began to reveal the contrasts in its altered social composition: "prominent citizens lived on it almost cheek-by-jowl with courtesans, groggeries and manufacturing plants."[8] Though the northern stretch of the Bowery, around the area of the village, retained its highly respectable antecedents, its southern terminus bordered on the first slum of the city, originally gathered around the industries of Collect Pond and later known as Five Points. Whereas the Bowery Village took on the reputation of being a pleasant summer resort and "domestic little community,"[9] Five Points became the immigrant breeding ground for the numerous yellow fever epidemics that raged through the lower portion of the city. This nascent polarization of class and urban space would characterize the Bowery throughout its antebellum period. With its contradictions of slum and aristocracy, the Bowery could be spatially likened to "a lady in a ball costume, with diamonds in her ears, and her toes out at her boots."[10]

Yet despite the contrary raiment, our lady would strike a steady gait in her attempt to unify the oppositions into one democratic body. The social structure of antebellum New York was more fluid and less divisive than in its period of post–Civil War expansion. Much more tolerant of its differences, it often gave the appearance of a homogeneous society by its tendency toward integration in activities and amusements. The Bowery Theater (established in 1826) was one such center of leisure which ushered in the democratic congregation. But once inside, the democratic experience became less a study of classlessness than a reflection of urban society's unraveled fabric. In the theater's pit were gathered the laboring classes and Bowery Boys, spectators with a vengeance whose eagerness for participation led at times to a continuous dialogue with the performers. Their vital presence could often make or break the evening's show, and the exuberant applause that issued from them, as Whitman recalls, was "one of those long-kept-up tempests . . . no dainty kid-glove business."[11] Above the pit, physically as well as socially, were the dress boxes, which seated the more sedate and respectable families of the Bowery. The third tier of boxes was cordoned off for the less decorous patrons of the arts, the prostitutes, and the gallery was given over to their gents, who blended with the other dandies and gamblers. Shouting matches were not uncommon between the various segments of the theater, lending a bit of confusion to the distinction between players and audience. As the gaslight shifted, the theater audience became the very stage for the display of social and economic differences; though drawn apart by position, the spectators were held together under one roof in an act of cohesion. The management played to this conflict between division and unity, varying its bill from Shakespearean drama to opera, dance, melodrama, and circus stunts. At times, any number of forms, from high to low, appeared on the same bill, and, during the 1830s, the contradictions were often eased by a little comic relief provided by T. D. Rice's performance of Jim Crow which closed each evening. This ritualistic evocation of the black experience was not without its scape-goat qualities, restoring a sense of harmony to the multitude by aligning them along racial lines.

As the processes of industrialization and urbanization began to exert their influence, the heterogeneity of the populace sought expression in separate institutions. After the 1830s, and more so following the 1850s, "the class lines dividing box, pit, and gallery were often transferred to particular theaters."[12] Along the Bowery, the upper class began to claim the more fashionable Park Theater while the middle class flocked to the Bowery Theater, leaving the Chatham Theater to the lower class. The democratic body, now disjoined, found regeneration in its parts.

New urban associations began to take hold of the Bowery that revealed the distinction between village and city forms of affiliation. Symbolically evincing a unique cultural identity, the Bowery Boy and Bowery Gal emerged as celebrated American types of working-class origin. They not only displayed a unique fashion and style of conduct but also gave vivid form and expression to the value of youthful peer groups and heterosexual associations on the Bowery. The leisure activities of Bowery Boys and Bowery Gals, both separately and in their liaisons with each other, demonstrated to the broader social structure of the city a growing working-class presence that cut across gender lines.[13]

A laborer, the Bowery Boy often relied on his hands as tools for his trade and as weapons in battle. The boy's mode was essentially a heroic one as demonstrated by his true-blue Americanism, honorable defense of womanhood, manly battles, and feats of bravery as a volunteer fireman. As a member of a volunteer fire company, he combined rivalry and conflict with cooperative and civic efforts. Again, his physical prowess was not only indispensable in manning the machine before the age of steam engines but also necessary in waging the numerous fights which often flared between competing companies. Many of the ensuing fights involved miniature armies of the night, with as many as one thousand contestants vying for conquest. The volunteer fire companies were events as well as associations which represented, all at once, political, social, and territorial allegiances. As organizations, they mediated relationships that were growing far too complex and distant and provided a sense of identity in concert with American ideals and the demands of urban life.

Personified by Mose, the Bowery Boy's heroic stature was elevated to mythic proportions.[14] An enlarged mimetic figure of the American type, Mose was a virtual Paul Bunyan displaced to a new urban reality. Though Mose stalked through city streets rather than the rolling fields of the republic, he still embodied simplistic rural values, such as strength, self-determination, and possession of one's resources—all at odds with his habitat. No obstacle could slow Mose's purposeful momentum which, in full stride, was nothing less than an object lesson in control, a hands-on manipulation of urban structures for the benefit of one man's revenge against battalions of neighborhood youths. The collision with the enemy was often magnified by his extraction of lamp posts and streetcars, which served as ready ammunition for the bout. Yet Mose's struggle was also a symbolic one which revealed the inflated existence of disintegrating republican values within a renewed setting of increasing city domination. In uprooting the material evidence of a growing urban context, Mose suggests the presence of a more encompassing enemy, one that could still be effaced in the return to an essential American past where larger-than-life individuals freely roamed.

This issue of control was reiterated by numerous street gangs that formed on and off the Bowery in response to the hardening of territories exacted by the divisions within a heterogeneous social system. The gangs functioned to assert themselves, along with their policies and beliefs, as separate entities in contention. Bowery gangs, such as the O'Connell Guards, Atlantic Guards, and American Guards, were, as the recurrent appellations denote, obviously on the defensive. They were protective nativistic associations which often vied for superiority with the Plug Uglies and Dead Rabbits, less assimilated immigrant groups. The general rowdiness and disruption of order that characterized these gangs were epitomized in the riot of 1857 between the Dead Rabbits and the Bowery Boys in which one thousand men clashed, leaving eight to ten dead and many more injured.[15] As with the bloody Astor Place Riots which preceded it in 1845, class tensions and political alliances provided the underlying turbulence for the gang warfare. In general, the riots of antebellum New York were symptomatic of a more regulated and self-conscious social structure, and, lacking the graceful sweep of Mose's aggressive statement, street gangs resorted to desperate tactics in order to voice their discontent and wage their futile wars of dominion.

Street gangs played their role in lowering the reputation of the Bowery. But its descent, long in the making, was hastened after 1850 by the rising popularity of Broadway, a neighboring parallel avenue which exceeded the Bowery in elegance and in the value of its retail establishments. The shipbuilding industry east of the Bowery and the expanding slum district of Five Points to the south also contributed to its decline. As the more wealthy quarter on the Bowery's northern end, Astor and Lafayette Place, began to dissolve, Irish and Germans, coming from the southern and eastern points of entry, assumed control of the thoroughfare. The Melodeon, opening in 1846, served as an early model for the tawdry amusements which rose at an almost exponential rate shortly thereafter. During this same period, the Bowery Theater was largely given over to sensational melodrama and farce, which played to the sentiments of the lower classes. German beer gardens and stores became conspicuous recreational and commercial enterprises along the avenue. In 1850, the Bowery played host to 27 oyster houses, 52 taverns, and 240 distinct yet varied trades, ranging from tailors and drapers to shooting and daguerreotype galleries.[16] The Bowery, and its residential vicinity of the Lower East Side, soon became a slice of New York hospitable to immigrant proprietors and families, thrifty shoppers, and venturesome tourists. Its cheap lodging houses also showed an urbane toleration for the life-style of transients and down-and-outs. As it moved into the post–Civil War era, the Bowery constituted "the cheapside of New York; the place of the People; the resort of mechanics and the laboring classes; the home and the haunt of a great social democracy."[17] With its emergent status as a separate urban entity within the city, a section complete in itself, the Bowery reflected a pattern of segregation and activity inherent in the very growth of urban culture.

The city's chief office, as Adna Weber defines it, "is the spectroscope of society; it analyzes and sifts the population, separating and classifying the diverse elements. The entire progress of civilization is a process of differentiation, and the city is the greatest differentiator."[18] This process of differentiation, which sorts the populace along such variables as class, occupation, race, and ethnicity, operates most efficiently when the fundamental conditions of urbanization have been met; that is, the existence of a large, highly concentrated population of various types and backgrounds. Though New York had met the criteria of a voluminous, dense, and relatively heterogeneous aggregate at an earlier period than most American cities, all these factors were greatly enhanced during the three decades following the Civil War. New York hustled into the period fully armed with a population that nearly tripled

in the twenty years between 1840 and 1860 (from 312,710 to
805,658). By 1880, the city's urban dwellers had exceeded 1 million,
and in 1890 the population of metropolitan New York had neared the 3
million mark. This tendency toward urban settlement was somewhat
exaggerated by the phenomenal rate of growth in New York. But the
city only emphasized an American pattern of development and distribution of population that rampantly shifted the center of control
from rural districts to urban centers by the close of the nineteenth
century.

The nineteenth century proved a catalyst for this transition. Born in
the spacious countryside, the century was laid to rest amidst a congested network of telegraph and telephone wires, steam-driven elevated railroads, tracks and electric trolleys, traffic snarls, crowds,
closely packed physical structures, a ganglia of pipes underneath the
paved streets, and the mixture of noise, soot, and smoke that lingered
overhead. The century bore witness to the steady rise of the city,
which, in 1800, numbered six and claimed only 4 percent (210,873) of
the country's population; by 1890, this figure had climbed to 29 percent, with over 18 million Americans jammed into 448 cities nationwide.[19] While urban dwellers increased their numbers 87-fold during
the span of the century, the population of the country as a whole
multiplied by only 12-fold.[20] And though rural areas still retained the
majority of the American people in 1890 (one out of three residing in
cities), the distribution of wealth belied the change in focus of national
life to an urban-centered civilization. As measured in property values,
the wealth of cities surpassed that of the rural districts by a ratio of 2
to 1.[21] The larger numbers scattered throughout the countryside
could not compete with the concentration of wealth possessed by the
cities. This more accurate index reveals the primacy of the city at this
time and the direction in which the nation's economic, social, administrative, and cultural life had taken.

The roots of urbanization lay in the new methods of production and
distribution which, nurtured by technological developments, took hold
in the fertile soil of industrial capitalism. During the post–Civil War
era, the growth of cities as prime manufacturing, commercial, and
service-oriented centers accelerated at a rapid pace, exerting a
centralizing effect on an already mobilized population. Steam-driven
power machinery fostered the redistribution and clustering of people
into large urban areas as a necessary and accessible labor force to man
the industrial apparatus and as a ready market for the consumption of
its goods and products. The development of factories and the exten-

sion of railroads provided the livelihood and means of migration for the depopulation of the countryside. When technological progress was applied to the farms, it reiterated this demographic tendency by intensifying production while leaving hands idle in the wake of the tractor's plow. The economic organization of industrialization, with its emphasis on the masses (from both production and market orientations) and its inevitable convergence in the city, rendered the formerly dispersed arrangement of the populace demanded by an extractive industry, such as agriculture, obsolete. Mechanization on the farms created both surplus food and surplus labor which helped to remove and remake the means of production and its many attributes for a new frontier.

The urban frontier was propped up by the powerful economic forces which effectively reorganized American society, guiding its transition from household or village economy to an international center of trade and finance in one swift century. Critics of the late nineteenth century attest to the complexity and potency of these altered conditions of American life by the various interpretive schemes they have employed to still the reverberations of the age. No other period in the chronicle of American history appears to have engendered so many designations. Known variously as the Gilded Age, the Age of Excess, the Brown Decades or Buried Renaissance, the Great Barbecue, the Mauve Decade (a luminous fragment), and, most recently, as a process of incorporation, the late nineteenth century has continued to live up to each appellation. [22]

The Gilded Age (to use Twain's and Warner's original formulation) was an era of generally unrestrained industrial capitalism best characterized by Alan Trachtenberg's notion of incorporation; that is, "the emergence of a changed, more tightly structured society with new hierarchies of control, and also changed conceptions of that society, of America itself."[23] The primary agents for this heightened sense of structure were the networks of transportation and communication. Railroad, telegraph, and telephone were a few of the major new industries which functioned to solidify incorporation and augment bureaucratic organization. These developments, along with the rise in advertising, created urban and national markets for the absorption of mass-produced goods. Other industries, such as copper, steel, oil, and iron, were attuned as well toward an economy of expansion and production under the control of unprecedented corporate bodies and monopolistic enterprises. Rockefeller's Standard Oil Company became a corporate paradigm in 1879, exemplifying the practice of vertical integration and conglomeration which served to eliminate competition while generating large pools of capital. Other social forms of economic consolidation soon followed, and, by 1893, 12 bullish companies manipulated a total capital close to $1 billion. The combinations flourished over the decade, increasing to 318 by 1904 with holdings of over $7 billion. [24]

The dynamic implicit in industrial capitalism vindicated Tocqueville's assertion that inequality of condition would enter through the gateway of a manufacturing economy. The hardening of class lines and the growing rift between capital and labor were accentuated by the social forms of monopolistic control and by the general drive toward acquisition, consolidation, and concentration of wealth into a select class of capitalists. The mechanisms which enhanced industrial productivity also worked to section off the social structure by the demand for a finely engineered division of labor which stratified and categorized, separating the rank-and-file workers from the middle strata of professional and organizational managers and both from the upper level of corporate business leaders. The incorporation of the industrial unit, which extended its mode of hierarchy to society and culture in the urban community, achieved efficient integration by exercising the principle of segregation.

Though the premise of economic unity through social division promoted a higher standard of national and per capita wealth, it also resulted in a skewed distribution of the nation's affluence which deepened the level of poverty while extending its range. The higher standard of living experienced during the Gilded Age was largely the result of overproduction and glutted markets, an Age of Excess which caused prices to fall while real wages remained relatively stable. [25] Though wages declined in periods of depression, they did not positively correlate with the more dramatic and continuous drop in price levels. The improved condition of the average laborer, as measured by the relation between wages and the margin of subsistence, offers some justification for the argument against the increasing immiserization of the urban proletariat at this time. Yet this situation was more a benign consequence of the internal dynamic within industrial capitalism, with its aggressive tendency toward mechanization and mass production, than an act of intervention on behalf of the system's benefactors. The higher standard of living was offset by many factors, such as high infant mortality rates, economic insecurity, technological and structural unemployment, accidents on the job, the oppressive hours of labor, and by an overall sense of exploitation that manifested itself most in terms of the degrading conditions in which the lower levels of society earned their minimal incomes and sought out their substandard shelters.

The improved standard of living was also counteracted by the disproportionate distribution of national income. G. K. Holmes's extrapolations from the 1890 census data base indicated that the distribution of national wealth was indeed skewed, for the top 10 percent of American families held 72 percent of the wealth (the very top 1 percent of the distribution retained some 25 percent of the wealth).[26] Among industrial workers in the 1880s, Trachtenberg estimates that 40 percent lived below the poverty line while 45 percent existed barely above it.[27] These figures substantiate a majority standing of poverty during the Gilded Age, further validated by the lack of ownership which parallels the movement from rural to urban settlement. In 1890, less than 7 percent of families owned their own homes in New York City; the far greater majority were tenants, and fully two-thirds of the families in the city were propertyless.[28] By 1900, the extent of home ownership increased only slightly to 11 percent, with the greater number of these properties outside Manhattan and the Bronx, the prime real estate areas.[29]

Incorporation had implanted a more pervasive condition of poverty within the very core of an affluent society. Similarly, the social and economic upheavals which attended the Gilded Age demonstrated a prevailing sense of dislocation and discontent amidst the centripetal momentum of urban-industrial regimentation. Strikes, depressions, protests, unionization, unemployment, and acts of violence indicated that American society could not be licked into shape without consequence or reprisal. Strikes, in particular, were common occurrences which brought about harsh lessons in corporate power and government alliance to the gathered workers, and depressions seemed to turn as cyclically as the seasons during the period from 1870 to 1898.[30] The worst depression yet experienced in the nation, a watershed of sorts, landed in 1893 and lasted until 1898. The depression caused widespread unemployment (20 percent of the labor force was without work), heightened conflict between capital and labor, contraction in both the industrial and agricultural sectors, an exacerbation of the transient problem, and the emergence of peripatetic "industrial armies" who marched on Washington to demand a relief program of public works. Ironically, by the end of the Gilded Age incorporation had spawned its very own forms of secession.

The economic insecurity and displacement brought on by the depression and by the period as a whole are best embodied in the tramp, a figure who represents the complete withdrawal from structure and the very folly of incorporation. Appearing *en masse* in the early 1870s, the tramp increased his numbers rapidly over the next three decades. The depression of 1893 contributed significantly to the tramp's presence as well as to the existence of his associates, the hobo and homeless man. Numbering over 45,000 at the beginning of the depression, the incidence of tramps and hoboes abroad within the country had reached an estimated 100,000 by its close.[31] The "industrial armies" of 1894, led by "Generals" Coxey, Fry, and Kelly, exhibited much less aimlessness in their wanderings than the tramp. These armies were comprised mainly of the unemployed who sought rectification for their condition, accepting the road only as a means for a viable reentry into the home. The paramilitary organization of these armies betrayed their desperate attempt to retain a semblance of good order which amounted to a strained compensation for its conspicuous absence.

The challenges to incorporation erupted from its interstices and only temporarily relaxed the tentacular network of its muscular hold upon the nation. In general, incorporation continued to flex and expand its grasp, particularly in shaping the center of its controlling body—the urban environment. It becomes apparent that the city's chief function of segmentation and differentiation of its social structure was preceded and given impetus by the economic processes already under way. They often worked simultaneously once the urban-industrial operation was in full swing to order American society into fine gradations which were then funneled into distinct urban spaces. Segregation in the workshop broadened itself to the neighborhood and marketplace, giving visible expression to its distended reach. "The processes of segregation," as Robert Park observed, function to "establish moral distances which make the city a mosaic of little worlds which touch but do not interpenetrate."[32] Economic specialization, fed by the density of population, forced such social fragmentation and the creation of vivid oppositions within the city limits. The splendor of Fifth Avenue with its palatial mansions and the stately curvature of Broadway contrasted sharply with the serried urban slums just off the Bowery and in its vicinity of the Lower East Side. Irish squatters in the more undeveloped regions uptown also attested to this direct connection between socioeconomic status and segregated urban space. As the culture of affluence fractured into subcultures of poverty, the prospect of unity was preserved through the rationalization of victimization in the world view of social Darwinism:

Those who were crushed by competition, regimented by machines, too poorly paid to keep up with the Joneses, were invited to find solace in the fact that their sacrifices were essential to national welfare, that without victims there could be no struggle for existence, that without a struggle for existence, there could be no progress, that without progress there could be no hope for perfection.[33]

The establishment of tenement quarters, especially within dense, overcrowded, and unsanitary slum districts, gave tangible evidence to the separation of the lower classes and ethnic groups from the more prosperous sections of the city. If victimization was an inherent concept of order, it was also a material and social condition; the ideal had found its correlative in the existence of subculture and poverty. From 1864 to 1890, the number and population of tenements throughout the city had more than doubled. In the latter year, virtually five-sixths of the city's residents lived in over 37,000 such structures.[34] On the average, the degree of overcrowding within these tenements was twice that of other urban dwellings and far greater in the dense immigrant enclaves bordering the Bowery. In 1900, three adjacent wards of the Bowery—the sixth to the south (Chinatown), fourteenth to the west (Little Italy), and tenth to the east (New Israel)—comprised the most overcrowded wards in the entire city, with the tenth ward taking precedence by packing an average of sixty-five people per tenement dwelling.[35] The mean number of persons per dwelling in the total city for 1890 is given as nineteen, a fact revealing the great division between slum conditions and housing in general.[36] These same Bowery wards were also high in the density of their regions. Again, New Israel surpassed all other wards in 1894 with a density of 702 people per acre, giving it the reputation of being the most congested area in the country if not the entire Western world.[37] High density and overcrowding in the Bowery wards blurred the boundaries of street, sidewalk, and residence. In contrast to the well-managed flow of pedestrian and vehicular traffic on Broadway, the streets of the Bowery, such as Hester, Henry, and Mulberry Bend, mixed marketplace, playground, and social center and stalled traffic into one enmeshed mass of disordered yet vibrant humanity.

In 1896, the total population of the immediate Bowery vicinity, from East Houston Street to Chatham Square, and four to five blocks deep on both its east and west sides numbered about 110,000 people collected in over 100 city blocks (the more extended boundaries of the Bowery included nearly half a million inhabitants). Though tenements were scarce on the Bowery itself due to its commercial nature, they

abounded along its transverse and parallel arteries. And if the Bowery
showed an industrious front to passersby, the remainder of its form
revealed the agglomeration of tenements which hemmed it in. Over
240 tenements alone existed on square Bowery blocks along its southern course below East Houston Street.

A typical cross section of tenement conditions just off the Bowery
was displayed in a cardboard model at the Tenement House Exhibition
of 1900.[38] The tenement block in question, bounded by Chrystie (an
immediate parallel street east of the Bowery), Forsyth, Canal, and
Bayard streets, included thirty-nine old-law tenement houses which
ranged from four to six stories in height. Within these structures were
605 apartments, or a total of 1,588 rooms, which housed 2,781 people. Close to 70 percent of these rooms were either completely dark,
with no ventilation, or received their only light and air from the minimal and stale source of airshafts. There was no bath in the entire block
and only 264 water closets, about one for every ten residents. The
incidence of disease on this block involved 32 cases of tuberculosis
during the previous five years and 13 cases of diphtheria in 1899. In
addition, 660 separate families had sought charitable aid (in another
ten-block section of the Bowery 4,000 families had made similar appli-
cations). In all, the rentals derived from this one-block sample
amounted to $113,964 per year. The purpose of the exhibit, which
showed models, poverty and disease maps, charts, diagrams, and
statistical tables, was to demonstrate factually to the public that "in
New York City the workman is housed worse than in any other city of
the civilized world."[39]

Massive immigration (over five million immigrants landed at Castle
Garden between the years 1869 to 1889) lent itself, by its concentration in urban districts, to the machinations of the tenement industry.
The privatization of social control, with entrepreneurs maximizing
profits through the intensive land use of crowded tenement construction, underlay the problem of slums and its intransigence to reform:
"The real cause both of slum conditions and of resistance by property
owners to the enforcement of any legislation to improve urban housing
was that old-style tenements in New York in the eighties, for example,
paid their owners an annual profit of 40 per cent."[40] Individual ownership of tenements, the rule rather than the exception, yielded to the
competitive demands of the market and to the interest in private gain
as opposed to social welfare. Owners of modest means, entrepreneurs were assisted in their capitalistic enterprise by the lack of substantial municipal intervention and by the original gridiron plan of the

city, which fulfilled its design by the erection of tenement buildings that efficiently covered anywhere from 75 to 90 percent of their stingy and squalid lots.

Tenements and urban slums grew into self-sufficient social entities, worlds of their own, which serrated the tissue of urban form even further, creating a sense of isolation and mystery between culture and subculture. "The tenement obstructed the reunification of an urban community in which the middle class lived physically, socially and culturally in a world apart from the immigrant working-class population."[41] Immigrant enclaves within the Bowery reinforced this separatism by lending an alien and strange Old World atmosphere to this region. In the Lower East Side foreign-born immigrants often exceeded native-born citizens, sometimes by a ratio of 2 to 1.[42] New immigrants from southern and eastern Europe, Italians, and Russian, Polish, and Hungarian Jews established their own pockets within the Bowery vicinity. Chinese, Germans, and Irish sought out their own separate territories as well. While this finer and more internal process of segregation functioned to counteract the urban tendency toward depersonalization and anomie by the retention of traditional folkways, it also intensified class, ethnic, and racial tensions both between culture and subculture and among the imploding dissimilar subcultures that lived side by side. Sequestered in their infamous rear tenements and intricate quarters, such as Bottle Alley, Baxter Street Court, and Bandit's Roost, these immigrant groups signified containment and secrecy (much like the inner compartments of cheap lodging houses which sheltered the homeless along the Bowery and like the interior spaces of the street's saloons, opium dens, foreign theaters, and bewildering amusement centers). Such sanctuaries both on and around the Bowery deepened the convolutions within the urban fold and magnified the paradox of social distance amidst physical proximity which characterized the city in general.[43]

By the turn of the century, the Bowery had earned its reputation for being, in Robert Park's phrase, a "detached milieu," complicating the above paradox by virtue of its layered textures. As one writer expressed the paradox, the Bowery is "a quarter to be visited, but never known; seemingly a vast, insurmountable social barrier, shutting off intercourse not only between the northern and southern parts of the city, but between its own eastern and western tributaries, so that these people living so near each other, having the same vital interests and opportunities, are yet as separate as though the sea rolled between them."[44] The process of segregation, which gave rise to sub-

culture, found reification in the phenomenon of social distance. Yet
distance would not end the process, for its very nature would heighten
a sense of mystery, inviting pursuit and eclipsing discovery.

As a detached milieu, the Bowery expressed its discontinuity with
urban culture. This was not only evidenced in the form of housing
conditions, but also in the very features which constituted the essential qualities of its subcultural identity: vice and deviance, poverty and
destitution, and commerce and entertainment. These forms, which
validated the urban process of segregation, institutionalized the divergent way of life that existed within the Bowery. They also worked to
widen the ever-present gulf between culture and subculture.

Though a subculture like the Bowery is indeed detached from its
cultural progenitor, it is by no means severed, and thus it exercises a
degree of retention modified by its fundamental act of contravention.
So while the basic tenets of industrial commercialism were incorporated into the Bowery's salable framework, they were often
caricatured or magnified in scale or accommodated to meet the level of
necessity among the lower classes. Just as New York had given over
every fiber of its commercial being to the activities of display, diver-
sification, distribution, and exchange, so too had the Bowery, and
more out of mimicry than direct ironic statement, though the latter
often seemed the unintended result.

Up until the mid 1880s, before the city's commerce expanded uptown to 14th and 23rd streets, the Bowery was the center of retail
trade and housed such department stores as Lord and Taylor, E.
Ridley and Company, and the original Atlantic and Pacific Tea Company. The Bowery then was a lively commercial avenue, with its elevated and surface transportation, glaring storefront lights, and throngs
of shoppers milling along the sidewalks. Especially on Saturday nights,
when the workers and their families were flush with the week's
wages, the Bowery established itself as a commodity carnival which
brought a sense of unity to culture and subculture by bringing them
together under its rainbow of clustered lights and illuminated signs.
The hues of gaslights were as varied as the articles for consumption,
and the Bowery, megaphone in hand, barked out its wares in a manner
that amplified the dominant values of an urban society and the bold
tactics for their communication.

To read the signs tentatively could not have been further from the
Bowery's slogan. Subtlety was not its mode of conveyance; rather
than evoke desire, it beat it out of the hearts of consumers. The
sideshow ambience lent itself to numerous gimmicks which an-

nounced, pushed, and shoved commerce down streets and alleyways in a desperate search for a deal. Some of the chicanery of mock auctions, pawnbrokers, and disastrous store sales was made manifest in the advertising technique of one Bowery department store, the Red House. By turning its barkers into harlequins who then performed as mountebanks in order to woo the crowd inward, the Red House symbolically evinced the very essence of the Bowery's *modus operandi.*[45] Less a *caveat emptor* than a mimetic display, the technique proved effective and showed the crowd's willingness to line up and be counted.

Although surrounded on all sides by poverty, the Bowery exercised its legerdemain by the illusory portrayal of affluence in shop windows. These windows became portals of style and elegance, enticing the populace while visualizing the stark differences between appearance and reality. The live model, "dressed in the most ultra mode," became the seductive yet unreal mediation between the realms of opulence and impoverishment. A fashionable signal of unlimited opportunity, he also exerted, by his contrived presence as advertisement, the dissemblance of possibility. Posturing on his pedestal, the model was but one isolated sign in motion, a concept without sequence, a symbol suspended from its context: "Sometimes he strolled to and fro in the window, sometimes he stood on a slowly revolving turntable. At intervals he would raise a slender, elegantly manicured and bediamonded hand and caress the mustache: and now and then he would turn his eyes towards the crowd outside and smile sweetly."[46] Such a dangling social proposition, which personified the translation of a commodity fetishism into terms of mobility and status, did as much to invoke the specter of control as evoke the image of desire disengaged from program.

The carnivallike reelings of the Bowery's rendition of consumer capitalism were reinforced by the open-air market which gathered in the shadows of the brightly lit facades of storefronts and down the less trafficked sidestreets. Poor vendors sought out the poorer clientele whose restricted means forced the patronage of a more personal array of barrows, barrels, stands, and carts. Here the insidious designs of enticement were absent, for mutual necessity alone exacted the commingling of buyer and seller. Vendors of meat, fish, fruit, suspenders, socks, picture frames, and flowers needed only to rely on a rough and coarse voice with minimal projection. The open-air market was perhaps the Bowery's indigenous form of commerce. Devoid of spurious

antics, the poor vendor and patron met on an equal footing reminiscent
of the medieval marketplace. Their plain sense of exchange linked
class and commerce into terms which could be well understood by
both partners. On the ground floor there were no illusions, only clear,
concise, and direct definitions.

During the 1880s, respectable businesses began to wane on the
Bowery as amusements and places of entertainment waxed sensational. Saloons, dime museums, concert halls, stale-beer dives, eating
houses, gin shops, beer gardens, theaters, and the like all conspired
to shift commerce away from retail to a more broad-based social
consumption of pleasure and vice. In 1891, one observer gave testimony to the profusion of such places along the Bowery itself by making
a count. Out of ninety-nine known places of leisure, seven were theaters, six museums, and four music halls; the remaining eighty-two
emporiums of joy, an average of six per Bowery block, were cheap
saloons or similar drinking places.[47] Overall, fully one-sixth of all saloons in the city and one-fifth of all pawnshops were situated within the
Bowery, while 27 percent of all arrests were made there.[48] Organized
crime had settled into the area by the turn of the century under the
aegis of "Big" Tim Sullivan, giving rise to a new breed of ruthless
gangsters who began to divide the territories and distribute the businesses of prostitution, graft, gambling, and robbery. Their organizational style, characterized by involved political networks, methodical
violence, and hired contracts, actually belonged more to the twentieth
rather than the nineteenth century, that is, more to the seasoned age
of a Meyer Wolfsheim than to the adolescent period of Mose the
Bowery Boy.

Though the upper classes, dining at Delmonico's or Sherry's or
strutting through Peacock Alley (that fashionable corridor of luxuriant
display in the Waldorf), looked askance at the "immoral" region of the
Bowery, the denizens of the subculture confronted their urban habitat
from an entirely different perspective. To those inside the Bowery, the
saloon was less an instrument of debauchery than a social mechanism
for class affiliation and solidarity. It was the meeting place for the
workingman, the unemployed, and the homeless, the truncated social
hierarchy of American society. The saloon not only sustained these
subgroups but provided them with a facility for social and political
engagements, such as labor union meetings, weddings, dances, and
christening parties.[49] The saloon keeper fulfilled as many roles as his
establishment, shifting from banker to business advisor, employment

The Bowery at Night, *1896, by W. Louis Sonntag, Jr. The New-York Historical Society, New York City.*

agent, political contact, publicity director, and messenger. In all, he was a social force in the community, an agent who made the subculture cohere and made his presence known to both insiders and outsiders.

Many of the saloons gained a popularity that extended beyond the subculture. McGuirk's place, known as Suicide Hall, and Steve Brodie's saloon best typified the kind of publicity seeking, adapted from Barnum, that drew tourists and slumming parties down into the Bowery to sample its widely acclaimed status as a netherworld of the city, a status literally enriched by such joints as the Plague, the Hell Hole, and the Inferno. Brodie's eccentric advertising stunt, an alleged leap from the Brooklyn Bridge, was represented in a huge painting above his saloon. The dispute over whether he had actually made the jump or not did not deter the curious from participating in the historical event every time they crossed the threshold into the bar. The sign had made the man, and the Bowery was learning quickly how to capitalize on its reputation.

The Bowery had attained a degree of self-consciousness regarding its social boundaries which reinforced the stereotypical perceptions of a naive culture. If culture could cloak the meaning of the Bowery in terms of immorality, wretchedness, depravity, perdition, and pure unadulterated Satanism, then the Bowery would comply—but for a price. The slumming trade was a profitable one, and the Bowery, playing its part in a mutual act of social duplicity, adapted itself to the preconceptions of the tourists which were largely gleaned from newspapers and magazines. Opium dens, for example, were a favorite stop along the touristic itinerary. Like our live model in the clothier's window, the opium den operated under the same synthetic principles of exhibitionism and concealment while inverting the cultural factors of class and status. The setting was completely staged, addicts posed euphorically, and imitation articles or accoutrements substituted for the genuine ones. Such a contrived snapshot satisfied the sordid expectations of the tourist and proved financially rewarding to the den's proprietor. Throughout, the real mysteries of class and subculture were preserved as if to guard the authentic against intrusion. By confronting the outsider with entrenched images, the Bowery withheld the true meaning of its context and identity. Thus dramatic differences within the social system were confirmed rather than comprehended, transforming social intercourse into a mystifying process which corroborated the paradox of physical proximity and social distance.

The more accessible entertainments on the Bowery reflected the complementary urban themes of segregation and assimilation. Built up as diversions, dime museums, variety houses, music halls, and theaters offered escape and distraction from the confusion and harsh circumstances of urban life. Yet inside the house, diversion often proved a redoubling of the city's shattered panorama. Fragmentation and specialization, conditions which accompanied the complex occupational organization of the city, found reiteration in the manifold and hybrid forms of Bowery entertainment. As legitimate theater scattered uptown, the Bowery increasingly gave expression to an admixture of melodrama, farce, pantomime, minstrelsy, burlesque, and vaudeville. The National Theater, a variety house, often combined minstrelsy, olio, and melodrama into one long program of discontinuity. But it was the rise of vaudeville that responded most energetically to the frantic pace of the city and the segmentation of its structure. It did so by imposing a decorous format which standardized the chaos into manageable categories. The intense activity of its variegated acts was industriously assimilated so that there existed "a sameness even about its infinite variety."[50] If unity could no longer be retained in the dissimilar contents of a secularized age, then it would be transferred to the focused and integrated structure of its medium. In this sense, "the vaudeville theater belongs to the era of the department store and the short story."[51]

Dime museums, such as the Gaiety and the Globe, also provided a set framework for a staggering assortment of freaks, marvels, and monstrosities. Divided among curio hall, human curiosities, and live performance, the dime museum stratified its displays into studied eccentricities. The congerie of live figures was loosely joined by virtue of their placement under one roof and on a particular floor. Yet their amazing feats and pronounced physical deformities lent a rough continuity of the grotesque to the menagerie. What else could possibly join that dazzling chain of sword swallower, glass eater, bearded lady, iron-skull man, armless wonder, living skeleton, turtle boy, man fish, and the speculative entity of "Zip, the what is it?" but the interconnecting links provided by irregularity, anomaly, and deviance, the very links which formed the circles of subculture within the city. The exhibits within the dime museum merely exaggerated the eccentric showmanship without, perhaps overstating the disfigurement of urban extremes but at least staying close to the spirit of its excesses.

The theatrical expression of immigrant groups along the Bowery often resisted this American tendency toward the assimilation of multiplicity. In extending the doctrine of segregation to its utmost limit of cultural pluralism, they attempted to retain the homogeneity of their national or religious experience. The Bowery Theater, more of an aggrandized variety house after the Civil War, was given over to German drama in the late 1870s and renamed the Thalia. Right next door was the Atlantic Gardens, a spacious German lager beer garden which held as many as fifteen hundred people. Like the German theater, the beer garden was a respectable, family-oriented center in which traditional customs were reenacted amidst music, song, and dance. The Germans were soon followed in 1889 by the Polish Jews, who turned the Thalia into a forum for Yiddish drama. In 1891, Yiddish drama was displaced by Jewish theater, and the Thalia once again adapted to the new tenants. In the remainder of its history, before burning to the ground for the fifth and final time, the Thalia (alias Bowery Theater) was theatrical home as well to the succeeding waves of Italian and Chinese immigrant groups. Though a consistent force for national pride and cultural integrity, the foreign theater only temporarily solidified a given immigrant group. Citadels of nationalistic identities could not hold their high ground on the Bowery. Each in turn was eventually leveled by the monolithic thrust toward Americanization; that is, toward the exchange of intimacy and community for mobility and anonymity.

Aside from manifesting the tensions between subculture and culture, division and accommodation, Bowery theater also provided an

arena for practical apprenticeship. It was on the Bowery, at Hoym's,
that Harrigan and Hart began their careers in musical comedy which
offered idealized treatments of poverty on the Lower East Side. Harry
and Al Jolson were launched at the Gaiety Museum, and Irving Berlin
started as a "busker" (a freelance performer) at Callahan's dance
saloon. Harry Miner's Bowery theater featured the four Cohans, Weber and Fields, and Eddie Cantor, who evaded the hook by taking first
prize on one of the amateur nights. Mixing highbrow with lowbrow, the
People's Theater and the Windsor gave an experimental flavor to entertainment that characterized Bowery fare in general. In all, the free-
wheeling Bowery theaters and amusements provided a valuable testing ground for young unknowns, a means to cultivate talent and gauge
the public interest. But success at the bottom of a social democracy
was far from being a pushover, for the Bowery audience, in turn,
shrewdly measured the neophyte performer, holding the very handle
of the hook's long but deadly reach.

Commerce. Entertainment. Vice. "However, . . . there was a collection of men to whom these things were as if they were not."[52] The
haunt and prophecy of the Bowery lay in its unassimilated subgroup of
the homeless. If the tramp embodied the folly of incorporation, then
the homeless represented its futility—a lingering antithesis to structure, organization, and integration. Living examples of social and economic decomposition, the homeless constituted the entropy of industrial capitalism.

As early as the 1870s, the homeless began to make their increasing
numbers felt throughout the city and, particularly, within the confines
of the Bowery. By the 1890s there were an estimated 60,000 homeless men and women on the streets of New York, with over 14,000
being lodged nightly in 200 to 300 private or public sleeping facilities.[53]
As many as 116 cheap lodging houses, ranging in price from seven to
twenty-five cents per night, were either on the Bowery or within its
immediate vicinity; the dormitories on the Bowery itself provided shelter for about 9,000 of the city's homeless population.[54] Though profitable for the proprietor in his lucrative struggle for existence, the
cheap lodging house embodied the patrons' faltering race for survival.
For the down-and-out who could afford a semblance of crude civility,
anything from a canvas string hammock to a double-decker bunk would
suffice for the night's lair. For a little extra, a room of one's own could
be had, a cell with a cot, chair, locker, and caged ceiling; the latter
feature made for a makeshift view, an interiorized window of one's
confinement.

A sample of one lodging house in the early 1890s revealed that the greater percentage of its homeless residents were unskilled workers.[55] In a review of nationalities which comprised the group, Germans led in numbers followed by the Irish and native-born Americans. In all, the average age of the sample was forty-one years, which indicated that the men were withdrawn from productive work somewhat prematurely. A separate survey of street beggars made around the same time confirms the high ranks of nationalities found in the lodging house sample, though arranged in a slightly different order.[56] The presence of native-born Americans in both, however, disclaims the popularized sentiment of the time that homelessness was an isolated phenomenon attributed to foreign populations and mass immigration. The condition of homelessness was far more encompassing and signaled a skeletal form of penury that extended beyond personal or nationalistic interpretations. This specter of misery and want was intrinsic rather than extrinsic to American society and thus called for a systemic definition of poverty to account for its nature and extent.

If the Bowery, as a distinct subculture, begins by an enumeration of contrast and discontinuity, it ends as a study in entrapment. The process of urban segregation reached the nadir of the homeless where social distance had descended into a faint presence of outline. The homeless were rendered increasingly invisible to the city by their relegation to the Bowery. Yet these outcasts would continue to enhance the mysteries of this region and, by eventually taking over the Bowery for their own designs, prove to all the powers of endurance.

The twentieth century has bequeathed the Bowery to the homeless, culminating the transition of this district from a heterogeneous urban slum to a more homogeneous skid row. Progressive reform in housing and municipal government, combined with upward mobility for second-, third-, and fourth-generation immigrant families, had helped to reduce the general level of poverty in the city as well as in the Bowery vicinity.[57] But as commerce evacuated the area for its sprint uptown, realty values on the Bowery dropped drastically. The opening of the Williamsburg and Manhattan bridges in the first decade of the new century had brought an influx of traffic to the street which breezed by en route to other destinations within the expansive metropolis. Amusements and entertainments, which had animated the Bowery's flamboyant character, were siphoned off by the growing popularity of the Tenderloin bounded by Seventh and Fourth avenues, from 14th to 42nd streets—an opportunistic center for graft and vice as well. The astonishing phantasmagoria of Coney Island also played a vital role in contributing to the Bowery's declining popularity. The movement from life to artifice was symbolically realized in Coney Island's reconstruction of "the Bowery with the lid off" (referring to the absence of the Third Avenue El) which became a part of Dreamland in 1903.[58] This open-air museum retained the memorable iconography of the original Bowery, replete with saloons, beer gardens, restaurants, casinos, and theaters and the honky-tonk thrills of its amusements. By transforming the Bowery, in its autumnal phase, into a realm of buoyant fantasy, "the Bowery with the lid off" represented abandonment and recovery, the replacement of the actual by dream and nostalgia. Preserved in its escapist historical encasement, the Bowery was frozen in the very moment that it stumbled into the twentieth century.

The transition of the Bowery into a skid row was often lamented at this time, making for headlines which echoed society's nostalgia for its vanished community: "Slowly the Bowery Passes into the Shadows of Tradition," "Things to Be Seen on the Old Bowery," "The Street That Died Young," "When the Bowery Was in Bloom." All invoked the bygone era of its heyday, a restoration of life amidst decay. As a subculture of the vanquished came to predominate on the Bowery, the street, reflecting the condition of its inheritance, lost both its productive activity and energetic pulse. It had indeed hit the skids, a slow roller following the circumscribed drift of homelessness.

> The Bowery is different. The other streets move purposefully through the city. Like the rods and pistons of some great machine, each has its definite and recognizable function to perform. The Bowery starts at the slope of Cherry Hill, picks up its decrepit way across the traffic of the Bridges, makes a weak curve toward the magnet of Broadway, and expires with a groan at Cooper Square.[59]

As if to seal the lid on the Bowery's fate, the Third Avenue El was reconstructed in 1916, setting up express and local tracks together in the center of the street (this was unlike the original design of 1878, which bordered the sidewalks and left the center open). This material change in urban transportation resulted in an oppressive sense of enclosure underneath the El and left the modern Bowery hidden in darkness. With the omnipresent structure overhead, the sights of the Bowery were now forced downward into the subterranean ground of its social being.

Yet, ironically, these changes renewed the meaning of the Bowery as a social and ecological base for the homeless within the city. The Bowery reconstituted its purpose and reputation by deepening the specialization that was forced upon it. As an institutionalized skid row, the Bowery had remade itself into a coordinated network of missions, flophouses, labor agencies, lunch counters, restaurants, used clothing outfits, cheap saloons, and pawnshops. Later internal developments, such as the Bowery Chamber of Commerce, *Bowery News,* and attempts to establish a Bowery College further cemented the framework of this context as a place of refuge and collective expression for the downtrodden.

As a skid row, the Bowery was virtually an all-male community, reflecting the domination of the labor force by men and acting as a barometer of their ebb and flow in times of economic prosperity and depression. For a time, the fluctuations of seasonal employment and casual labor demands also contributed to the male-oriented nature of skid row and to its role as a reservoir of cheap labor. But, for the most part, that restless breed of hoboes and tramps, readily associated with periods of industrial expansion, was beyond the verge of extinction, dissolved in yellow harvests, black boxcars, and neon lights. Their worn heels were already one step over the horizon. In passing, they had given way to the sedentary existence of the "home guard" who stood fast to the certainty of his urban bedrock.

In the early 1900s, close to twenty-five thousand men were lodged nightly along the Bowery.[60] Their numbers increased during 1914–15, a period of widespread unemployment. A study of fifteen hundred homeless men conducted by the city-run Municipal Lodging House at this time revealed the obvious economic factors responsible for their plight. It was found that the majority of men were clearly willing to work if given the opportunity or requisite medical attention.[61] Such was the case during the 1930s when economic collapse had forced the unemployed into urban skid rows as a last resort to starvation and isolation. Homelessness and joblessness were so closely linked at this time that the extent of occupancy in the Bowery's Men's Shelter proved, in fact, a reliable index of the rate of unemployment in the manufacturing industry.[62]

Improvements in the conditions of labor mandated by the New Deal and a state of economic recovery largely stimulated by wartime industries and recruitment promoted a more widespread national and per capita affluence. From the 1940s on, skid row responded by becoming less a direct consequence of capricious labor market forces wrought by an unregulated system of industrialization. Yet the homeless were still prevalent on the Bowery and in other skid rows throughout the country, lending substance to an abiding state of disenfranchisement in the midst of national prosperity, middle-class suburbanization, urban renewal, and corporate hegemony. The rising American standard of living had resulted in a minority status of poverty in which the homeless constituted its base component. But though the extent of homelessness had diminished, the intensity of its condition had not. As one Catholic Worker volunteer observed, skid row represented "perhaps the bitterest, most physical and obvious poverty that can be seen in an American city."[63]

The population of the Bowery's skid row dwindled from 13,675 in 1949 to 3,000 in 1971, a contraction of more than three-fourths of its community.[64] By the late 1970s, the number had dropped to about 2,000; by 1987, it was down below 1,000. Though reduced in magnitude, the structured, institutionalized context of the Bowery still served throughout to order a well-defined subculture. But as of today (fall 1988) there are only two bars, one liquor store, one municipal facility, nine flophouses, one lunch counter, one coffee shop, one mission, and three social service agencies along the Bowery. This faded setting exists within an overshadowing array of restaurant and office equipment supply shops, lighting fixture stores, crockery outlets, hardware concerns, banks, and jewelry exchanges. But more than its modern commercial or residential features, it is the automobile traffic along the Bowery that conveys a sense of fluidity amidst the broken, statuesque figures of the homeless gathered on median strips and street corners. At best, when delayed by traffic lights, the cars offer a means of livelihood for these reduced entrepreneurs who, unsolicited, bring out their bottles of window cleaner and worn rags to clean windows in an industrious appeal for some change. The demise of the Bowery as a traditional skid row and its ascent as a residential street has been aided by the process of urban renewal. The influx of artists and other city residents into this area has been made possible by the availability of cheap rents and high vacancy rates in loft and warehouse buildings. The rapid gentrification of neighboring SoHo as an art center, prime living area, and urban playground has extended its reach into the Bowery vicinity, giving rise to experimental and traditional theaters, restaurants, rock clubs, art galleries, and enhanced real estate values.

The altered factors and dispersed condition of homelessness in New York City today, during the late 1970s and throughout the 1980s, while leading to the further destabilization of the Bowery as a skid row subculture, have worked to distribute rather than diminish the number of homeless throughout the city. The decline of skid row has not caused the disappearance of homelessness; instead, it has signaled a reconceptualization of its renewed force and decentralization. Contemporary homelessness, extensive (an estimated 36,000), scattered, and incohesive, has proven to be a diffused and disoriented way of life far beyond the ordered community of skid row.[65] In flight from its territorial base, homelessness has transgressed the geographical boundaries of skid row, but in doing so it has not retained the subcultural identity endemic to its structure and affiliative network of supports. In its most recent development, homelessness has become uprooted, unearthing a subculture clinging to the arcane remnants of the Bowery like a vine to its fallen arbor.

2 / MYSTIFICATION

I unroll the scroll of new revelations.
—*T. DeWitt Talmage*
The Masque Torn Off

The Bowery, as an embodiment of urban poverty in the late nineteenth century, gave form and substance to the process of spatial segregation within the city. This segregation of the working immigrant class and the destitute homeless underclass translated into the condition of social distance which shrouded poverty with a sense of the unknown, inexplicable, or secret; that is, with the mysteries of the great city. Mystery induces detection, and the *mise-en-scène* of the Bowery vicinity became the luring context for the sleuths of culture in their apprehension of subculture.

Yet the conspicuous investigation of subculture was from the beginning foreshortened by a style of mystification which served as attitude and adjustment to the novelty of urban poverty. As a guiding conceptual orientation, mystification constituted the clues to social action which tended to make the conditions and causes of poverty obscure or mysterious. The result was not a penetration of mystery, but rather the reinstatement of its mystifying presence and the elevation of poverty to urban spectacle. Thus the strategy of mystification as a mediation between culture and subculture sought to encompass the latter's social ground by a deflection of its hidden meaning. The secret was kept intact, as were the dominant cultural values of the era, through the exercise of a mode of detection characterized by grand social deception. As the agents of culture retreated from their forays into the Bowery, irresolvable boundaries, differences, and stereotypes were reaffirmed instead of genuinely understood. Social intercourse and subcultural explication were subjugated to a culture emphatically aligned to the basic premises and forms of industrial capitalism in all of its repercussions. And though unsettled by the consequence and prospect of urban poverty, the agents of culture balanced their need to know with their counterstatement of mystification. They had descended only to throw dust into the eyes of American society.

The hermeneutical device of mystification was informed by an idealized world view associated with traditional Christian morality and the transmutations of Protestant theology. Melodrama was perhaps the best expression of the ideal, which upheld divine providence as a vehicle for a benevolent moral order that rewarded good and punished evil. Character prevailed over social phenomena, and even in a period of wrenching social change, such as the Gilded Age, the historical forces which shaped lives, institutions, and urban conditions were concealed behind the bloated posture of the ideal. As such, the religious paradigm hovered incongruously amidst a growing secular matrix.

Accordingly, a dominant view of poverty, guided by an individualistic and moralistic interpretation, framed the problem in terms of dependency and adverse character traits.[1] The social factors of slums, unemployment, homelessness, and the like were considered less a condition of poverty than an accompanying correlative to the personal deficiencies of the poor to compete successfully within a system of laissez-faire economics. This entirely personalized view of poverty was also given impetus by antebellum values, which stressed republican virtues such as the Jeffersonian ideal of free labor and independence—a program derived from the Enlightenment's creed of democratic individualism. The fact that a decentralized agrarian economy was the requisite situation for such values did not diminish their powerful impact and endurance in an era of centralized urban industrialism. Unable to objectively and analytically codify the dramatic changes in American civilization during the Gilded Age in terms of social, economic, and historical forces, Americans characteristically reverted to the sunlit commonplaces of a prior and obsolete moral order for their sense of the present. And when a modern system of knowledge such as Darwinism was embraced to lend vision, it was readily incorporated into this preexistent moral idealism in order to justify it. Social thought would come out right in the end as long as science, in the altered form of social Darwinism, led us back to our idealistic origins rather than forward to the realities of an age circumscribed by materialism.

Evasion is the motif of mystification, a fixed tropism away from American actualities as shaping determinants of the visible disparity between poverty and affluence in the great city. Lulled into an attitude of optimistic acquiescence, the mystifiers of urban poverty obfuscated the conditions and dynamics of its social import by an unfailing reduction to moral individualism, the picturesque, or the "dangerous classes." For the most part, the mystifiers entertained no serious social evaluation or criticism of the broader context in which poverty was situated, for the communities of poverty were severed from any integrated network of causality.

The three representations treated in this chapter—the sensationalistic genre, the urban picturesque, and the realism of William Dean Howells's fiction and Jacob Riis's reportage—tend toward different degrees of mystification and thus leave intact the social cleft between the worlds of culture and subculture. As embodiments of mystification, all three formalized approaches worked to repress the broader social and historical meaning of urban poverty. Because of this propensity for concealment, which ultimately upheld a static and fragmented bourgeois world view, these approaches can, in fact, be seen to reflect an ahistorical position. The various strategies of concealment which these mystifying representations advanced effectively eclipsed the shaping processes of the era. Whether the occlusion of societal sphere of activity and process was cultural, ideological, economic, political, or juridical, the net result was a reification of social thought and perception and a virtual obliteration of historical perspective. Though each representation's inherent strategies differed in style and sophistication, the underlying assumptions which produced such an effect can be summarized in an overall agent-scene orientation to social life. Such a framework, whether wedded to idealized Christian morality or to an ethical conviction of the universe, viewed the individual as a sort of free agent, a controlling force which (with rudder firmly intact) navigated through and dominated the rough seas of environment. In the world of social phenomena, this heightened reduction to individual character seemed sufficient for a delineation of both the condition and the cause of social inequality. The consequent social attitude, manifested to varying degrees in the above forms of mystification, was an affirmation of the social order wrought by the economic organization of industrial capitalism and the related ideological content inherent in its dominant culture.

Yet to one looking historically at its various forms, mystification appears as processual rather than static and can be placed on a continuum with social distance and social intimacy (reflected in the demystifying strategies of critical realism) at the opposing ends. All three of the aforementioned representations can be arranged on the continuum to illustrate the progression from the social distance/mystification terminus, best expressed by the sensationalistic genre, to the transition to critical realism, embodied in Riis's and Howells's realism, which marks the juncture between social distance and social consciousness. The progression signals a gradual and unwitting movement by outsiders toward a more genuine discovery of the objective circumstances and subjective qualities of urban poverty which would finally be realized in the thrust toward critical realism.

The sensationalistic genre, for example, was aligned in the most extreme manner with the antipode of mystification. Assimilating the traditional Christian perspective of morality and the cultural form of melodrama, this genre, which laid claim to the conquest of mystery, reinstated the stark bifurcation between social classes and, relatedly, between culture and subculture through its highly distancing and mediational strategies of condemnation, conjecture, righteous indignation, and the police lantern. In combination, these strategies transfigured the reality of social event into moral spectacle and Christian ideal. So, while culture became immanently linked with the good, pious, just, and sacred order of society, subculture became inextricably associated with the reverse; that is, an evil, wicked, unjust, and profane eruption of disorder. Framed in this manner, the proponents of this genre were able to preserve the unknown (social process) while also justifying the asymmetry of power characteristic of the era.

Since the urban picturesque school was more secularly conceived than the sensationalistic genre, moving out from the Christian soul to the human senses, it slid slightly farther away from the extremity of mystification. But although the school's penchant for observation and impressionistic description led its members to an initial level of encounter with subculture, the results were diluted by atmospheric renderings, stereotypical treatments, and shallow picturings of the "other half." Essentially motivated to fix on the picturesque qualities and eccentricities of urban existence, the representations of this school displayed a lack of confrontation with the conflictual nature of the dialectic between culture and subculture and thus remained suspended on the plane of superficiality.

The realism of Riis and Howells continued the secularization of mystification accelerated by the urban picturesque writers. Riis's and Howells's more refined methods of social observation and analysis were accompanied by their more progressive modes of discourse, which found expression in photography, reportage, literary sketches, and the novel. Their preference for a more experiential encounter that would help to discover the "real" and "true" factors behind the unsettling conditions of American life makes them transitional figures, occupying the midpoint between mystification and critical realism on the .continuum. This ambivalent position for Riis and Howells is appropriate, for it also comments on their general inability to fully embrace either the orthodox view of their cultural past (reflected in romantic idealism) or, due to their inescapable moral screen, the future movement of the era (reflected in scientific materialism).

Though all of these formalized approaches were undoubtedly aligned on the mystifying side of the continuum and its underlying construct of social distance, their representations of the Bowery vicinity treated in this chapter ironically paved the way for a spirit of skepticism and inquiry into the social factors and processes of urban life. As the pioneering spokesman for critical realism and progressive advocate for its translation into social reform, Parrington viewed this new movement as the "slow decay of . . . romantic optimism."[2] We might naturally extend that definition to include the dissolution of mystification as well.

In invoking Parrington and the use of his term, *critical realism,* my intent is not only to pay a debt to the spirit of revolt which characterized his thought but to expand in a more contemporary manner upon the useful foundation that he set as an intellect who emerges from within the period under consideration. Although I view critical realism in the general context of literary naturalism, I do not regard the former as an inherent part of the doctrinaire theory and practice thought to be exported from the Continent. Within this study, critical realism, though encouraged by the spirit of naturalism, is more meaningfully seen as an indigenous American development, a strategy formulated as a corrective response to the social structure engendered by industrial capitalism and its cultural ethos of mystification. Critical realism thus emerges from within; that is, through its dialectical relationship with mystification in the contention between culture and subculture in American society.

As a strategy of demystification, critical realism resides at the opposite end of the continuum from mystification, pushing the dialectic to the limits that defined it for the late nineteenth century. The participation of this movement in the dialectic was characterized by a confrontational style which challenged the relationship between man and environment. This challenge, as posed by Theodore Dreiser and Stephen Crane, is best understood apart from the paradigm of literary naturalism which accompanies it. In these writers' unmediated mode of inquiry (descent and discovery into the otherwise concealed realm of antistructure), critical realism disrupted those strategies of containment established by the followers of mystification. As the ensuing chapters will show, Crane's and Dreiser's interest in relating the spatial extremes of the social spectrum reclaimed the value of social process as an essential aspect of a historical perspective. Thus, their works of critical realism did not replicate the basic assumptions of cultural ideology but instead exerted an autonomous force which both evaluated and negated that context in which mystification flourished in order to readjust and reconstruct anew.

The gradual demise of mystification, however, proved a difficult undertaking, for it had found structured expression in two of the major industries of New York City—journalism and book publishing.[3] Even before the Civil War the book-publishing industry had been dominated by the accomplice of mystification, the sentimental domestic novel, which was contained largely within the feminine middle-class culture.[4] The phenomenal growth of daily newspapers, in particular, resulted in the formation of corporate enterprises devoted to the purveying and dissemination of mystification as well as to the institutionalization of social distance.[5]

> Thus, the dailies dramatized a paradox of metropolitan life itself: the more knowable the world came to seem as information, the more remote and opaque it came to seem as experience. . . . Assuming separation in the very act of seeming to dissolve it, in their daily recurrence the newspapers expressed concretely this estrangement of a consciousness no longer capable of free intimacy with its own material life. The form in which it projected its readers' assumed wish to overcome distance concealed its own devices for confirming distance, deepening mystery, and presenting the world as a spectacle for consumption.[6]

The translation of information into spectacle—yellow journalism— was accomplished by the means of shock and sensationalism. Hearst's *New York Journal* was the shrewdest exploiter of the techniques of the spectacular for a mass audience of readers. The techniques served inadvertently to raise the readers' threshold for arousal. As a momentary stay against desensitization, each issue would have to surpass the previous one in its lurid details of crime, poverty, vice, and the generally horrendous. "The Modern Editor and His Boss," a full-page color cartoon which appeared in an 1890 issue of *Puck*,[7] satirically comments on the rage of yellow journalism that was then in full swing. The cartoon shows a troubled editor sitting at his desk with pen and paper in hand. He is dwarfed from behind by a tall, looming figure—the god of sensation—who, completely attired in shocking tabloids, directs the editor's thoughts by the sheer brutality of his presence and stapled

"The Modern Editor and His Boss," January 1, 1890, *by J. Opper in* Puck.
The New-York Historical Society, New York City.

messages. Tabloids such as the "Morning Shriek," "Daily Disturbance," and "Evening Howl" are redundantly amplified as the big boss,
drum and cymbal slung around his shoulder, blows through a brass
horn. As the *Puck* cartoon reveals, the editor's office had become the
parade ground for an ostentatious display of words performing as if on
a bandstand and for a rhetorical style of persuasion that operated
under the guidelines of gluttonous banality.

This penchant for sensation and self-advertisement extended to the
newspapers' involvement with the poor during the depression years
1893 and 1894.[8] During this time of widespread unemployment, the
New York *Herald, World,* and *Tribune* contributed to urban relief
programs by soliciting funds for the supervised distribution of free
bread, clothing, and coal. Aside from being criticized by fastidious
charity organizations for the practice of indiscriminate aid, the three
dailies were scrutinized for the publicity race they were engaged in to
dramatize the plight of the poor and their noble efforts at amelioration.
The ulterior motives of each paper, aggrandizement and enhanced
circulation, became apparent to more critical observers. As "The
Spectator" for the *Outlook* summarized the situation, each daily was
"doing its alms with its left hand and letting the world know about it
with its right."[9]

In terms of sensationalism outside the realm of popular literature,
mystification had found concrete form in commodities (as diversified
and arranged in department stores), the booming medium of advertising, the general act of consumption, and the experience of the city as a
jumbled series of unrelated parts to a whole that functioned despite
the irregular fit and isolation of its attributes. Mystification had per-
vaded many aspects of American culture and society, ranging in scope
from the lofty sermons of pulpit bearers to the quotidian activities of
men and women making their urban rounds. Yet mystification would
perhaps reveal its nature best, become in fact transparent, in its
dealings with the subculture of urban poverty. The unfamiliar turf of
the Bowery region would prove a sort of acid test to the supremacy of
ideality and the longevity of its transformation into exhibition. Over
time, it would be the very pressures of neglected American realities
that would invert the attitude of mystification into the perspective of
critical realism.

The sensationalistic genre of urban and sub-urban investigation was
advertised to the public in a thrillingly Barnumesque style. As early as
1849, popular and touristic accounts, such as George Foster's *New*

York in Slices,[10] began to respond to the fragmentation of urban space. Conceived as slices of the whole, the disparate sections of the city became known for their distinctive institutions and social life. From the financial activities of Wall Street to the haunts of the Bowery, writers sought to popularize the divisions and thereby reduce the abstraction of the city into a randomly perceived collection of concrete manifestations and peculiarities. This earnest desire to explain the variegated city to itself produced another generation of writers who simplified the manifold differences into stark oppositions which revealed the bifurcation of social class and the growing interest in the city as composed of distant places of mystery occupied by the "other half." Books brandishing titles of vivid contrast, such as *Sunshine and Shadow* or *Darkness and Daylight,* virtually became generic appellations for the Gilded Age's diurnal rhythm of piety and wickedness. *The Secrets of the Great City, The Nether Side of New York,* and *The Dangerous Classes of New York* boldly announced the delineation of an alien, underworldly quality to city life which threatened a complacent social structure. And the proposed conquest of this seamy side of urban life, the mysteries and miseries of crime, poverty, and vice, was undertaken by such intrepid proclamations as *Metropolitan Life Unveiled, The Masque Torn Off,* and *New York's Inferno Explored.*[11]

The sensationalistic effect of these titles was often reinforced by the pictorial designs on the books' covers or inner flaps. J. W. Buel's *Metropolitan Life Unveiled,* for instance, greets the reader with hosts of large and small red devils, either pulling back the veil or hiding beneath it, menacing pitchforks, fire, and potions. Commissioner Booth's *New York's Inferno Explored* highlights the inferno with ghostly blood-red lettering dripping against a black background. The book's alliterative and associative subtitles—"scenes full of pathos powerfully portrayed—Siberian desolation caused by vice and drink—Tenements packed with misery and crime"—mimic the big dailies' strained but nonetheless juicy headlines.[12]

For the sensationalistic genre, the city proved an image of danger worthy to be feared and an incarnation of evil that must be avoided at all costs. This equation of danger with sin became a fervent warning to middle-class culture in its relation to the subcultures of poverty, vice, and crime. What was at stake among the popular writers of the genre was the safety and perpetuation of an integrated system of property rights, moral values, and political control—a sense of good order that could be upset by reprisal from the lower classes. The "dangerous classes," as Charles Loring Brace feared, might follow the example

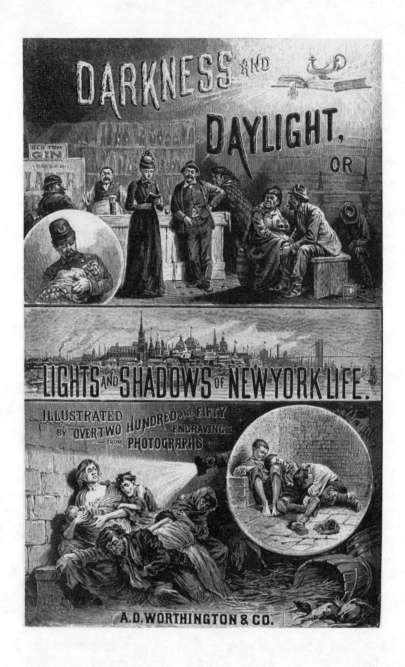

Illustration from the inside flap of Darkness and Daylight, or Lights and Shadows of New York Life, *1891, by Helen Campbell et al. The New-York Historical Society, New York City.*

set by the recent Paris Commune and explode in violent communistic
action against the custodians of culture and society.

Simultaneously enticed and repulsed by the existence of urban subcultures, these writers' advertisements of their penetration into the
unfamiliar were at odds with the superficial results they delivered,
which reaffirmed rather than minimized social distance. Prompted by
fear and buttressed by the maintenance of the status quo, their tren-
chant expositions of social mysteries and miseries were diverted into
class-serving homiletics. T. DeWitt Talmage's boast of "excavation and
exposure" proved nothing more than Buel's frank admission of purpose,[13] that of "wholesome revelation":

> While the descriptions are devoted to unmasking social evils,
> they are not prompted by pessimistical reflections, but rather to
> show the dark and ominous sides of national life, that the beauties
> of refinement and purity may appear nobler by comparison. . . .
> My motive is none other than a wish to enlighten the public upon
> matters which, if universally understood, would be a blessing to
> all humanity, by mitigating misery, restoring domestic and social
> confidence, and by keeping pure the morals of our youth.[14]

Buel's prologue betrays the real focus of such mystifying exposés: a
deflection of the conditions of the lower classes into a glorification of
self-absorbed middle-class verities. As such, virtue prevails over vice,
for the descent ultimately reflects upon the ascendant class and solid-
ifies its unexamined position of social and ethical superiority.

If any semblance of demystification did ensue from these stunted
explorations into low life, it was one aimed toward nurturing vigilance
among the public. To citizen and tourist alike, the warnings were
sounded and chicanery laid bare so that one could better navigate the
strange streets of the city without being duped, swindled, or infected
by moral contagion. It was precisely in this reversed sense that misery
was revealed and alleviated.

So the mysteries of the city were unveiled only to reveal the more
formidable vestiture of social perception layered in the textured folds
of language and attitude. The language of condemnation, for example,
summarized an ideology toward the subculture of poverty which effectively denied and distorted its experience by keeping realism at bay,
accentuating distance, and exerting the force of domination. Archaic
and pejorative expressions served to tag the poor with the abstract
and easily recognizable conventions of melodramatic stylization. Tenement conditions were "pictures of wretchedness," Owney Geoghe-

gan's sportsman's bar on the Bowery became a "mundane Hades" filled with the "hissing fumes of villainous whiskey," lodging houses were frequented by "fetid odors" and "pestiferous smells," and New York nightlife in general laid out its "ventholes to perdition."[15] Writers exploring the depths were often given to fustian prose which was sufficiently generalized to avoid specific description and the colloquial. If description was resorted to, it was usually suffused with emotionally laden nouns and modifiers to cement the author's transgression of the taboo and his resultant contact with pollution and filth. In such cases, the relentless cadence of condemnation reiterated the obloquy in which the offensive encounter was met with and its reflection in the descriptive content. One writer's rendition of his visit to the "Blind Men's Hotel," in Blind Men's Alley in the vicinity of the Bowery, works by a poetics of the bestial to reestablish the realm of the taboo, a realm that he has just violated. Inside the hotel, he presents to the reader one of its degraded wonders:

> A frightful, sightless, withered, paralytic old man, who crouched in his seat like one of the Acquarium [*sic*] chimpanzees in its straw, wrapped from neck to heels in a filth-encrusted army over-coat, gibbering and grimacing, lapping his pendulous, alcohol-swollen lip, with his loose tongue. His face and his palsied hands were the only things about him that moved. And it seemed a fortunate thing for humanity that they were all of him that was left alive.[16]

Incidentally, the publisher's preface to the volume in which this passage appears assures the reader beforehand that "there has been no attempt at coloring or sensational writing, and, while the truth has been told, it has been presented in a chaste but vivid manner."[17]

The act of condemnation tended to commingle person and setting into one depraved mass of destitution. As a tactic of mystification, it either blamed character outright or indirectly through a denunciation of environment. True to the tenets of an individualized interpretation of poverty, the act turned a description of an impoverished setting into the epiphenomenon of intemperance and indolence; thus character was censured rather than the dynamic social forces of industrialization and urbanization. The mystifying finger of condemnation always landed on the obvious and delimited sphere of the personal. It was unable to dislodge itself and circle the much larger perimeter of social responsibility; that elusive sphere was still beyond the planets.

This moral-religious view of poverty, brought home by the rhetoric of condemnation, was the natural frame of reference for evangelical missionaries throughout the city who, by profession, trafficked in salvation and regeneration. The gospel temperance workers at the Bowery Mission and Young Men's Home who ministered to the poor and homeless indeed believed them to be victims, but of "appetite, passion and crime" rather than social or economic constraints.[18] In this sense, victim is equivalent to a culprit gone wayward along some slippery path. Retrieval, religious reform, and rehabilitation were basic to the program conducted by the Bowery Mission. Services, including song, prayer, sermon, and testimonials, were practiced every evening of the week. In order for a homeless man to seek help and shelter inside the mission, he was obliged to attend these services and go through the motions. If ardent for nothing short of conversion and redemption, he would not only accept the daily ritual but, more significantly, the imposed definitions of his very condition. In other words, reform was premised upon the assimilation of deceptive cultural standards and traditional modes of perception regarding the sinful causes of poverty or homelessness. As the following testimonial reveals, the outsider's moralistic frame of reference was internalized by a former insider: "On the 9th of September I came to the Mission, a miserable homeless wretch, believing that there was no hope on earth for me, having been cast out from home, wife, friends, society, through the influence of strong drink. But I was met by kind and sympathetic friends who spoke encouraging words to me, and told me that there was still hope for me."[19] In extending the middle-class notion of condemnation without the social reckoning, this man testifies that he has made the perceptual leap from the derelict streets of subculture into the cradle of culture.

The language and attitude of social condemnation were complemented, especially in religious discourses and tracts, by the tone of righteous indignation and a conjectural posture toward the problem of poverty. Though these supplementary styles differed from the manner of strident damnation, they worked toward the same effects and operated under shared assumptions. As a distinct mode of apprehension, the conjectural pose, soon to be examined, misrepresented the announcement of genuine encounter proclaimed by its practitioners. Conjecture, that affecting response to the spectacle of urban poverty, can be viewed as a pose for dealing with the anxiety of the unknown by fleeing into the familiar oratorical effusions of the hypothetical. The pose was frequently exercised as a fervent stay against a more penetrating style of objective observation and analysis. By drawing the grand inference and often framing it into a series of questions which accommodated the external experience of poverty to the internal template of Christian culture, the reliance upon conjecture precluded any semblance of meaningful encounter between culture and subculture. The hidden purpose of conjecture (as we shall soon see with Talmage) was to function as a pose in order to deflect social involvement and thus reinforce the polarization of affluence and poverty in urban society.

The conjectural pose often accompanied the strategy of righteous justice which Rev. Fred Bell, the "singing preacher," deemed "the grandest invention ever discovered."[20] Though Rev. Bell did not directly explain either strategy or phrase, perhaps we might probe the unexplicated politics implicit in such a useful and widely practiced strategy through his descriptive elaboration. "New York," Rev. Bell asserts, "is rotted by certain sorts of human vermin that infest its dark places, who live by preying on human prosperity, womanly virtue, and human souls." Having begun his spiel on the poor classes of New York, Rev. Bell continues his diatribe by adding the omniscient and divine arbiter of righteous justice which gives the language of condemnation a blessed aura of vindication. Without skipping a beat, the reverend makes an abrupt transition:

> Oh, the dark, shameful things that night frowns sadly upon, and the dark places of the day hide from human eyes. Oh, the sad muffled groans smothered by rough hands, and dark noisome dens under the sidewalks; in the back cellars; up the noisome stenchful alleyways. Oh, the shameful injustice, the robbery, violence and crime, perpetrated by brutal fiendish beings in the form of men; the number of which is lost to man, and which makes one feel relieved when he knows there is an "Eye" that sees, and a rectoral justice that marks; and, so exact is the record, that groan for groan, and shame for shame shall be the tare.[21]

The strategy of righteous justice was surely grandiose in scope and style, but as invention it implemented a method of apprehension marked by evasion and the seeming resolution of moral ambiguity. When fused with sentiment and pity regarding the plight of the poor, the strategy gave the appearance of social encounter—that of concerned ministers forsaking the pulpit for the streets in an attempt to grapple with the devilish consequences of industrial capitalism. But in reality these very proponents of social responsibility and justice were rescued from the self-implicating entanglements of such action by the redemptive adoption of a moral screen. Hence they took to the streets in fulfillment of an ethical obligation but returned to the pulpit no more enlightened as to the social, economic, or political causes of the phe- nomenon they had cautiously brushed against. In fact, they returned to their churches steeped even further in the precepts of their Christian theology: the location of social evil in character and a plea for charitable impulses aimed at salvation and regeneration of the poor. Conjecture, as we shall see, and righteous indignation thus constituted the politics of avoidance, the arousal of a sense of pitiful injustice extravagantly portrayed in sentimentalized treatments of the poor combined with the inevitable flight from social incrimination. This elusive strategy not only preordained the quest but justified the retreat into moral certainty as well.

The Reverend T. DeWitt Talmage, the renowned pastor of the Brooklyn Tabernacle Church, [22] exemplified this devious methodology for explaining the problematic province of poverty. His revelations are inscribed in his series of discourses entitled *The Masque Torn Off*. His program for tenement reform amounted to a lack of confrontation with the historical process that had contributed to the very existence of such conditions. Given to denial of social forces and motivated by the idea of division, the logical though caricatured extension of the principle of segregation, he advocated the destruction of tenements and the disorganization of their subculture. With the setting eradicated, its former inhabitants could then be shipped out to a preindustrial setting of colonized farms which would satisfy the need for productive work and domestic felicity. Only under such an illusive remedy—a beneficent scapegoat theory—could the city be purified of its undesirable qualities and harmony restored.

In his excursion into the scenes of urban poverty, Talmage conjoined cursory observation with haphazard conjecture. Aroused by a specimen on the streets, he responds:

> Hark! What is that heavy thud on the wet pavement? Why, that is a drunkard who has fallen, his head striking against the street— striking very hard. The police try to lift him up. Ring the bell for the city ambulance. No. Only an outcast, only a tatterdemalion— a heap of sores and rags. But look again. Perhaps he has some marks of manhood on his face; perhaps he may have been made in the image of God; perhaps he has a soul which will live after the dripping heavens of this dismal night have been rolled together as a scroll; perhaps he may have been died for, by a king; perhaps he

may yet be a conqueror charioted in the splendors of heavenly welcome. But we must pass on. We cross the street, and, the rain beating in his face, lies a man entirely unconscious. I wonder where he came from. I wonder if any one is waiting for him. I wonder if he was ever rocked in a Christian cradle. I wonder if that gashed and bloated forehead was ever kissed by a fond mother's lips. I wonder if he is stranded for eternity. But we cannot stop.[23]

Talmage and his associates truly "cannot stop" and ponder too deeply over these witnessed scenes or lend a helping hand, for there is only time for self-preoccupied guesswork. After the eternal litany of the unknown has been spent, a tentative escape into the sealed hypothetical refuge of Christian possibility and wonderment, Talmage "must pass on." He possesses no other analytical or critical equipment in which to meet and evaluate the events other than the all-encompassing framework of romantic affectivity and the *reductio ad absurdum* of Christian apologetics. If he had stalled in that silent moment between the incantation and the abandonment, Talmage might have faced a specter even more dreadful—that perceptual alternative of realistic appraisal. After the moment, he must pass on.

When the conjectural pose had served its purpose, Talmage reverted to the standard fare of righteous indignation to evoke the tandem emotions of the unworthy and the just. It is the army of homeless children which elevates the pitch of his sentimental piety: "Oh! what a pale, coughing, hunger-bitten, sin-cursed, opthalmic throng—the tigers, the adders, the scorpions ready to bite and sting society, which they take to be their natural enemy." And again, in response to the sight of poor newsboys huddled under a stairway, but this time with a concluding plea for salvation to ward off the regiments of civil disruption:

Look at them! Now for a little while they are unconscious of all their pains and aches, and of the storm and darkness, once in a while struggling in their dreams as though some one were trying to take the papers away from them. Standing there I wondered if it would be right to wish that they might never wake up. God pity them! There are other regiments in this reserve corps—regiments of rag-pickers, regiments of match-sellers, regiments of juvenile vagrants. Oh! if these lads are not saved, what is to become of our cities?[24]

In light of all these marching regiments, one wonders whether or not Talmage would have truly preferred a nocturnal paradise for these legions of homeless youth. In a typical line of eloquent defense, Talmage alters a sense of pity with the preservation of the morally right and incumbent office of culture.

In a general sense, and for all advocates of this stylized attitude, the cultural fortification against the surge of subculture was provided by the foundation of righteousness, the established standards of the just and right, and the mortar of indignation, the requisite anger with which the socially unworthy were regarded. Under the guise of sentimentalism and pity, emotionalism became the battle cry and sorrowful grief the sympathetic reparation. Taken in its entirety, the strategy outlined an ideological slaughter which obliterated social realities, amputated reason and realism, reclaimed social distance, and forced the condescending peace of judgment severed from social responsibility and action. Thus it was that culture existed in support of society.

This collusion between culture and society in their unqualified acceptance of industrial capitalism was expressed by the very nature of the encounter which brought culture and subculture together. For writers of the sensationalistic genre, their encounter with the "other half" was, as a rule, mediated by the legal authority of police officials. Policemen or detectives became the public agents who introduced subculture to culture. In doing so, these agents offered protection and guidance to eager though estranged explorers and lent a degree of influence that opened doors otherwise closed to them. The role of the police as go-betweens necessarily determined the nature of discovery and prevented an unmediated personal experience between the realm of culture and the forbidden terrain of subculture.

The descent into the unknown was thus mollified by the formidable presence of the police lantern, which scouted out and illuminated the scenes of investigation. As a practical tool, particularly in an age of gas lighting, the police lantern led a path of sight into the prevalent shadows which enveloped the urban streets at night. Yet aside from this pragmatic feature, it symbolically directed one's encounter by the entrenched association of the bull's-eye with crime and detection. "Carefully keeping in the little track of light cut into the darkness by the lantern, I followed,"[25] recounts one writer in his tour of Gotham Court, a tour defined by submission and allegiance to the leadership of social authority. In this way, the police lantern motif implicitly certified that one's experience with urban poverty was legitimately rendered.

As a motif of discovery, the police lantern tour often combined its act of legal mediation with the preestablished condition of social distance and a pervading sense of mystery. Representatives of *Frank Leslie's Illustrated Newspaper* speak to this admixture in their quest for material, which resulted in the series of articles, "Our Homeless Poor," or "How the Other Half of the World Lives."[26] Near Baxter Street, just west of the Bowery thoroughfare, the party found themselves in "a region that many of us, bred and born in New York, had never seen before": "Here Mr. George Van Buskirk, a detective, took charge of our party, and two extra policemen walked within sight—a proceeding that was not calculated to give us a hilarious sense of the neighborhood we were entering. Never within our remembrance have we seen so many sharp angles and narrow, almost interminable lanes. . . . Into one of these we plunged, double file, lighted dimly forward by the policeman's lantern."[27] The logical progression is from distance, with its accompanying emotions of fear, peril, and danger, to protective mediation, which mitigates the precipitous plunge into the mysterious. Here the region of mystery is given concrete form as the labyrinthine image of urban poverty is internalized in city space. The party follows its winding course until it ends up near Five Points, in the "dreary enclosure" of Donovan's Lane, the *axis mundi* of their involuted sojourn. The eerie, chiaroscuro effect of the police lantern highlights the momentary encounter, which amounts to nothing more than a visual tone of social contrasts: the lantern threw out "lurid gleams on the black and broken walls each side. Now and then a dark figure met us, and pressed itself against the wall as we passed by, then disappeared like a shadow in the darkness."[28]

Later, in the party's visits to cellars and lodging houses, the police lantern cuts a bit more light into the condition of the homeless. But, on the whole, the illuminated scenes are still steeped in the surrounding shadows, which threaten to extinguish the portraiture of lighted forms. In a typical visit, the officer enters as if the keeper of poverty and misery making his nightly rounds. Holding up the lantern, he discloses the scene and singlehandedly brings the life composed within it into being. This gesture marks an instantaneous transition from darkness to light, absence to presence, and permits a detailed description of the interior setting and its inhabitants. But the disclosures are fleeting, much like the apparition of that figure pressed briefly against the wall who slips back into the void from whence it emanated. The police lantern is unable to fix on the specimens of poverty and hold them under the examining light. Instead, it offers temporary and superficial flashes as it swings in random directions through the night's panorama of suffering, illuminating now a ragged face, now a crowd huddled in massy folds, now the maddened stare of a man being taken by surprise, and so on. The police lantern casts an ephemeral lighting of the context which fades as soon as the transient party leaves for another errant visitation. Obscurity is built into the nature of this hit-and-run technique, which substitutes a faint glow for a brilliantly sustained illumination of the poor and homeless. Ultimately, the apprehension of poverty as both fact and concept is obviated by its sure drift into darkness, into the perpetuated mystery of absence.

More than a motif, the police lantern also served as a trope which expressed this method of inquiry and style of social perception. As trope, the police lantern was at once the vehicle for perception as well as its vanishing embodiment. This procedure of lighting and shading the scenes of poverty, disclosing and dissolving, incarnated an attitude of mystification which became a paradigm for followers of the sensationalistic genre. Together, as motif and trope, the police lantern provided a practical means of entry into the labyrinth of subculture along with an effortless way out by virtue of its interpretive legerdemain. In its instrumental and symbolic value, the police lantern reiterated the interworkings of culture and society in the retrenchment of subcultural encounter and explication.

In *The Masque Torn Off*, Talmage exploited the trope of the police lantern to further illustrate the major symbolic contrasts in the social system. By translating them into the melodramatic display of the magic lanterns of police and home, a sort of primitive slide show verbally rendered, Talmage opposed a principle of moral order to that of social disorder. The elevated framework for these views of culture and subculture was none other than the conventional lesson of virtue paired with vice, a sense of hallowed structure set against the intrusion of antistructure. The magic lantern of the home was shown brightly on affluent middle-class culture as manifested in the insulated life of the family. Unity, joy, and domestic bliss were held in focus as the "family gathered around the argand burner. Father, feet on ottoman, mother sewing a picturesque pattern."[29] The children, romping and frolicking, offered their night prayers to protective guardian angels. The whole picture of purity and social respectability was consecrated from above and identified with a providential cosmos which insured harmony and safe passage. In the magic lantern of the police, the sacred sphere of the home was replaced by the profane and desecrated life of the streets, where groups of outcasts roam, "intoxicated and wrangling, cursing God, cursing each other." Expelled from a morally sanctioned structure, subculture resides on the externalized ground of the street or in its anarchic extension into the tenement. Here the "dark, bat-like wings" of vulnerability supplant those of angels "that spread wings of canopy over the trundle-bed." Harshness, struggle, and the disorganization of family life are the rule among the tenement dwellers: "Children fleeing from the missile flung by a father's hand. Fragments of a chair propped against the wall. Fragments of a pitcher standing on the mantle. A pile of refuse food brought in from some kitchen, torn by the human swine plunging in the trough."[30] The last slide cements the notion of disaffiliation and anonymity in life as well as death as a poor waif is laid to rest in Potter's Field.

The moral lesson is thus brought home by a repeated alternation of these studied contrasts, and, like the effect of Buel's "wholesome revelation," culture is ennobled in the end. In accordance with traditional melodramatic structure, the magic lantern of the police—the social ills of poverty—is thrust into the foreground in an act of apprehensive trespass. But the magic lantern of the home—the force of social innocence and Christian order—subdues this villainous positioning and manages to restore itself and affirm its cherished world view. A just culture prevails over an unjust subculture, a heroic pattern written into the very chapter title in which the oppositions between affluence and poverty appear. The title, "Under the Police Lantern," reflects less on those subjects under the beam of investigation than on the motives of the investigators themselves. The heading betrays the wedlock between legal and Christian authority and clearly suggests the cherubic wingspan under which Talmage was guided.

Talmage's reliance on melodramatic display to confirm the ideals and values of culture is a telling device, for it invokes the prevailing literary form of the age. As social allegory, melodrama had formalized mystification into an inherent principle of coherent structure and perception. The form not only summarized the thematic armature—denial, distance, and domination—of sensationalism's strategies (condemnation, righteous indignation, and the police lantern motif), but it also contained the armature as an integral aspect to its broader moral vision and ideological purpose. Preoccupied as it was with the middle-class verities of romantic love, feminine purity, the sanctity of motherhood, male dominance, and the reputable domains of home and society, melodrama signified an idealized representation of culture. This representation etherealized the encroaching realities of social conflict

and division by its enveloping "aura of unreality," thus steeping melodrama in "an existence within a world of its own upon which 'real life'
touched mainly through established channels."[31] The allegorical quality of melodrama villified the invasive nature of social realities not
outright, in terms which would claim validity to the impact of condition
and environment, but obliquely through their personification in villainy.
Hence, social reality conformed to the insular world of melodrama by
its translation into character and its polarization into vice confronting
and testing virtue but inevitably being vanquished under the latter's
putatively divine aura. In this fashion, the category of melodrama,
underwritten by the spokesmen of culture, preserved an individualized interpretation of broader social concerns and social problems.
By turning social event into moral spectacle, the melodrama, with its
penchant for happy endings, succeeded in reinstalling the ideal providential partnership of class and Christian faith.

Two Bowery melodramas illustrate these general principles. *On the
Bowery*, a grand scenic melodrama equipped with specialties, first
appeared at the Fourteenth Street Theatre on September 10, 1894.
The melodrama, an adaptation of R. N. Stephen's original play by
Thomas H. Davis and William T. Keogh, was altered to feature Steve
Brodie's celebrated status as saloon keeper and infamous bridge
jumper. The spectacular quality of the melodrama was thus enhanced
by the exhibition of Brodie's mannerisms and heroics. In Act II Brodie,
the "king of the Bowery," appears both outside and inside his saloon
going about the usual business with his motley assemblage of Bowery
clientele. Inside his saloon, Brodie bursts into song with a rendition of
"My Pearl, the Bowery Girl," an idealized depiction of Bowery femininity. In Act III, he takes the awaited dive from the Brooklyn Bridge,
reenacting his own inimitable feat and at the same time rescuing the
proverbial young woman betrayed and doomed by her villainous lover
in the unfolding of the plot. Brodie returns in Act IV just in time to
save the heroine once again from a burning house set aflame by the
persistent villain. The murderous plot is thus foiled and in the final act
the culprit apprehended. In the end, the love affair of two innocent
sufferers, almost destroyed by the machinations of the villain, is reinstated. The happy ending is both confirmed and manifested in Brodie's
final lines of the play: "Mr. Drayton, at last that man is pinched, and
we'll have a wedding to wind up the night we started on the Bowery."[32]

Just as *On the Bowery* belies its title by having little to do with the
actual conditions of Bowery existence, such was the case with Theo-

dore Kremer's melodrama, *The Bowery after Dark*, produced at the Star Theatre on December 25, 1898.[33] Kremer's play emphasized the themes of male dominance and Christian faith and conversion. The final scene discloses a "heathen" Oriental in an act of supplication as he kisses the cross before dying. In promoting its major themes, the play submerges the gallery of Bowery types beneath the thrust of upper-class wealth, romantic conflict, and adventure. Though the "authentic" Bowery characters are protective and helpful agents for the cause of righteousness, they are peripheral to the play's dramatic tension. Their representation in the action mimetically retains the structurally inferior position they fulfill in the broader social structure. Placed in insignificant and spectator roles, their marginal status highlights the significant patterns of interaction among the superior agents of social prestige. At best, the Bowery characters stereotypically embellish the subcultural scene, but they are impotent as actors on the cultural stage of dramatic action. Except for Brodie, this ancillary role for Bowery characters applies as well for *On the Bowery*.

If the transformation of social event into moral spectacle ensured the ideal, it also asserted the reclamation of social mystery and the negation of a ruptured social system. In its formal thrust the melo-drama embodied the ideology of mystification and proved itself an allegory that preferred to be read as a moral fable rather than a social parable. As an ordered metaphoric expression of the sensationalistic genre, the melodrama incorporated its attitudes, strategies, and con-clusions; it was the purple mantle which cloaked the genre's already encumbered vestiture of social perception, a mantle which enshrined the dogma of mystification.

The urban picturesque school of writers was more "realistic" in its treatment of poverty than the sensationalistic genre. This was pri-marily a result of the school's focus; that is, a study of the picturesque qualities of urban poverty rather than the reassertion of its mysterious presence. A preoccupation with the picturesque had the advantage of putting writers in the first level of encounter with poverty, an encoun-ter that naturally dwelt upon the sensuous details of person and place. The highly stylistic nature of the quest necessarily forced a heightened sense of description regarding the appearance of urban poverty in contrast to the vague generalizations and uninformative abstractions characteristic of the sensationalistic genre. This concern with the technique of description encouraged a representation that functioned socially to acknowledge the existence of the lower classes within their urban enclaves. Though this proved a distinct progression in the social perception of poverty, the mere observation and acceptance of condition did not precipitate a process of discovery that would extend and deepen the further levels of encounter. Limited by such an adamant allegiance to its florid focus, the urban picturesque school could not get beyond the introductory formalities of its newly acquired relationship. Thus it remained in a perpetual state of strained acquaintanceship with the conditions of urban poverty.

As a wing of the much broader local color movement, the urban picturesque approach to "low life" shared much of the movement's interest in the relationship between writer and regional context and its emphasis on cultural diversity and the richness of setting. During the 1890s, the urban picturesque wing closed in on its own confined region, applying the notion of verisimilitude in capturing the ambience and dialect of poor immigrant groups residing in the Bowery vicinity, urban toughs, beggars, and social institutions. As with the local color movement in general, the urban picturesque existed and became, in fact, transfixed on the continuum between the moralistic reductions of the sensationalistic genre and the more fully developed secular inquiry embodied in the realism of Riis and Howells. Both the local color movement and the urban picturesque explored commonplace themes as particularized in community life, observing and detailing the interaction between event, character, and unique setting. Yet the prevailing interest in "color" or "picturesqueness" among many writers (perhaps branded by Bret Harte's sentimentalized treatments, which actually miscolored his subject matter) led to the exploitation of milieus for their exotic attributes.[34] This finely selective handling of environment suggested its inertia as an overall shaping factor for the development of community and society. As such, the movement became an integral aspect of what Larzer Ziff refers to as "the business of beauty; the business of idealizing daily activities to make the American scene one with the court of Arthur and the Palestine of Jesus."[35] The local color movement and its urban wing were thus more truly defined by their "surface realism": "Generally the term local color has denominated a surface realism delighting in oddity, whimsicality, idiosyncrasy, and in those stubborn, inbred character traits which lend themselves to comic treatment or caricature. . . . The chief limitation of local color, in practice if not as a genre, is its frequent unwillingness to front some of the unpleasant facts of life."[36]

Substituting flirtation for confrontation, the local color and urban picturesque styles tended, by design, to be too heavily atmospheric so that the narrative framework became virtually "a skeleton upon which to festoon scenic effects."[37] The urban picturesque school in particular retained a capricious attitude toward its topical interest in poverty among immigrant groups and the homeless. Its writers not only dallied but wallowed in the descriptive intoxicants of sights, sounds, smells, tastes, and the general feel of "the other half." This fundamental attitude precluded a sober, more encompassing and incisive outlook concerning the parameters of urban poverty and the critical relationship between culture and subculture. The literary products which ensued from such a fanciful activity were none other than, as Stephen Crane aptly put it, "pink valentines."[38]

The typical representational form of the urban picturesque was the brief sketch or vignette. Essentially ornamental and decorative, the form was infused with a narrative style marked by subtlety and refinement and thus likened, by Brander Matthews, to "an urban calendar of times and seasons."[39] In the hands of such writers as H. C. Bunner, Brander Matthews, Richard Harding Davis, and Julian Ralph, all members of New York society and representatives of the genteel tradition, the form of the urban picturesque was given a unifying strategy. Its aesthetic was, of course, a concern with the quaint outlines and the soft focus of the picturesque. The point of view, primarily personal and subjective, with priority given to narration, suggested an epistemology which stressed momentary perception and impressionistic observation. And, well adapted to the flourishing commercial periodical market of the day, with mass market outlets such as *McClure's* and *Scribner's Monthly*, the form was not without its equally significant economic considerations.[40]

Bunner, editor of the humorous magazine *Puck* from 1877 to 1896, provides a classic example of how one's association with a periodical specializing in brevity and the anecdotal tale can influence one's style accordingly, for Bunner transferred these literary strengths to his treatment of the Bowery. Appropriate to the genre he worked in, Bunner's fascination with the area was piqued at a young age by some lithographic prints he had seen which portrayed an early Bowery. These pictures were supplemented by tales of the Bowery's modern development, which fed Bunner's youthful imagination with the grandeur of Mose, the Bowery Boys, and the stage of the Bowery Theater. Thus for Bunner, the Bowery had become "one long avenue of romance, mystery, and thrilling adventure."[41]

Though drawn to the Babylon of nationalities which comprised the Bowery vicinity (Polish Jews, Hungarians, Chinese, Bohemians, Russians, and Irish), Bunner, an "ardent collector of slums,"[42] found the Italian quarter to be the most interesting and picturesque of all. His office overlooked the main stem of the Italian slum, Mulberry Street, and it was here that Bunner developed his "fellow-feeling of vulgarity with the mob."[43] He was impressed by the turbulent swirl of crowds, vendors, objects, festivals, processions, and, above all, the heady "pure arsenical tones" of reds, greens, and yellows in the apparel and foodstuffs: "bright, cheerful colors . . . that you could warm your hands on."[44] For Bunner, the overall impression of the Italian quarter was "festal," the happy home of "friendly poverty": "The stranger who enters Mulberry Bend and sees the dress-goods and the candies is sure to think that the place has been decorated to receive him."[45] Although effective in rendering a blithe sense of place, Bunner's treatment of Mulberry Bend and the Bowery in general remained touristic in its surface quality of broad brush strokes and blotches of color. Moreover, it served to stimulate the delights of spectators in their own picturing of the scene so that knowledge of condition was supplanted by the sketchy and flattened visual appearances.

Matthews, also a critic, editor, essayist, and novelist, was an ardent admirer of Bunner and, in fact, the two of them collaborated in 1884 on a collection of short stories, *In Partnership*. They also collaborated in living arrangements, sharing the same apartment building on 17th Street and Stuyvesant Square, a dwelling that would later house William Dean Howells. Matthews inherited Bunner's attraction to the alluring low life of Mulberry Bend. In his vignette "In Search of Local Color,"[46] Matthews charts his journey to the spatial center of the Italian tenement district. The quest's physical point of origin begins at the broad intersection of Bowery and Rivington, where Matthews, in the guise of Rupert De Ruyter, a journalist with "the Kodak eye of a reporter,"[47] runs into John Suydam, a University Settlement worker in residence for the summer. Though familiar with the smart set, wealthy clubs, literary soirees, theater, journalistic adventures, and the masses-at-large, De Ruyter confesses to his guide that he knows nothing about the poor tenement dwellers. This motivating perspective of social distance is reinforced but at the same time justified by the use of Dutch names and the invocation of the truly native New Yorkers, whose patriarchal claim on city life is understood by virtue of their descent from the original claimants of Manhattan. To a representative of this privileged lineage, the current influx of immigrant groups can be considered as distinctly "other," worthy perhaps of investigation but not of equal ownership of the city. The use of Suydam, a fledgling social worker, provides the means of access into the subculture, a distinct movement from the mediation of police authority to that of humanitarian reformers.

Guide and novice set off, following the labyrinthine structure of the Italian quarter, moving from the broad expanse of the Bowery to narrower side streets, lanes, and alleyways. De Ruyter takes note of salons, Italian ices, fruit vendors, furniture wagons, and handcarts with "gayly colored calicoes":

> Everywhere . . . were noises and smells. The roar of the metropolis was here sharpened by the rattle of near machinery heard through open windows, and by the incessant clatter and shrill cries of the multitude in the street. . . . But over and beyond the noises and the smells and the bustling business of the throng, Rupert De Ruyter felt as though he were receiving an impression of life itself. It was as if he had caught a glimpse of the mighty movement of existence, incessant and inevitable. What he saw did not strike him as pitiful; it did not weigh him down with despondency. The spectacle before him was not beautiful; it was not even picturesque; but never for a moment, even, did it strike him as pathetic. Interesting it was, of a certainty—unfailingly interesting.[48]

In sum, the narrator tells us nothing; in trying to transcend the picturesque sensations, he arrives at a dumbfounded spectacle which is, at best, "unfailingly interesting." The reduction to "interest" becomes a device which deadens further interpretation and analysis while documenting that there is actually nothing beyond those impressionistic sights, sounds, and smells worthy of regard. If poverty is neither picturesque nor distressing, then it must be dismissed by a trifling touristic discount. As Rupert De Ruyter tells his guide, while pondering the sculpted faces and classical profiles of passersby, "I haven't found anything so Italian as this for years."[49]

De Ruyter and Suydam eventually reach their spatial center, a rear tenement building. Holding his breath to ward off the stench, De Ruyter glimpses a gang in the cellar playing cards and drinking the dregs of beer kegs. He then makes his way upstairs to view several overcrowded apartments. In one room he finds "Italian Pete," who "has an eye like a glass stiletto." After Suydam converses with Pete, the party leaves the tenement for the open air of the streets and their way out of the district. In passing a police station, they learn that "Italian Pete" is being hunted for the murder of his wife. After pointing the officers in the right direction, Suydam turns to De Ruyter and inquires as to whether he had seen anything interesting on their search: "'Oh yes,' is the answer. 'I've got lots of color; just what I wanted. And that Italian whose wife was *mort*—he's copy, I'm sure. Yes . . . that completes the picture. I can get a good *mot de la fin* now.'"[50]

That *"mot de la fin"* clinches the contrived nature of the vignette, which proved essentially picturesque after all. It not only rounds out the sketch but validates the ultimate search for color and copy, turning experience into a marketable product for the dailies. Without the final turn of events, the vignette would have floundered in the nondescript entity of mere interest. Instead, and through a reporter's good fortune, it was raised to the level of spectacle. The recovery insured De Ruyter's hold on the familiar stuff of copy and thus overshadowed the utter lack of transformation that distinguished his uneventful journey into the labyrinth. The rushed visit through the Italian quarter is diminished by the sensationalistic stroke of the end result, an affirmation of boundaries and stereotypes, a story which any contemporary reader of the press could not only recognize but relish.

Matthews's failure of perception into social process and discovery can also be evidenced in "The Vigil of McDowell Sutro,"[51] a vignette which approaches the problem of impending homelessness. Sutro, beset by hunger and the need for shelter, the two primal correlatives of homelessness, is forced to spend the night on a park bench in Union Square with its more seasoned habitués. The loneliness and deepening desolation of his vigil are set against the background of city life with its intense activity. Restaurants, saloons, variety shows, theaters, vehicular and pedestrian traffic, and the like surround Sutro but remain tauntingly inaccessible to him. The contrast is effective, as well as the stalled sense of time and restlessness which besiege our would-be victim. But dawn brings the vigil to a close and mystification to its rise as the new morning grants Sutro a reprieve in the form of an awaited letter with an enclosed check and promise for work. When viewed against the permanent and progressively deteriorating state of homelessness, Sutro's brief stay is an instance of content reflecting form, for the urban picturesque itself, as style and strategy, can only glimpse this undesirable life. Both writer and genre can go no farther and are thus spared a substantial or sustained point of entry into this social condition. At best, a vigil can be held as a gesture to the leap of perspective which resides at the farther shore of critical realism.

Perhaps the most picturesque sight of all in the city was not Mulberry Bend or Union Square but, rather, the peregrinations of Cortland Van Bibber, the uptown aristocrat attired with gloves, a gardenia in his coat, and a cigar that protruded from a finely discriminating mouth. A creation of the newspaperman, short story writer, and novelist Richard Harding Davis, Van Bibber was a thinly veiled replica of Davis himself in his socialite role as the ideal American male: chivalrous, attractive, adventurous, a respectable member of Society, and a keeper of its code of manners and noble conduct. Unfamiliar with the urban territory south of Washington Square, Van Bibber was far more at home in the refuge of his club and amidst the exclusive isolation of his class. The distance was essential to his sense of decency, privilege, and social proprietorship. Fortified by this select social space, Van Bibber would venture forth now and then into the throng of the streets below the dividing line of Washington Square North.

One of these sojourns is given in "The Hungry Man Was Fed," an account of the collision between Van Bibber and a street beggar. After giving the beggar, "a miserable-looking, dirty, and red-eyed object,"[52] a quarter to buy food, Van Bibber retraces his steps in order to find him again. In doing so he loses his bearings but, always composed and in control, Van Bibber discovers the recipient of his sport. Not recognizing Van Bibber, the beggar hits him up again for some money to buy food. Van Bibber takes the request literally and escorts the beggar into a cheap restaurant for a huge breakfast, much to the tramp's displeasure. Threats of exposing the imposter to the police humble the beggar into forcing down the multicourse meal. He is not only made to eat it against his will but to pay for it as well, including the tip. The poverty of the beggar is thus made sport of, and Van Bibber makes a mental note to recount the incident, as part of his vast repertoire of adventures, for the benefit of his fellow club members later in the day. The manipulative element of the prank and the act of submission would no doubt find an appreciative audience.

The cohesion of Van Bibber's upper class, apparent in "The Hungry Man Was Fed," is temporarily threatened in the allegorical tale "Eleanore Cuyler." Much to the disapproval of her New York Society associates, Miss Cuyler abandons her uptown apartment and exiles herself into the lower station of the College Settlement on Rivington Street, just east of the Bowery. Here she begins an apprenticeship of service to the poor slum dwellers, reading the Bible in German to half-blind and elderly women. Disappointed with the dull task assigned to her, Miss Cuyler goes about her duties somewhat uninspired and with the troubled sense that "the good she did . . . was in no way proportionate to that which her influence had wrought among people of her own class."[53] Behind the self-sacrificing motive is also the unspoken love for a Mr. Wainwright, who is abroad and, as Eleanore soon learns, engaged to an Englishwoman. In the wake of this knowledge, sacrifice turns to self-remorse and pity, which her work among the poor tends to justify.

Van Bibber enters the scene months later as an intrusive but nonetheless crucial agent for the rescue of Miss Cuyler and the more significant restoration of class unity. After an evening's lark at the People's Theater on the Bowery, Van Bibber takes a pleasant stroll down that "Thieves' Highway." Suddenly, "the hurrying figure of a girl of his own class who passed in front of him down Grand Street brought him, abruptly wondering, to a halt": "What a girl, well-born and well-dressed, could be doing at such an hour in such a neighborhood aroused his curiosity; but it was rather with a feeling of *noblesse oblige*, and a hope of being of use to one of his own people, that he crossed to the opposite side of the street and followed her."[54] After realizing her destination, the College Settlement, Van Bibber is momentarily relieved. But on noticing another man following Miss Cuyler and one with far less benevolent and honorable intentions, he is once again put on guard. The district near Orchard and Rivington streets, with its distinguishing signs of immigration and labor, becomes utterly foreign to Van Bibber. Yet character dominates the baffling environment as the resourceful Van Bibber recovers just in time to step out of the darkness and in between the other man and Miss Cuyler, who are now face to face on the sidewalk. As the man makes a move to touch Miss Cuyler, Van Bibber intercedes, striking him in the face with a stick: "He was very cool and determined about it, and punished him, in consequence, much more effectively than if his indignation had made him excited." A hidden group of East Side waterfront toughs, of which the follower was a member, descends on Van Bibber and what ensues can be seen as a visible and emblematic class struggle. As one tough exclaims to Van Bibber, "'You needn't think you can come down here and run things—you—'"[55] Describing each pugilistic feat of the ferocious battle for the benefit of the reader, Van Bibber succeeds in single-handedly trouncing the opposition. He thus validates the tough's complaint in extending his invincible domain.

Afraid of a scandal, Miss Cuyler asks Van Bibber not to mention the incident. But, driven by pubescent one-upmanship, Van Bibber tells all to his close friend Travers, who was to have been with him that evening, thus placing the joke on him for not having been "in it." The translation of event into story happens almost instantaneously and the news travels throughout the club and into Mr. Wainwright's unsuspecting ears. Wainwright, having recently returned from England, bolts for the College Settlement upon hearing the scandal. Eleanore, by now dissipated from her ministrations to the poor, whom she comes to view as "unrepentant and ungrateful," is ripe for rescue and recovery. Wainwright and Eleanore disclose their love for each other and take flight from the Bowery in his awaiting hansom. Their wedding concludes the story and rectifies the sense of class segregation which Miss Cuyler had breached. The internal conflict dissolves into harmony as the wedding carriage departs with a clear sense of direction. Van Bibber and Travers, ushers to the ceremony in a real and symbolic way, ponder the mended unity. As the carriage picks up momentum, Travers blandly comments: "'They don't think the wheels are going around, do they? They think it is just the earth revolving with them on top of it, and nobody else.'"[56]

Van Bibber's feeling of *noblesse oblige* toward one of his own class is vindicated in the end by Cuyler's marriage to Wainwright and by her consequent reentry into Society. She is once more a part of the chosen "they," proving, after all, that her utmost usefulness resides in an unstinting allegiance to wealth and privilege. Davis's message here is more than picturesque; it is basically thematic, a romantic fable which struggles earnestly to maintain the social distance between classes and the purity of upper-class culture. The reincorporation of class is granted by an attitude which fixes the alienation between classes. When not making sport of subculture, Davis is at pains to kick it off the exclusive urban map and so lighten the load of that revolving sphere. As there is no more room at the top for anyone else, Davis ejects the burden of social consciousness and propels the levity of an illusive social orbit.

Julian Ralph, also a journalist and short story writer, brings us back into that context of subculture which Davis had so thoroughly obliterated. As a New York *Sun* reporter on the scene for twenty years, Ralph's assignments frequently took him into the Bowery tenement districts to cover weddings, wakes, funerals, picnics, and social activities. The tales in his book, *People We Pass: Stories of Life among the Masses of New York City*, were actually witnessed by Ralph in his role as newspaperman. This formal association by Ralph with Bowery life naturalized Ralph to the context of subculture and lent his investigation more depth than those of other members of the urban picturesque genre. Ralph's characters, as opposed to Davis's Van Bibber and Miss

Cuyler, are not outsiders to the setting but, rather, intrinsic to it.
They are residents of the tenement communities who animate a more
familiar sense of place with their dialect, customs, political associations, social roles, and institutions.

If these insiders could have ambushed the narrative designs of their
literary executor, a significant contribution to the phenomenology of
poverty might have resulted. But, instead, Ralph remained the un-
affected and supreme formulator of his material. Although populating
his stories with insiders, Ralph offset his gains by a wholly externalized treatment which glided on the surface of tenement conditions
and social life. Most of his stories, such as "Love in the Big Barracks,"
"Dutch Kitty's White Slippers," "Petey Burke and His Pupil," "The
Line-Man's Wedding," and "Low Dutch and High," are infiltrated by
the traditionally idealized themes inherent in romantic sentiment. Subculture is thus represented in terms of dominant cultural values and
genteel perception, which convey a strategy of social control and
mystification. Under this strategy, the typical young girl becomes "an
ideal daughter of the tenements." She is "so inoculated with self-
respect that evil will pass her by." And the notion of poverty itself,
true to the urban picturesque creed, is presented only to be subse-
quently negated. Ralph assures us that poverty does not reside in
situational determinants but in individualized acts of misperception.
The tenement slum dwellers, in fact, "are not so poor as most of us
think. Many are not poor at all; many are poor only as they make
themselves so. . . . The rent of each flat is little; the cost of food is
less than most of us would believe possible, for these people only eat
to live."[57]

If not denied outright, poverty, with its marginal level of sub-
sistence, is accepted into the cultural framework by making it seem a
normal adjustment to those who freely choose its spare diet. The
social and economic deprivation of the impoverished is beyond the
scope of Ralph's "surface realism." Measuring the quality of tenement
life by biological survival, he obscures the real issues of human dignity,
worth, and purpose, which are all beyond the meager budget of the
poor. What life entails past the point of satiation is thus rendered
meaningless, for it does not exist. Yet, in accordance with this double
standard, the life of culture actually begins once the beef has been
digested. The double standard allowed Ralph to firmly situate himself
within the picturesque and sentimental traditions so that, despite the
potential of his material, he remained a venerable host at the banquet
of social innocence.

The urban picturesque genre is probably best defined by its glaring omissions concerning the submerged details of poverty. Unwilling to chart the life of the poor from the factory to the tenement, its exponents were unable to deal with the construct of poverty in terms of want and suffering. The alienation of labor and the distress of tenement existence were phenomena beyond the range of the genre's circumscribed discovery; an unfailing search for color and an obsession with the picturesque denied writers access to deeper layers of social process and perception. Even more involved thematic treatments tended toward mystification by serving established cultural precepts at the expense of subculture. The urban picturesque writers were unwilling and unable to confront the descriptive analogues of poverty, such as hunger, desensitization, hopelessness, dependency, and withdrawal. They could not hit on the antidote to their style and write, as did their contemporary J. W. Sullivan, regarding the degradation of a poor immigrant tailor, "Every day of his life he died; for every day brought its insults, its oppressions, its heart-quakings lest he be deprived of his miserable chance of getting bread, and each day made less a man of him and killed him by just that much."[58] In comparison to the urban picturesque genre, Sullivan's humanistic passage is truly an act of transcendence, effectively bypassing the stock stereotypical treatment of ethnic poverty. In deepening the level of encounter between culture and subculture and in letting the latter breathe, Sullivan surely gives renewed meaning to Ralph's adage that the poor "only eat to live."

The above passage is taken from one of Sullivan's sketches entitled "Not Yet: The Day-Dreams of Ivan Grigorovitch." Ivan's daydreams of socialistic, cooperative schemes centered round work and housing reflect the author's own political allegiance. Active as a socialist, Sullivan was sympathetic to the cause of immigrant labor and improved living conditions for the urban proletariat. "Not Yet" perhaps acknowledges Sullivan's own sense of forbearance, as Ivan's socialistic visions are delayed by his untimely death from fatigue and heart failure.

Though influenced by picturesque qualities, Sullivan was capable of surpassing their limitations. "Not Yet" acknowledges the dominant force of the factory and its menacing extension into the street and barracklike quarters of the working class. Ivan, a Russian immigrant, takes refuge from this distress and humiliation by "imagining the beauty that might be in a poor man's daily life instead of the misery that is." For Ivan, the factory, as representative of urban-industrialism, is the source of his discontent, while the daydreams are the mechanism for his escape. Yet the escape is taken as a utopian pathway into the future of humanity rather than a momentary wish to satisfy material or selfish needs. The cues for Ivan's daydreams are not only his immediate and dismal surroundings but the public account of the world at large: "Newspaper accounts of the acts of man in his present undeveloped nature—stories of war or famine, of petty crime or brutal deed— would by way of contrast bring to his mind's eye, and then to his paper, plans and pictures of what men might do in the better environment of the future."[59] Through Ivan, Sullivan expresses his interest in the condition of poverty and in the constructs of environment and socialist intervention. The numerous daydreams, whether of vending machines to dispense newspapers (thus freeing street vendors for higher pursuits), or cottage and garden communities uptown, or cooperative farms and factories, or the "boulevardization" of the avenue, all stress the alteration of physical, economic, and social environments. The essential structure of the dreams remains the construction of a harmonious and egalitarian social system characterized by a strong sense of solidarity. Before Ivan collapses and his dreams give way to the hard, concrete facts of the pavement, his vision of "golden times" reoccurs with people assembled at the dining table of a handsome central house in the midst of a cooperative farm/factory. The people are lifted from the former drudgery of their lives, "all glowing with kindliness, sympathy, sincerity, intelligence—each animated with the religion of humanity."[60] After his fall and death, Ivan's daydreams are sharply contrasted with the reality that is—the morgue, Potter's Field, and an anonymous burial.

In several of the other sketches in his *Tenement Tales of New York* ("Threw Himself Away," "Luigi Barbieri," and "A Young Desperado"), Sullivan repeats the focus on the struggles and sacrifices of the ethnic working classes. Though the socialist theme is missing and the style weaker in the aforementioned sketches (due to the interweaving of allegory and realism), Sullivan succeeds in exposing ethnic prejudices, class barriers, and the environment of poverty. "A Young Desperado," in fact, renders an exposé of urban poverty by a reversal of the Horatio Alger formula; moving from riches to rags, Raymond, a seven-year-old who has just moved with his wealthy family from Connecticut to New York City, becomes lost and homeless in the streets. Almost overnight, Raymond descends to the lowest class of the homeless—a poor street urchin. The device allows Sullivan to present a sweeping panorama of urban poverty and slum conditions while at the same time highlighting his environmental perspective; that is, the significance of situation over that of character. Raymond is so visibly transformed from his experience in poverty that even his father cannot readily identify him in the lodging house.

Though Sullivan corrects for those glaring omissions of the urban picturesque group, he does employ some of the stylistic qualities. His concern with the environment of poverty puts him in the company of Jacob Riis, but Sullivan's socialist program for amelioration, though vague, is at odds with Riis's underlying assumptions. And Sullivan's brand of Christian socialism is far more assertive than Howells's creed. To finalize this displacement of Sullivan, his literary style anticipates the proletarian fiction of the 1930s in terms of its reliance on allegory, exaggeration, polarization, and working-class struggle and sacrifice. Though critical in intent and execution, the level of realism attained (except for "Not Yet") lacks the qualities of dimension, depth, and complexity.[61] Withal, Sullivan exists as a sort of purposeful anomaly, removed from the grip of mystification, looking in the direction of Riis's and Howells's realism, gazing backward to Edward Bellamy's utopian visions, escaping into the future of socialist fiction, and bypassing the complexity of critical realism along the way. Sullivan is a writer who does not flow in one smooth direction. He is best understood as an effective antidote to the urban picturesque writers, though not necessarily a clearly defined transitional figure to Riis and Howells.

In the movement toward the midpoint on the continuum, realism in the representation of urban poverty marked a transitional phase between the obscurity of mystification and the clarity of critical realism. The kind of realism typified by Jacob Riis's reportage and William Dean Howells's critical essays and fictions sought out that middle ground between the two extremes. Although fundamentally bound to the traditional values and genial optimism of democratic individualism and to the middle-class verities of Victorian gentility, Riis and Howells also revealed, by the nature of their treatments, a more clearly objective and analytical approach to the problematics of social experience. Allied on the one hand to the tenets of metaphysical idealism (a religiomoral faith in teleology, human perfectibility, and divine progress), they were, on the other hand, drawn to the factual and worldly basis of scientific materialism (a rising attitude of skepticism, discriminating inquiry, and mechanistic determinism).[62] Caught in the midst of such an ambiguous allegiance, truly betwixt and between two eras, these agents of realism inherited the legacy of mystification but also served as unwitting midwives to the cultural mutation of critical realism. Both

Howells and Riis sought to resolve this ambiguity by a fusion of the older ideals of American society with its new, dramatically altered factors of social existence. Howells's struggle to champion the credo of realism in his essays and fictions attests to this synthetic effort, as does Riis's overriding concern with the environmental role of the tenement in his discussion of urban poverty. Ultimately, the nature of the ensuing synthesis in both cases, though promoting the advent of naturalism and progressive ideology, weighed heavily in favor of its birthright—those values descending from the Enlightenment and inherent in the development of genteel culture. In their transitional role, Riis and Howells thus document that, though ahead of their time, they were not beyond it.

As a police reporter for the New York *Tribune* during the 1880s, Riis utilized this official relationship with the newspaper to sanction his extensive investigations of Bowery slums. It was at the *Tribune* that Riis perfected his anecdotal slum vignette, a style defined by stereotypical depictions of immigrant groups, dramatic portrayals of tenement poverty, and brief pleas or proposals for reform. His office was located on Mulberry Street, right across from police headquarters. Whereas Bunner and Matthews breezed through this same locale in a carefree search for local color, Riis remained a firmly planted observer who underwent an apprenticeship here as police reporter. This apprenticeship to the press entailed covering everything that meant trouble raised to spectacle: murders, fires, suicides, robberies, and tales of poverty and woe. This relationship to context and subculture, though qualified by Riis's professional association with the *Tribune*, was far more involved than that experienced by the urban picturesque writers. More than an observer or reporter on the scene, Riis also functioned independently as an agent for nocturnal exploration, social documentation, and impassioned reform.

Riis's job as police reporter strengthened his level of encounter with urban poverty by providing the means for direct experience and self-discovery. Riis worked at night, and, though at times accompanied by police or Health Department officials, he more often than not made his rounds through the slum districts alone. Even off duty, Riis extended his experiential perambulations through the Lower East Side, undaunted by the hour or the publicized dangers of the vicinity: "My route from the office lay through the Fourth and the Sixth wards, the worst in the city, and for years I walked every morning between two and four o'clock the whole length of Mulberry Street, through the Bend and across the Five Points down to Fulton Ferry. There were cars on the Bowery, but I liked to walk, for so I saw the slum when off its guard."[63]

But even before his assignment with the *Tribune*, Riis had become familiar with the harsh life of city streets and country lanes through his own personal necessity and misadventures. After arriving in America in 1870, Riis spent several futile years of work and wandering, tramping and homelessness. Once penniless in New York City, he slept in a doorway on Chatham Square and in the Church Street Police Station Lodging House. For food during this travail, he received meat bones and rolls from a sympathetic French cook at Delmonico's. After weaving through a number of odd jobs in the Northeast (carpenter, coal miner, farm hand, railroad gandy dancer, lumberjack, salesman, peddler, and telegrapher), Riis finally landed, via luck and timing, a job as a reporter for the New York News Association. This brought a close to Riis's own sense of economic dislocation, a dislocation which testified to the turmoil of his era. From the News Association (at that time he was living in a Bowery boardinghouse), Riis went on to bigger and better things. He became the editor and later owner of the political organ, the South Brooklyn *News*, a reporter for the *Tribune*, a member, for a while, of the New York *Evening Sun*, then freelance reporter, author, and reformer.

Riis's success as a newspaperman, editor, and author can be attributed in part to his well-rounded education. But it is also a result of his knack for exploiting opportunity, for turning hard-earned positions into a case study for upward mobility. Riis became, in Theodore Roosevelt's words, a "ideal American citizen"[64] largely through a fervent embrace of those values which defined Americanism: diligence, assimilation, competitive struggle, love of God and country, and an exercise, as Frederick Jackson Turner once put it, of "that dominant individualism, working for good and for evil, and withal that buoyancy and exuberance which comes with freedom."[65] Riis's rising star was from the beginning hitched to the commonplace struggles of immigrant life. Yet despite his broad-based experience from the bottom up, Riis showed little empathy for those whose conditions he once shared: immigrant hardship, homelessness, economic insecurity, and the forced idleness of tramping. His faith in democratic individualism led him to expect from other ethnic and subcultural groups the same level of success that he had attained. Displacing reality with ideals, Riis had failed to see himself as an exception to those debilitating conditions from which he arose.

Riis's widely publicized book, *How the Other Half Lives*,[66] was a culmination of his investigations into tenement slum conditions during the 1880s. The title, though copyrighted by Riis around 1889, was a conception that extended beyond his own individual ownership; it had been brewing in the cultural ferment since the early 1870s and by 1890 had become a facile device for concocting the urban contrasts among social classes.[67] Though the title and its subject matter, urban poverty, were not entirely novel by the time of Riis's publication, his leanings toward factualism in description and analysis did serve as an original contribution to his approach. His documentary exposition of tenement conditions, ethnic enclaves, pauperism, poverty, and child and adult labor was reinforced by statistical information and photographic representation. In relying on written and pictorial evidence, Riis offered incriminating proof for the disturbing existence of urban poverty which justified his efforts at explication and reform.[68]

But throughout Riis did not let these interspersed factual accounts subvert the basis of his interpretive designs. Instead, the facts were deftly assimilated into Riis's own ideological position, a fixation on tenement conditions themselves as the singular cause of pauperism, begging, crime, tramping, distress, moral destabilization, intemperance, and a vengeful proletarian class. All the problematics of urban poverty inevitably found their root explanation in the elastic tenement: "And so it comes down to the tenement, the destroyer of individuality and character everywhere," Riis concluded.[69] In taking the shadow for the substance, Riis isolated tenement conditions and their consequences from the broader historical and socioeconomic processes to which they were inextricably connected. This suspension from process and context provided the key to Riis's own sense of mystification, a disregard of antecedents and an uncritical examination concerning the impact of industrial capitalism and urbanization.

Yet, paradoxically, Riis's condemnation of the tenement as the cause of urban poverty also attested to the strength of his position, for the focus on environmental factors led Riis away from the older, solely individualized interpretation of poverty and toward a more modern awareness of condition and situation as determinate variables. In his treatment of the Jewish Ghetto and tenement sweatshops, in which he outlines working conditions, low wages, meager budgets, and other economic features, Riis shows that, momentarily at least, he is on the verge of a new and more inclusive interpretation of poverty. His animus against "landlord despotism," "enormous rents," and "miserable wages" led others to further advance the cause of tenement and labor reform.[70] Though Riis could not go all the way, bound by his transitional role and ultimate commitment to private enterprise, he nonetheless paved the way for more progressive critiques regarding the impersonal factors of poverty and their placement within an encompassing social, economic, and political configuration.

As much as Riis proved a harbinger for progressivism, he also echoed the moralistic preconceptions of the past. His mystifying attitude toward tenement life was rendered by a merger of righteous indignation with a tour-guide motif. In combination, tone and motif constituted that degree of distance essential to middle-class perspective and encounter. But for Riis, the guided tour supplanted the extraneous police lantern as a mediation between culture and subculture. Its use, though keeping distance intact, modified the act of social perception by lending a more personalized approach to the representation of poverty. Riis's style was direct, sensual, and dramatic, a language of social access sufficiently inoffensive so as to benefit the vicarious experience of his readers. His tour, though externalized and spotty, offered a panoramic view of slum life, spanning in several pages the various locales of Cherry Street, Penitentiary Row, Gotham Court, Blind Man's Alley, and the Jewish Ghetto. This device permitted Riis to bring the whole context into rapid view; and if each episode was somewhat sketchy, the overall effect was that of a related entity unfolding before the reader. Riis filled in the gaps with anecdotal tissue, and his stroll was confident and casual, for he knew his way around the maze of back alleys, stable lanes, and hidden byways of the Bowery district.

In rediscovering that grand invention, righteous indignation, and in adapting the mediation of the guided tour, Riis chaperones our encounter with the tenement. Surrounded on all sides of his controlled descent by the vista of tenement blocks, Riis announces:

> Enough of them everywhere. Suppose we look into one? No—
> Cherry Street. Be a little careful, please! The hall is dark and you
> might stumble over the children pitching pennies back there. Not
> that it would hurt them; kicks and cuffs are their daily diet. They
> have little else. Here where the hall turns and dives into utter
> darkness is a step, and another, another. A flight of stairs. You
> can feel your way, if you cannot see it. Close? Yes! What would
> you have? All the fresh air that ever enters these stairs comes
> from the hall-door that is forever slamming, and from the windows of dark bedrooms. . . . That was a woman filling her pail by
> the hydrant you just bumped against. . . . Hear the pump squeak!

It is the lullaby of tenement house babes. . . . Here is a door. Listen! That short hacking cough, that tiny, helpless wail—what do they mean? . . . Oh! a sadly familiar story—before the day is at an end. The child is dying with measles. With half a chance it might have lived; but it had none. That dark bedroom killed it. . . . We grope our way up the stairs and down from floor to floor, listening to the sounds behind the closed doors—some of quarrelling, some of coarse songs, more of profanity. . . . Come over here. Step carefully over this baby—it is a baby, spite of its rags and dirt—under these iron bridges called fire escapes, but loaded down, despite the incessant watchfulness of the firemen, with broken household goods, with wash-tubs and barrels, over which no man could climb from a fire. This gap between dingy brickwalls is the yard. That strip of smoke-colored sky up there is the heaven of these people.[71]

The tenement conditions are thus known through one who has been there. The details arise or appear from Riis's own experience and obtrusive retelling of it. As guide, Riis's purpose was to draw readers into the unexamined interior of tenement life and bring them into contact with the sensual and moral abominations of the tour. The nature of this travelogue, dotted with declamations such as "Listen!," strives to arouse the senses and conscience of visitors as they stumble across the "other"—mothers, fathers, and children, real specimens of the tenement. Riis reduces the threatening element by the round-trip ticket to and from the tenement and by his ever-present moral screen. His mystifying attitude is also conveyed through his ideology of suspension and containment. Enclosed by the tenement, readers walk amidst the very walls of urban poverty rather than through its manifestation. Recall that, for Riis, the infant suffering from measles is killed by the dark bedroom rather than the larger and more pregnant forces of social injustice and class victimization. Riis can thus righteously hold the tenement accountable for poverty, in this case infant mortality, by a disposal of inductive reasoning and an adherence to the language of the concrete. Freed from such potentially self-incriminating logic, both Riis and his readers can remain on safe ground, even within the tenement, for the nature of the tour condemns condition, and to a certain extent subculture, while exonerating middle-class culture. Steeped in the myopia of detailed specificity, Riis can well afford to get his ire up and to let his Christian conscience expand.

Riis's use of a language of the concrete to conceal social process extends to the visual medium as well. His flash photos, mostly taken during the 1880s, are impressive documents whose suasive powers reinforce the moral and ideological position of his written text in *How the Other Half Lives*. In terms of social utility, Riis's photographs satisfied his compulsion to make the reader bear witness to the Dickensian quality of urban poverty in America. As an integral complement to his tour-guide narration, the photos brought the reader into visual relationship with scrubwomen, homeless lodgers, tenement districts, yards and alleyways, "street Arabs," tramps, newsboys, black-and-tan saloons, growler gangs, criminals, sweatshops, Potter's Field trenches, and the like. Though Riis pioneered with the camera for its social utility, the results appear to us now as distinctly artistic, thus fusing the social with the aesthetic.

The fusion of aesthetic and social qualities, however, lent stylistic unity and ideological coherence to Riis's overall strategy of containment, which featured the tenement, its inhabitants, and immediate surroundings as the *fons et origo* of urban poverty. The powerful and dramatized photographs which appear in the text bring us into contact not only with slum conditions but also with another significant aspect of Riis's social utility—his vision of mystification. In photographs such as *Gotham Court, Blindman's Alley, Bandit's Roost, Mullen's Alley, Bottle Alley*, and *Bone Alley as It Was*, Riis further concretizes his condemnation of environmental conditions through his narrow yet extremely focused perspective. All of the above photos, as their designations attest, show highly restricted and confined zones within the very core of tenement slum districts. *Mullen's Alley* in particular is a photo whose formal qualities reiterate Riis's social vision. The photo takes a long view of an alleyway whose opening is narrow to begin with (seven feet in width) and tapers inward to a claustrophobic point at the other end which can be easily spanned by a man's casually outstretched arms. The ragged children and adults who reside in the photograph are tightly framed and, near the end of the alley, squeezed in by the converging tenement structures on either side of them. The scene is darkened by virtue of the enclosure, though some light still lingers before its escape through the V-shaped shaft at the top of the picture. The overall effect is a heightened sense of containment wherein the residents are being vanquished by their very own means of existence—the tenement slums. As with Riis's verbal medium, the visual representations certify that condition is equivalent to process and

process equivalent to condition. The tautology arises from Riis's extremely delimited perspective, which disconnects the situation of poverty from the driving social forces of the era. Even the condition of
poverty is displayed in fragmented and unrelated pieces, thus not only
isolating poverty from affluence but alienating poverty from itself,
keeping its political identity unknown and its social purpose mute. In
terms of the relationship between culture and subculture, the result is
a realization of the urban paradox: social distance amidst physical
proximity. Although Riis's photos bring you into focused contact with
poverty, they draw you inward to the point where you are entrapped
by their vagrant and reified space, thus engaging your eye with the
striking presence of the various subjects while at the same time diffus-
ing your social perspective into the pleasant aura of mystification.

Aside from the inadvertent projection of ideology into the visual
scene of the composition, Riis also took a more direct role in arranging
his photographic representations of slum realities to align with his
social vision and personal prejudices. This was accomplished by composing several scenes, such as the haunting and forbidden atmosphere
of *Bandit's Roost, Baxter Street Alley, Home of an Italian Ragpicker* (a
sentimentalized and pauperized treatment of a madonna and child), and
The Tramp. The Tramp, for instance, illustrates the contrived picturing very well. Riis's visual portrait of the tramp as one of studied
insolence is buttressed by his narrative analysis, thus fusing both the
visual and verbal media in order to support an ideological position. In
the written text, Riis reduces the tramp problem to the moral considerations of ill-applied charity and idleness, and his photograph of a
tramp in a Mulberry Street yard renders this social attitude. Riis's
retelling of the encounter which prefaced the photo is a telling study in
the reciprocal manipulation between culture and subculture:

On one of my visits to "the Bend" I came across a particularly
ragged and disreputable tramp, who sat smoking his pipe on the
rung of a ladder with such evident philosophic contentment in the
busy labor of a score of ragpickers all about him, that I bade him
sit for a picture, offering him ten cents for the job. He accepted
the offer with hardly a nod, and sat patiently watching me from
his perch until I got ready to work. Then he took the pipe out of
his mouth and put it in his pocket, calmly declaring that it was not
in the contract, and that it was worth a quarter to have it go in the
picture. The pipe, by the way, was of clay, and of the two-for-a-

cent kind. But I had to give in. The man, scarce ten seconds employed at honest labor, even at sitting down, at which he was an undoubted expert, had gone on strike.[72]

Riis, by the way, was compelled to give in because the pipe conveyed the essential detail that he was after. It was pictorially equivalent to Matthews's *"mot de la fin,"* a final touch that signaled the slothful and shiftless posture of the tramp.

Riis's interest in directly picturing various scenes of urban poverty found more dramatic expression in his magic lantern lectures, a sort of primitive slide show with an eerie chiaroscuro effect. This performative vehicle allowed Riis to arrange the fragmented scenes and compositions of his pictures into a concise, clear, and melodramatic message. The vivid contrasts in social condition and attitude of the photos were, in many cases, true crowd pleasers. The magic lantern lectures led the audience into a reasonably vivid though distanced encounter with urban poverty while at the same time reaffirming genteel, middle-class values and virtues. As in his tour-guide narrative, Riis led his audience in and out of the scenes to arouse their senses, indignation, concern, and sentimentality relative to the "other half." Yet there was little enlightenment built into the program. The moment Riis's visual projection of poverty was presented it was subsumed into a higher and more righteous order so as to explain, minimize, and deflect the social ramifications, thus leaving the audience affected yet vindicated. Consider the following juxtaposition, with its conditioned melodramatic response, as a case in point: "In Washington, D.C., a hush fell over the audience when he [Riis] showed a picture of an abandoned little girl, and they [the audience] broke into cheers and applause when the next slide showed her in the care of Sister Irene's Home for Children."[73]

Though powerful and penetrating testaments to the existence and prevalence of urban poverty in America, Riis's photos, whether packaged in a slide show, directly composed, or spontaneously selected, are deceptive in that they are aligned with his overall strategy of mystification. Although this strategy claimed a total grasp of the situation, it in fact only cordoned off a section of its broader meaning, thus curtailing the reach of Riis's social inquiry.

Riis's observation and social analysis are also foreshortened by his middle-class prejudices against tramps, new and more radically visible immigrant groups (Italians, Jews, Chinese, and blacks), street beggars, the homeless, and the urban proletariat.[74] His chapter "The Man with the Knife" draws all these elements of the dangerous classes

Mullen's Alley, *ca. 1890. Jacob A. Riis Collection, Museum of the City of New York.*

together into one symbolic individual, driven by a senseless rage to avenge his oppression by destroying the property and morals of middle-class culture. To forestall this eruption of violence, Riis appeals not only to his culture's sense of justice but also to its vested interests and preservation of social control. Justice and reform become, in fact, instrumental to the perpetuity of society. Rather than promote a fundamental rearrangement of the social fabric which would close the rift between poverty and affluence, Riis opts for a measure of reform

Bandit's Roost, *39 1/2 Mulberry Street, ca. 1890. Jacob A. Riis Collection, Museum of the City of New York.*

consistent with his ideology. "The ultimate and the greatest need, . . . the real remedy," Riis asserts, "is to remove the cause—the tenement that was built for 'a class of whom nothing was expected,' and which has come fully up to the expectation."[75] The tenement is thus not only the cause of urban poverty but its solution as well. Riis's attitude of containment completes its circularity and, in doing so, excludes the larger context of slum conditions. For Riis, tenement reform does not imply a sequence of gradualist measures that would combat the negative effects of industrial capitalism and laissez-faire economic policy. There is no program beyond his advocacy of "philanthropy and five percent,"[76] a reference to the construction of model

Tramp in a Mulberry Street yard, ca. 1890. Jacob A. Riis Collection, Museum of the City of New York.

tenements built and managed by conscionable members of the private sector inspired by voluntarism. Municipal ownership of housing and related industries, redistribution of wealth, national regulation of monopolies, and adult labor or unionization laws that would reduce the economic exploitation of the working class are all beyond the scope of Riis's constricted moral critique. His fixation on the tenement as both cause and solution of urban poverty severs environment from its political and economic base. In arranging his critique as such, Riis absolves culture and affirms his own strategy of mystification, thus insuring his untarnished reputation as an ideal American citizen.

With an intensity equal to Riis's argument for tenement reform, William Dean Howells, the spokesman for literary realism, led a crusade against the prevailing bulwark of idealized and romanticized fiction which had continued to dominate the publishing market. From his own perch, as editor of the *Atlantic* and later *Harper's Monthly*, Howells disseminated his counterviews concerning literary style and attitude. His promotion of realism, the principles of which were always somewhat vague and often reduced to "that fidelity to experience and probability of motive,"[77] was largely advanced by virtue of his animus against the suspect standards of the opposing camp. Howells's strident and relentless criticisms were not aimed at romantic aesthetics but, rather, at their perversion into a popular medium which trafficked in outdated virtues and obsolete ideals. The machinations of popular romances, featuring the gothic interplay of heroes, heroines, passions, chivalry, high romantic agony, and a display of the marvelous and impossible, conspired against the realities of the Gilded Age by a regression to a sentimentalized and feudal mode of existence. Howells reproached this competing ideology for its falsification of experience and aversion to the commonplace motives, impulses, and struggles which defined American society:

> It appears to us that the opposite position is one of the last refuges of the aristocratic spirit which is disappearing from politics and society, and is now seeking to shelter itself in aesthetics. The pride of caste is becoming the pride of taste; but as before, it is averse to the mass of men; it consents to know them only in some conventionalized and artificial guise. It seeks to withdraw itself, to stand aloof; to be distinguished, and not to be identified. Democracy in literature is the reverse of all this.[78]

For Howells, realism satisfied the requirement of "democracy in literature," a truth to life as it presented itself in the circumstances of modern existence. Even though Howells's creed of realism projected a divine purpose into that life and concerned itself for a while with the "more smiling aspects" of American society, it nonetheless functioned to heighten the writer's awareness of social conditions, values, and responsibilities.[79] Though drawn to the moral imperatives of genteel culture, Howells was also attracted to the great social upheaval of his era. At the one end, he espoused the ethical preconceptions which

underlay Emersonian optimism and, at the other, influenced by the
events of the Haymarket Riot, he embraced the cause of Christian
socialism.[80] Like Janus, Howells presided over the gates of culture,
looking out in both directions. His fight for realism, however, kept the
body of his thought centrally located in an attempt to accommodate
the disparity of his vision. In seeking a fusion between the ideals of the
past and the actualities of the present, Howells bridged two widely
diverse eras. Accused by one generation of ushering in a seamy realism, "a miasmatic breath blown from the slums," as Thomas Bailey
Aldrich characterized it in disparagement, Howells was also criticized
by a later generation, nurtured by Dreiser, for his "quiet reticences"
and "obtrusive morality."[81] The middle ground of Howells's literary
landscape was thus outflanked from both directions. But if, eventually,
the center did not hold, it at least provided that necessary step in the
progression of a cultural dialectic. In all fairness, as Parrington writes,
"Howells was the reporter of his generation—the greatest literary
figure of a drab negative age when the older literary impulse was
slackening, and the new was slowly displacing it. He marks the transition between the earlier idealism and the later naturalism."[82]

In his relationship to the realities of urban poverty, Howells reas-
serted his role as a transitional figure and, in doing so, proved himself
a better prophet than practitioner. While Howells was open to a critical
examination of social problems and social inequities, certainly elevat-
ing the level of discourse on the subject of poverty, he was hampered
in his efforts at observation and analysis by his moralistic and genteel
heritage. Howells's adoption of the social distance between culture and
subculture qualified his realism. He writes:

> The whole spectacle of poverty . . . is incredible. As soon as you
> cease to have it before your eyes,—even when you have it before
> your eyes,—you can hardly believe it, and that is perhaps why so
> many people deny that it exists. . . . When I get back into my
> own comfortable room, among my papers and books, I remember
> it as I remember something at the theater. It seems to be turned
> off, as Niagara does, when you come away.[83]

Howells's unfailing honesty regarding his own sense of cultural distance is one quality of his treatment which he does not mystify. The
perceptions of poverty which ensue from his class position and ethical
posture, those of spectacle, incredulity, and disavowal, are given freely without hesitation or a sense of concealment. Howells states his
attitude plainly, avoiding the guises of righteous indignation and senti-

mentality. In being truthful about the impact of subculture upon culture, Howells discloses the attendant perceptions of his class.

In reflecting the cultural attitude of his time, Howells espoused the invidious distinction between the deserving and undeserving poor. His fear of pauperizing the poor through indiscriminate charity brought his roles as good citizen and good Christian into conflict. The Christian in him wanted to give freely to the pleas of the downtrodden, but, as a citizen of the republic, Howells believed that such unreasoned impulses would demoralize the recipients and deepen their sense of dependency. This conflict played itself out one day when Howells passed a poor stump beggar on the street who was seeking alms. [84] At first, Howells passed him by but then returned, bothered by his Christian conscience. After searching his pockets for coins, Howells could only produce a fifty-cent piece. Now his qualms regarding his role as a good citizen arose. The coin was too much to give, so Howells deliberated among his competing voices. Citizen Howells won out and quickly ducked into a nearby restaurant to get change for his fifty-cent piece. But, embarrassed to ask for change without a purchase, Howells bought a pack of cigarettes for ten cents, thus ensuring his respectability as a consumer. The purchase was wasteful, for Howells did not smoke cigarettes, but it satisfied his intellectualization nevertheless. He returned to the stump beggar and dropped fifteen cents into the cup, a neat though laboriously worked out compromise. Perhaps bothered by his ridiculous maneuverings in such situations of face-to-face encounter, Howells offers an equally ludicrous rationalization, which begins by way of social acknowledgment of the phenomenon and ends by way of a class disclaimer: "If we know by statistics and personal knowledge that there are hundreds and even thousands of people who cannot get work, and that they must suffer if they do not beg, let us not be too hard upon them. Let us refuse them kindly, and try not to see them; for if we see their misery, and do not give, that demoralizes us. Come, I say; have not we some rights, too?" [85] Such advice inverts the focus of victimization so that members of culture are the ones truly beset by moral pauperization. In stating the sufferings of the middle class, Howells turns the screen of social distance into a program for sanctioned inactivity. This advocacy of segregation between culture and subculture thus quiets those unsettling tribulations which arise from the act of charity. Reasoning thus, Howells can walk away from his emblematic stump beggar with his Christianity and citizenship in peaceful coexistence.

But Howells was too curious a social observer to be permanently

self-exiled from the spectacle of urban poverty. He returned to it time
and again and, though always a distanced spectator, he sought to
dislodge himself somewhat from the contentment that his social position naturally offered. The pattern of Howells's encounter with the
subculture of poverty can be defined by its facile movement in and out
of the scene of inquiry: the cautious subjection of his mind to the
turbulence of ideas and perceptions engendered by the encounter was
complemented by his subsequent reveries, which not only insulated
his experience but paved the way for his escape back into the cultural
arena.

In his sketch "The Midnight Platoon," the Howellsian character,
attired in fur overcoat and traveling through the city in a sheltered
coupé, happens upon a sight that he had long heard of—the bread line
of the poor stretching from the corner of Fleischmann's Bakery awaiting their midnight dole of loaves. He orders his driver to make a close
inspection of the scene, hoping, in fact, to get out and mingle among
the "Broadway coffle." But his conjectural posture soon takes over
and reiterates his claim to distance. His interest becomes purely subjective, a display of speculative consciousness. After attempting to
pick out the imposters in the crowd, he turns from social observance
to the inward drift of his mind:

> How early did these failures begin to form themselves for the
> midnight dole of bread? As early as ten, as nine o'clock? If so, did
> the fact argue habitual destitution, or merely habitual leisure? Did
> the slaves in the coffle make acquaintance, or remain strangers to
> one another, though they were closely neighborhood night after
> night by their misery? Perhaps they joked away the weary hours
> of waiting; they must have their jokes. Which of them were old-
> comers, and which novices? Did they ever quarrel over questions
> of precedence? Had they some comity, some etiquette, which a
> man forced to leave his place could appeal to, and so get it back?[86]

The series of conjectures, which compensate for the utter lack of
experiential knowledge, are suddenly halted by the character's sense
of his own "representativity" among the crowd. "He stood to these
men for all the ease and safety that they could never, never hope to
know. He was Society: Society that was to be preserved because it
embodies Civilization." The reciprocal symbolism of the scene freezes
the inherent separation between lower and upper classes. Humbled by
this awareness, the character drives off, somewhat troubled but nonetheless reassured by his concluding conviction: "What we are and

what we do is all right. It's what they are and what they suffer that's all wrong."[87] Though this seeming maxim provides Howells's moralistic departure and sense of recovery from the silent accusation of subculture, it fails to suggest that what is good and just might very well implicate the social misery that is wrong. The evasion of responsibility preserves the difference between classes by implicitly attributing the contrast in conditions to some ineffable source.

Separated from the experience of urban poverty by his sense of social distance, Howells was also confined by this position's logical aesthetic consequence, the picturesque. But though Howells was drawn to the picturesque qualities of poverty, he recognized their defections, their "false air of gayety,"[88] and so tried to overcome the superficiality of such perspectives. The results, however, were hardly convincing, for his insights could not seek expression in a style commensurate with a more profound level of awareness. As Howells strolls through the "wretched quarters" of tenement districts, his perceptions are initially fastened to the picturesqueness of the close neighborhoods. He is attracted to the impressionistic sweep of tenement facades, with their iron balconies and winding fire escapes, to the banners of laundry hanging in backyards, to the social life of poor families which animates the streets, and to the discordant sounds of peddlers and hucksters selling their wares. "In a picture," Howells comments, "it would be most pleasingly effective, for then you could be in it, and yet have the distance on it which it needs." But Howells is not satisfied with the mere picturing of the scene and so attempts to thrust the reader from the gallery into the life which is lived in the scene's interior:

> But to be in it, and not have the distance, is to inhale the stenches of the neglected street, and to catch that yet fouler and dreadfuller poverty-smell which breathes from the open doorways. It is to see the children quarrelling in their games, and beating each other in the face, and rolling each other in the gutter, like the little savage outlaws they are. It is to see the work-worn look of the mothers, the squalor of the babes, the haggish ugliness of the old women, the slovenly frowziness of the young girls. All this makes you hasten your pace down to the river.[89]

"But to be in it" should more accurately read "but to move through it." Howells's claim to an intimate depiction of the scene is offset by its remaining the appraisal of an outsider whose pace quickens with every perception. Readers are thus led out before they have a chance to

truly penetrate the distance of the scene's picturesqueness. The distance, though modified somewhat by Howells's presentation of the
unpretty qualities of tenement life, is still apparent in those intrusive
sights, sounds, and smells which he highlights. Unable to transcend
his style so as to assimilate an interiorized presence in the scene,
Howells resorts to the language of shocked morality. Such stock
phrases as the "fouler and dreadfuller poverty-smell," "the little sav-
age outlaws," "the squalor of the babes," and the "slovenly frowzi-
ness" of young girls work, as a whole, to supplant the distance of the
picturesque with that of a moral screen. Rather than convey a close
and familiar understanding of urban poverty, Howells's passage defies
its intention. At best it removes readers from the gallery and into the
picture's culturally molded frame.

In his most accomplished feat of literary realism, *A Hazard of New
Fortunes*, set in New York City during the late 1880s, Howells displays
once again the restraining force of the picturesque upon him. As editor
of the literary periodical *Every Other Week*, Basil March, a slightly
concealed projection of Howells himself, is frequently struck by the
"Neapolitan picturesqueness" of the impoverished Bowery vicinity. In
walking through the districts, March's recurrent concern is to work up
some local color sketches for his magazine with the accompaniment of
an artist. Yet in other episodes throughout the social novel March
professes to have surmounted the "purely aesthetic view" of the picturesque.[90] During these moments of dismissal, March replaces his
picturesque notions with philosophical and satirical raptures regarding
the variant conditions between poor and middle-class cultures. In attempting to move away from the picturesque and toward a closer
approximation of urban poverty, March proves, in the process, that he
too is not "in it." His stance is as remote as the picturesque treatment, for which he feels a simultaneous attraction and repulsion. Protected by his refined social observances and sophisticated commentaries, March is equally shut out from a deeper level of encounter with
the subculture of urban poverty. By translating condition into subject
matter, March does not enter the scene of inquiry as much as he
elevates it to suit his taste for disinterested discourse.

March's encounter with the "gay ugliness—the shapeless, grace-
less, reckless picturesqueness of the Bowery"—leads him to an inspection of this setting's nationalities, deprivations, and uncontrollable
energies. His interest in immigrant groups is more in the line of
construing personal histories rather than entertaining "public-spirited
reveries" involving the import of their condition for political economy.

This individualized focus extends itself to March's piecemeal examination of the Bowery itself. In reading the jumbled signs of the Bowery's appearance, March isolates its arbitrary interplay of harsh forms, loud colors, hideous dime museums, the "erasing line" of the El obstructing facades, ornate stations, and the varied width of the avenue "always in wanton disregard of the life that dwelt" in its midst. The frenetic panorama brings March to the threshold of a new perspective, which is built up only to be erased in the end. The pattern of his thought is much like the result of that insolent line of the El obscuring and diminishing edifices:

> Accident and then exigency seemed the forces at work to this extraordinary effect; the play of energies as free and planless as those that force the forest from the soil to the sky; and then the fierce struggle for survival, with the stronger life persisting over the deformity, the mutilation, the destruction, the decay, of the weaker. The whole at moments seemed to him lawless, Godless; the absence of intelligent, comprehensive purpose in the huge disorder and the violent struggle to subordinate the result to the greater good penetrated with its dumb appeal the consciousness of a man who had always been too self-enwrapt to perceive the chaos to which the individual selfishness must always lead.[91]

Howells's nascent awareness of the amoral nature of the Bowery and of society in general seems to push his thought into temporary agreement with the ethos of naturalism. But Howells's notion of a Godless universe, one without "intelligent, comprehensive purpose," is clarified in the conclusion to his passage by a moralistic discount; that is, the reduction of chance and lawlessness to "the individual selfishness" which produces the conditions of chaos. By reestablishing this law of selfishness and thereby implying both the exploiter and the exploited as bound by this base motive of humanity, Howells preserves his ethical interpretation of the universe. The specter of amorality is thus eliminated by a moralistic conviction.

The passage must be taken as a whole in order to catch the drift of Howells's conflictual approach and avoidance—his movement forward, in seeming transition, to the tenets of naturalism and then back again to the point of origin, moral idealism. In sliding to and away from the new world view which he dangles before the reader, Howells's passage becomes a perfect expression of his ambiguous social and intellectual position. The nature of his compromised synthesis is to bring the new forces, "accident and then exigency," under the encompass-

ing control of a still operative ethical code. In evaluating social forces in
terms of individualized conduct, this code subverts the sociological
imports of events by assimilating them into the moral dictum of personal integrity, or the lack thereof.

The mystification which results from Howells's attempt to dissolve
the tension between the old and the new is apparent in both the
content of the message and the manner in which that content is
formed into expression. Confused and evasive, the structure of
Howells's passage betrays his own struggle to subordinate the encroachment of the amoral to a residual but dominating perspective—
"the individual selfishness" which is man. The entire anatomy of the
passage rests upon this moralistic foundation, which undermines those
negative social qualities previously constructed. As the passage spi-
rals down to seek its interpretive ground, the negative is exchanged
for the affirmative, thus merging attitude and style into a compositional exercise in mystification.

The "vague discomfort" which follows from March's nebulous recognition of social forces and moral formulations is also a discomfort
conveyed by the narrator in his structural embodiment of such contradictory perceptions and conclusions. To suppress the discomfort,
Howells leads March out of the quagmire and back onto the solid earth
of the picturesque, to the colorful material presence of the Bowery
and to some of its resident social fixtures, such as the quaint appearance of a shabby-genteel ballad seller. This return to the diversionary
fancies of the picturesque rescues both March and the narrator from
their specious forays into the unknown conditions and conceptions of
urban poverty. Though courageously given to such ventures, character and author inevitably come back to embrace the techniques and
attitudes from which they tentatively embarked.

Howells's investigation into the realities of urban poverty was hin-
dered by the net of genteel, Victorian middle-class culture in which he
was caught. Thoroughly domesticated by the values of this culture,
Howells could not forsake his household and loiter, like an orphan open
to possibility, in that rough and vulnerable domain of subculture. Perhaps this is why Howells devotes much of the first hundred pages in *A
Hazard of New Fortunes* to the March family's search for a suitable
apartment. Securing a respectable home is one way of reconstituting a
frame of reference, a requisite mooring to the mannerisms of culture,
which both precedes and anchors an assessment of one's turbulent
encounter with urban life. Howells's social position kept his creed of
realism and his search for truth always in moderate proportion. His

concern with the commonplace aspects of culture prevented his social consciousness from carrying its momentary insights to their ultimate crises. This lack of development, the breach between Howells's restless observations and his complacent conclusions, leaves the vision of his realism stranded, where Parrington spotted it, in "the indecisions, the repetitions, the whimsical descriptions, the drifting talk" of those conventionalities of culture. The restraint of Howells's creed and the narrow circle in which his quest for truth resided "are all true to life, but they are not essential or vital truth."[92]

Yet Parrington would be one of the first to agree that Howells's dedication to his art and craft, his critical enterprise, and his sense of social interest all helped to bring about that "slow decay of . . . romantic optimism" which paved the way for the more critical perspective of succeeding naturalist writers. Like Riis, Howells's strategy of mystification restricted his relationship to the subculture of urban poverty. But in comparison to the sensationalistic genre, with its reinstatement of mystery, and to the fixed posture of the picturesque treatment, which affirmed the pleasantries of poverty, Riis and Howells offered a more balanced and sophisticated style of description and analysis. Their search for realism in the encounter between culture and subculture brought the ideology of mystification to that juncture between social distance and social intimacy. Though both agents were confined by that transitional chasm between the opposing modes of activity, they succeeded at least in charting its ambiguous territory. If the social and ideological purpose of their representations did not exchange distance for intimacy, it nevertheless left that possibility perilously open. In retrospect, both Riis and Howells prove invaluable keys to the transformation of a cultural equation which, by way of summary and prospectus, moves mystification along to its ultimate conclusion: if segregation, then distance, if distance, then mystery, if mystery, then the parallel strategy of mystification. And with the advance of mystification the need arises for critical realism, for that competing alternative of "essential or vital truth."

3 / DESCENT AND DISCOVERY

Life is the model, truth is the master,
the heart of the man his motive power.
—Hamlin Garland
　Crumbling Idols

Critical realism, as a new literary strategy for the 1890s, was not merely an extension of Howells's creed of realism. Though Howells provided the point of departure for a new generation of writers and remained an avuncular figure for his successors, especially Crane and Dreiser, a qualitative and decisive break in attitude and outlook separated the critical realists from their towering predecessor.

Disentangled from the conventionalities of genteel culture, the critical realists were far more uncompromising in their vision of man's position in nature and his relationship to society. Critical realism embodied a general consensus to shed the timidities of a moralistic and idealized view of the universe so as to more boldly and directly confront the conditions and values which governed American realities in the 1890s. Writers such as Crane, Dreiser, Norris, Fuller, Garland, Frederick, Chopin, and Cahan sought to come to terms with the turmoil of a decade that exaggerated the cumulative tensions of American life since the Civil War. The 1890s offered up social conflict in plenty—agrarian dissent, rural bewilderment, labor struggle in the cities, economic uncertainty (particularly during the depression years of 1893 and 1894), tramp armies, the continued disenfranchisement of blacks and women, and the persistent increase of tenement slums and homelessness. Such adverse consequences of American progress made it increasingly difficult for writers of the 1890s to respond in accordance with the Jeffersonian world view of democratic individualism. The romantic notion of the world as ethically and morally justified and of man as situated in a providential order was challenged by the cycle of disillusionment and revaluation experienced by critical realists. The sharpened contradictions between objective condition and cultural ideal produced the necessary conflict for the generation of new appraisals, which contested the prevailing image of man as centered in the radiance of divine purpose, a fixed moral agent of his destiny. Critical realists found it less tenable to frame their literary strategies around the optimistic model, which stressed the perfectability of the species, the purposeful direction of American society, and the transcendence of man. Older narrative devices did so despite the evident social disorder because they were guided less by American conditions than by moral precepts which emphasized the unlimited possibility of man and society. And when social conflict was represented, as with Howells, it was apologetically deflected by an interpretive reliance on individualism and morality.

Critical realism displaced the ethos of a conservative Christian morality, drawn from on high and supportive of the status quo, and offered a new, decentered image of man circumscribed by determinant conditions. Both the conception and language of critical realism, as capsulized by Crane, viewed the universe as simply indifferent, "flatly indifferent."[1] The alternative ethos of critical realism at its extremity is probably best depicted in Crane's short masterpiece "The Open Boat," in the drift of Crane's dinghy splashing recklessly about, and in his poetic lines which view this drift of man and nature as enclosed by "a horizon smaller than a doomed assassin's cap."[2] In "The Open Boat," Crane presents not only a narrative but a naturalistic image of man, reduced, minimal, his human project shrunk by the impersonal expanse of nature: "A high cold star on a winter's night is the word he feels that she says to him. Thereafter he knows the pathos of his situation."[3] This pathos is rendered by the notion that the universe, once benign and protective, is now mute, no longer intermingling its designs with the destiny of man. It exists beyond him, in spite of him, orbiting in its own sphere of disregard. The open boat: this, we must remember, is no ark. Here man is exposed, uncertain, tenuously housed amidst a terrain that dwarfs and nullifies, leaving man to his own humble resources, complaint and hope. The underlying attitude of critical realism is also ably evinced by Crane's "rudderless ship," his desert as parched and enveloping as Rimbaud's, and his preference for darkness rather than radiance, as evidenced in the following lines from *The Black Riders*: "I stood musing in a black world, / Not knowing where to direct my feet."[4] These lines of Crane, unsparingly Godless in design and intent, provide a fine preface for a literary project that freely accepted "accident and then exigency"—a conception that sent Howells scurrying back into his hulk of moral certainty.

Though naturalism informed the works of critical realists, it would be unwise to exaggerate its impact as both theory and model for American writers of the 1890s. Naturalism, as Parrington summarized it, is a "pessimistic realism, with a philosophy that sets man in a mechanical world and conceives of him as victimized by that world."[5] The movement's doctrinal accompaniment, amoral determinism, asserted the scientific emphasis of the new age—historical materialism (Marx), biological evolution (Darwin), and mechanistic physics (the Newtonian cosmogony). As a theory which translated these incontestable forces into the enterprise of literature, naturalism viewed the narrative in the harsh empirical terms of cause and effect. But except for Norris, an avowed student of Zola, naturalism, as a mechanistic philosophy and literary model, was less compelling for the eclectic array of representations that characterized American fiction at this time: "While in Europe realism and naturalism grew out of the positivism of Continental thought and the conviction that one literary movement had subsided and another was needed, realism in America grew out of the bewilderment, and thrived on the simple grimness, of a generation suddenly brought face to face with the pervasive materialism of industrial capitalism."[6]

A comparison of such writers as Crane, Dreiser, Norris, and Frederick shows how greatly they varied in stylistic technique, methods of composition, regional interest, and choice of subject matter. No singular influence can be said to have theoretically predetermined their selection of material and thematic design. Crane, in particular, was often at pains to rectify the attribution of his literary sources to French naturalists. The results of such efforts, however, were often appropriately ironic. In a letter to Huneker posted from England, Crane recounts the following incident: "I told a seemingly sane man at Mrs. Garnett's that I got my artistic education on the Bowery and he said, 'Oh, really? So they have a school of fine arts there?'"[7] It would have been futile indeed for Crane to have explained to this Englishman the importance for him, and for Dreiser as well, of the collaboration between literature and life in their encounter on native grounds.

Yet underneath the manifold differences that existed among the critical realists, a general foundation might be set forward which would cohere these diverse writers whose realism was basically critical (that is, highly evaluative of the relationship between man and environment) without necessarily being programmatic. On the whole, critical realists tended to invert the agent-scene ratio which had prevailed in melodrama, the sentimental novel, and, to a certain restrained extent, Howellsian realism. Rather than view man as an unbridled and heroic moral agent, a dominant and controlling self, they saw him struggling as a victim of some contestable determinant condition or circumstances. Hence, the pessimism. In general, the moving principle was reversed to that of scene-agent; that is, something working on man which was beyond his free and uncluttered self-determination.[8] The hindrance could be external (environmental determinism), ideological (the incorporation of cultural values false to experience), internal (physiochemical), or those inscrutable forces of fate and chance. In all, and despite the various strategies, victimization was often the result. Depicting man as shaped, or often entrapped, by determinant conditions, this result was neither tempered by divine intervention nor alleviated by a complacent moralistic reduction. In reversing the accepted intellectual orientation which had preceded it, critical realism undertook to contest, subvert, or simply expose the predilection toward mystification and thus to reveal the rupture between American fact and American ideal. In short, critical realism aimed to write of things *as they are*, without adornment, redemption, or moral rectitude, however problematical that proposition may prove in the interaction between subject and world. The shift in directional priority, from agent-scene to scene-agent, also paralleled the growing movement of logical positivism in the social sciences and the interest in advancing a systemic definition of poverty among progressive reformers. Essentially skeptical, these writers put into question the ideological forms which had inscribed themselves in the cultural products of literature, forms which were guided by a habitual acknowledgment of a former world view inadequate to the historical development of modern existence.

This change in outlook does not imply that critical realists were amoral writers, literary neuters without purpose or passion slavishly engaged in that most improbable of all efforts—mere transcription of the empirical, the starkly given matrix of events. Though these writers confronted the "pervasive materialism" of the era, they were neither bound nor absorbed by this sense of engagement. "The primary goal of the late nineteenth century American naturalists," Donald Pizer writes, "was not to *demonstrate* the overwhelming and oppressive reality of the material forces present in our lives. Their attempt, rather, was to *represent* the intermingling in life of controlling force and individual worth."[9] To be sure, some more than others accepted the amoral stature of nature, but that position only worked to thrust one back upon one's own haunches, to see quite nakedly the activity of man in his collectivity—society. "Naturalism," Pizer generalizes, "reflects an affirmative ethical conception of life, for it asserts the value of all life by endowing the lowest character with emotion and defeat and with moral ambiguity, no matter how poor or ignoble he may seem."[10] The ethical convictions of critical realists derive in part from their renewed interest in historical conditions, social institutions, systems of value and belief, social struggle, and environmental constraints. In these efforts of engagement and evaluation morality was not dismissed; rather, it had been recontextualized, taken from the pulpit and placed onto a new secular foundation—the streets. "Culture in its true sense," Crane wrote, "is a comprehension of the man at one's shoulder."[11] We may speak in a similar way concerning a more lateral morality as well, one aligned with the liberal and humanitarian strain of thought which gained popularity during the 1890s.[12] The notion of amoral determinism would, after all, much better serve the conservative keepers of a vertical culture, apologists content in the rationalization of a given, irreversible social order. Though the ethical convictions of critical realists were often implicit protestations of social realities (implicit, not quietistic, and arranged so as to avoid the moral preachiness and absolutism of a former style), they were nonetheless significantly apparent and interwoven aspects of a text. The readiness of critical realists to grapple with neglected issues and crises, such as the inequity of poverty and affluence in metropolitan culture, rural disintegration, religious and middle-class hypocrisy, and social violence, attests to the force of moral principles radically adjusted, principles residing in the contestable world of man rather than the impenetrable realm of nature.

The critical realism of Stephen Crane and Theodore Dreiser, as it bears upon urban poverty and the Bowery, sharpens an understanding of a literary movement which is perhaps better illustrated than categorized. In many of Crane's Bowery sketches and in Dreiser's immortal Hurstwood, both writers sought to come to terms with the relationship between culture and subculture and the false consciousness which separated each into immutably given social entities. Each writer helped to demystify the strategies of containment concerning middle-class perceptions of urban poverty as advanced by the melodrama and sensationalistic genres, the picturesque pastels of low life, Riis and his tenement, and Howellsian gentility. These strategies of containment provided narrative paradigms that organized social perceptions concerning slums, the immigrant working class, and the homeless. Taken together, they worked to repress the larger social meaning of poverty as shaped by the historic development of industrial capitalism and, in turn, constructed its reification, which naturally extended to that of social class as well. "Manipulation leads, again and again," Lukács cautioned, "to seeing conditions as a final ontological form of existence, while the real ontological form of existence is the process."[13] The *reductio ad absurdum* of this activity, the perfection of its social attitude, might be likened to Marx's ironic diagnosis: "Want is here derived from *pauverté.*"[14]

Crane's and Dreiser's focused penetration of urban space breached the reified social distance between culture and subculture and resulted in a heightened awareness of the Bowery as both condition and process. Their emphasis upon unmediated experience proved each writer's willingness to descend to the objective and existential ground of urban life. The descent, unaided by police lanterns or moral screens, constituted the essential mode of being for a discovery that could only be rendered from the inside, from the point of view which approximated that of subculture. In this sense, the critical realism of Crane and Dreiser resembles the experiential premise and holistic cultural strategy of traditional ethnography.

The critical realism of the Bowery sketches and the portions of *Sister Carrie* to be examined here derives meaning from the social processes which accompany each work's pattern of descent and discovery. As opposed to the detached moral assertions regarding the nature of poverty which upheld the basic anatomy of American life, Crane's and Dreiser's representations allowed these writers to slip through the social system and, in doing so, to discover urban man *in extremis*. In substituting social intercourse and intimacy for social distance, they also came to exchange structure for antistructure, the latter being the legitimate realm for their artistic query.

In his biography of Stephen Crane, Thomas Beer relates an incident, a slice out of the young writer's life, which, when magnified, provides the reader with an image of the whole—a perspective of incongruity, to borrow a phrase from Burke. At the behest of William Dean Howells, Crane, along with others, attended one of Howells's formal dinner parties. Crane, who had borrowed a friend's suit for the occasion, entered the "Dean's" sanctuary with a literary reputation that was still in a state of potentia. He had recently completed *Maggie: A Girl of the Streets* and published it himself under the pseudonym Johnston Smith. But outside of his select Bohemian circle, the writer's first novel had landed as inconspicuously as the shadow of a footfall down some tenement alley.[15] Howells and Garland, who both championed Crane's style of realism, became spokesmen for the writer and tried to lift *Maggie* from obscurity and into the critical limelight. During the course of Howells's dinner party, the "Dean" of American letters did not miss the opportunity to direct some of his discerning literary chatter to the man in the borrowed suit. Beer recalls that Howells "presented Crane to his other guests with, 'Here is a writer who has sprung into life fully armed,' and followed that music by saying, while Mark Twain was under discussion, 'Mr. Crane can do things that Clemens can't.'"[16] After their repast, Howells then brought out a collection of Emily Dickinson's poetry and began reading some aloud. For Crane, these poems were perhaps even better encouragement than Howells's praise, for they would inspire him to work up some inimitable lines of his own, *The Black Riders.*

What with all the praise and poetry swimming in his head, this must have proved a red-letter evening for Crane. How would he work out the excess energy engendered from such an event once the evening was through? Would he perhaps continue the social affair on his own with a cocktail at Sherry's or Delmonico's? Or, seeking a more modest celebration, would he call on one of his artist friends to join him at the Buffalo Mud, where he could flaunt his reception amidst familiar Bohemian atmospherics? Or would he simply retire to his journal and inscribe the prophetic words verbatim for future generations? Crane did none of these things. Instead, as Beer relates, "He did not stop to let his mind bask in all this; he walked over to the Bowery and spent the rest of the night watching drunken negroes play poker in the rear room of a saloon."[17]

From the sanctuary of culture to the profanity of subculture, Crane sought out the antidote and not the elixer. Evidently he had learned well where to direct his feet and rest his eyes. On this occasion, they led him out of the comfortable light of literary society and into the haunt of one of the Bowery's intimate spaces.

With Crane in the back room of a Bowery saloon and Howells ensconced in his study, we have a picture of American literature in transition. What, after all, was the meaning of realism in American life and letters if one could not freely loiter in the company of drunken Negroes, bums, opium addicts, prostitutes, malcontents, tenement dwellers, Bohemians, or the urban proletariat and in such sordid vicinities as the Tenderloin and Bowery. With all due respect to the moral and aesthetic complexities of the art of Howells and James, realism was, when devoid of this content, dulled by its thematic restrictions and enclosures, its bourgeois preoccupation with ethical crises, and its ignorance of the provocative depths of life and literature when allied with the generative realm of subculture. One might have inquired of Crane upon seeing him emerge from his Bowery haunt that night, Is there really anything at all to learn from below? And to this Crane might have responded with a sardonic grin illuminating his passage.

Crane's observations of and participations in New York City street life are contained in his "Bowery Sketches" (also known as "Midnight Sketches" or "The New York City Sketches"). These were written mostly between 1893 and 1894 while Crane lived in the city and worked as a freelance contributer to various New York presses and literary magazines. Viewed in their entirety, the sketches seem a literary apprenticeship. Though they contributed to Crane's artistic development during his productive New York period,[18] they are also important in their own right for their range of urban encounter, depth of social awareness, thematic inventiveness, and technical precision. Despite their energetic youthfulness, these sketches were carefully arranged studies which often aimed at the demystification of urban space. Through the use of the conventional journalistic form, the sketch, Crane achieved highly unconventional results. He did not use the sketch to dabble in the picturesque scenes of New York street life; instead, he employed the form to subvert its stereotypical associations with low life and local color. By doing so, Crane penetrated the superficial precepts of pietistic sentimentality and sensationalism and rendered standard urban material anew. The purpose of his submersion in the life of the Bowery homeless, for instance, was to lead his readers through the rhythms of departure and exposure, which intensified their sense of urban place and encounter. Much like the broad strategy of ethnographic realism, this method of departure and exposure was designed to dislodge readers from their enclosure in the certainties of cultural preconceptions, from the notion of the "other" as wretched. As such, they were not offered reassurance but, instead, uncertainty and the opportunity for a readjustment of position. By disclosing the presence of subculture and in capturing its own point of view, Crane sought to draw readers inward and, above all, to make them see. It is in this sense that Crane attempted, through the medium of the press, to educate the public through his acute literary and perceptual talents, talents which, as Berryman notes, have "the effect of obliterating with silent contempt half of what one thinks one knows."[19] Through his sketches, Crane took subculture from the streets and into the living room, not to enhance the joys of the fireside, to petrify "the eternal mystery of social condition,"[20] but to dampen the coals and so effect a climate that would cause readers to look around and take notice.

Crane's submersion in the social world of the Bowery homeless is represented in two of his sketches, "An Experiment in Misery" and "The Men in the Storm." The former sketch is the result of his experience one night in a Bowery lodging house, while the latter reflects his presence on a Bowery breadline.[21] Both sketches are experientially rooted in the social ground of Bowery existence, in a fragment of social life that, Crane attests, can not only be visited but known as well.

"An Experiment in Misery," originally published in the New York *Press* on April 22, 1894, and its companion piece, "An Experiment in Luxury," which appeared one week later in the same publication, reveal Crane's interest in relating the extreme social divisions of urban life. His purpose was to bring the extremities into contention, whereas the conventional representations of such contrasts invariably worked to mystify each antipode into discrete and disconnected threads of the social fabric.

Crane's narrative strategy for "An Experiment in Misery" is one clearly premised upon descent and discovery. The strategy seeks a disengagement from the normative boundaries of social structure so as to assert the ontological value of social process. In the sketch, the ritual pattern of descent is presented as a requisite action to a deepened level of encounter with the Bowery homeless and as a means for a reevaluation of social perception concerning their condition. The strategy can be stated quite simply: how does one overcome the social distance between culture and subculture and, in so doing, truly enter the life world of the homeless with genuine understanding?

In the 1894 edition of the sketch, which appeared in an envelope structure, the opening frame begins with the studied posture of mystification. "Two men stood regarding a tramp. 'I wonder how he feels,' said one reflectively."[22] This statement of distanced superiority and detached speculation deftly introduces the purpose of the experiment: to deconstruct the idle and conjectural stance of social distance so as to "discover his [the tramp's] point of view."[23] The distance established by mystification is thus replaced by the more searching objective of critical realism.

To align purpose with method, Crane, or the young man who narrates his experience throughout the sketch, involves himself in a rite of passage by which he gains access to the sacred interiors of the Bowery homeless: the saloon and lodging house. Though the nature of the rite provides entry and intimate association with the physical correlates of homelessness, its value is not limited to mere spatial intrusion. The rite of passage undertaken by the youth is more significant in its symbolic value, in the declensional progression of his social being as he is initiated into the condition and consciousness of the homeless. The epistemology which inheres in the various phases of the rite (disengagement, liminality, and reidentification) paves the way for the youth's own epiphany and for his extension of individual motif to the larger social process of homelessness which seals its social existence. Crane's insights into both process and condition are visually attended by his tightly controlled and patterned imagery. His impressionistic sensibility and reliance upon the techniques of contrast and chiaroscuro not only add depth to the experience of his passage but aid in the incisive depiction of its meaning as well.

The rite of passage thematically reinforces the geographically circular structure of the sketch. It commences its first stage, that of separation from structure, with the youth, alone, trudging down toward City Hall and attired in the symbolic vestiture of the homeless. His purpose is simply stated: "He was going forth to eat as the wanderer may eat, and sleep as the homeless sleep."[24] But by the time he reaches the sketch's physical point of departure, City Hall, he already begins to feel the ritual humiliation brought on by the poor quality of his clothing. Shouts of "bum" and "hobo" directed at him immediately begin to strip him of a former identity. As the normative grip of his prior status recedes, the youth is suddenly thrown into a "most profound dejection" (p. 27).

The time referent for the youth's separation, accelerated by the ritualistic value of clothing and labeling, is that of night, an appropriate period for withdrawal and illumination, as given in the tradition of a night journey. From City Hall, the youth loiters down Park Row, the southern extension of the Bowery, and seeks commiseration with others of his kind. There "in the sudden descent in style of the dress of the crowd he felt relief, and as if he were at last in his own country" (p. 28). The pathetic stillness of the youth's homeless compatriots is sharply contrasted with the image of the city in vibrant movement. But the misty atmosphere of a rainstorm seems to take the structure of the city, with its cable cars and processions of people, away on its wing. The technique thus works to evoke and dispense with the motion of the city in order to isolate its antithesis. Only the elevated railroad remains, transformed into a grotesque metaphor, as a forceful suggestion of social oppression and enclosure: the El station, propped by "its leg-like pillars seemed to resemble some monstrous kind of crab squatting over the street" (p. 28).

The youth's stage of separation and realignment is deepened by his entrance into a Bowery saloon, his first encounter with an intimate space. His passage is ceremonious. "The young man allowed himself to be swallowed" by the devouring imagery of the saloon, personified as "smiling in some indescribable manner as the men came from all directions like sacrifices to a heathenish superstition" (pp. 28–29). The sacred quality of this sacrifice is also located in the duties of a waiter "presiding like a priest behind an altar" over the meal (p. 29). This symbolic slaughter of the homeless as they take their daily bread amounts to a dark communion, a degenerative transubstantiation commensurate with their path of descent. Crane's tone throughout this passage is somewhat ironic, though, conveying a sense of mock sacrifice surrounding the debauch of drunkenness. Seen in the light of his successive stages, it is perhaps a final remnant of his sense of distance and detachment, the lingering of his naturalistic interest in retaining the objective rendering of events.

Once outside the saloon, the youth finds his "assassin," a foreboding Bowery figure whose "eyes peered with a guilty slant" (p. 29). After some typical Bowery maneuverings regarding the price of a bed, the habitué, with all the grace of an accommodating foot servant, guides the novitiate down a "dark street" and into the "gloom shrouded corridor" of the lodging house (p. 31). Here, in the most interior region of the subculture, the youth examines the "dark and secret places" of its heart (p. 31). His naiveté first leads to a preoccupation with the smells of the room, noisome impressions "that assailed him like malignant wings" (p. 31). But soon his more profound sense of sight begins to predominate his awareness, attuned to the Dantesque play of "tumbled shadows" about the place. As the youth takes his cot, which he likens to a slab, he prepares his own bed in this grave of social existence amidst men strewn about, "lying in death-like silence" (p. 32). His separation is complete.

The second or middle stage of the youth's rite of passage is that of liminality, a state of suspension in which the initiate is betwixt and between a former and future social identity or status-sequence. In this provocative phase of ambiguous allegiance the novice is free to enter the domain of the unknown, "to juggle with the factors of existence," as Victor Turner writes.[25] By thrusting one into spatial uncertainty, liminality engenders the possibility for renewed insight, transformation, and depth of involvement in the intercourse between self and social context. Yet the result of a liminal experience, whether or not it leads in the direction of ritual elevation or ritual degradation, is largely dependent upon where one finds oneself as it takes hold. Since the stage is often attended by symbolic imagery of death and rebirth, we should qualify the passage from the grave to the womb in light of our youth leveled in a Bowery flophouse. For in this context, grave and womb become one and the same opening, co-equals in a closed circuitry of social death.

As the youth settles into his lair, his liminal experience is aroused by his visual contact with another who lies beside him in the morguelike room:

> Within reach of the youth's hand was one who lay with yellow breast and shoulders bare to the cold draughts. One arm hung over the side of the cot and the fingers lay full length upon the wet cement floor of the room. Beneath the inky brows could be seen the eyes of the man exposed by the partly opened lids. To the youth it seemed that he and this corpse-like being were exchanging a prolonged stare and that the other threatened with his eyes. He drew back, watching this neighbor from the shadows of his blanket edge. The man did not move once through the night, but lay in this stillness as of death, like a body stretched out expectant of the surgeon's knife. (Pp. 32–33)

The initiate is thus drawn into the symbolic value of the room through the primacy of his perception engaged in an act of intersubjectivity. His encounter with the imagistic death of the "other" threatens in its evocation of the youth's subjectivity in which the external becomes internal, affecting a conversion which is awareness itself, intimately conceived. The objective rendering of events is vanquished by the "prolonged stare," an aperture of renewed attentiveness for the youth's own vision of the moribund room, where human forms appear "statuesque, carven, dead" (p. 33).

The essential presence of the place becomes apparent to the youth, who, in the merger of consciousness with setting, now begins to translate the meaning of the room through the wail of another's dream.

> To the youth these were not merely the shrieks of a vision pierced man. They were an utterance of the meaning of the room and its occupants. It was to him the protest of the wretch who feels the touch of the imperturbably granite wheels and who then cries with an impersonal eloquence, with a strength not from him, giving voice to the wail of a whole section, a class, a people. (P. 33)

The symbolic message of the youth's epiphany, the import of his dis-covery, is the attempt to deindividuate the perception of poverty regarding the homeless and relocate it in the social framework. Stated as such, an eccentric shriek is transfixed into a social cry of protest, a voice, not of one man alone, but of an entire subculture positioned in the posture of victimization underneath the crushing weight of a social order. The social system, like the grim image of the El station, exerts its hierarchical force from above, while the Bowery men, the recipients of its cutting edge, amplify the suffering of their social death from below. The significance of Crane's metaphor is to relate the condition of subculture to its more suggestive social processes of oppression.

Accentuated by his view of "vast and sombre shadows that, like mighty black fingers, curled around the naked bodies," the young man's epiphany produces an eerie insomnia in which he "lay carving biographies for these men from his meagre experience. At times the fellow in the corner howled in a writhing agony of his imaginations" (p. 33). The youth's experiment is now entirely within his own self, be-traying the positivist title of his intended study. The dissolution of subjective and objective realms into a single consciousness demar-cates the transcendence of social distance. The succeeding attitude, instigated by the youth's transitional phase of liminality, is one of initiation, an act of identification with the subculture of homelessness.

Although the morning after breaks the spell of his epiphany, it does not diminish the depth of his insights. His discovery lingers in his mind like a stigmatized master code which enables the condition of subcul-ture to unfold on its own terms. In the mundane light of daybreak, the youth observes the men as they move from a dignified state of nature into an emblematic state of social being: "Here and there were men of brawn, whose skins shone clear and ruddy. They took splendid poses, standing massively, like chiefs. When they had dressed in their un-gainly garments there was an extraordinary change. They then showed bumps and deficiencies of all kinds" (p. 34). Sublime in their humanity, deprecated in their sociality: here the descent is consoli-dated. Dishonored by their social being, the homeless bear witness to the deprivations of their inferiority, the defects of their status. For the youth, this signals the end of his liminality and the advent of his altered state, a participant in the common rounds of Bowery life. The ritual labor of social death thus engenders itself anew.

The final stage of the youth's rite of passage marks his reidentifica-tion with the subculture of homelessness. Rather than being reaggre-gated into the social structure from whence he departed, his experience of ritual degradation furthers his descent to the point where it is transfixed into a structurally inferior status.

Accompanied by his companion, the "assassin" (who symbolically assists in the annihilation of the youth's prior self), the young man returns to the "unholy atmospheres" of the street. "He had forgotten all about them, and had been breathing naturally and with no sensation of discomfort or distress" (p. 35). Together, the youth and his assassin engage in some typical conversations, a mixture of banter and cordiality, which attests to the nature of social interaction on the skids when in good, familiar company. They then walk into a basement restaurant and, over breakfast, exhume the assassin's disembodied memory, which unwinds in a peculiarly telegraphic form of degenerative thought: "South no good. Damn Niggers work for twenty-five an' thirty cents a day. Run white man out. Good grub, though. Easy livin'," etc. (p. 37).

When they leave for the street and City Hall Park, that precise point at which the initiate's journey began, he is no longer referred to as a young man but simply as a wanderer. The label of wanderer is the impress of his new identity, one which signals his exclusion from society and his complementary assimilation into the insurmountable boundaries of subculture. So though the initiate physically comes full circle in terms of the narrative structure of the sketch, psychologically he arrives not at the untainted origin of his passage but at its contaminated terminus. Structure and theme thus combine as a testimony to the profound impact of the rite's developmental stages, to the transformational value of social processes when locked in a pattern of descent. For the youth, situated once again at City Hall, does not return in a recaptured moment of his past, that of anticipation or studied curiosity, but as a dramatically altered embodiment of his experiment's fruition. He is, quite literally, down and out, an abject specimen of social misery. The cyclical structure of the sketch is thus not only representative of the continuity of poverty, of monotonous despair, but, more significantly, of the nature of social descent itself, which issues from the rite's passages. The rite concludes its movement through the context of homelessness in the punitive transformation of social being and consciousness, thus giving linear depth to a circular form of narrative presentation.

Back at City Hall Park, the initiate might as well be in another country. Now the city is reconstituted so as to contrast structure with antistructure and to express the concluding convictions of the experiment's stigmata:

The two wanderers sat down in the little circle of benches sancti-
fied by the traditions of their class. They huddled in their old
garments, slumberously conscious of the march of the hours
which for them had no meaning.

The people of the street hurrying hither and thither made a blend
of black figures, changing, yet frieze-like. They walked in their
good clothes as upon important missions, giving no gaze to the
two wanderers seated upon their benches. They expressed to
the young man his infinite distance from all that he valued. Social
position, comfort, the pleasures of living were unconquerable
kingdoms. He felt a sudden awe.

And in the background a multitude of buildings, of pitiless hues
and sternly high, were to him emblematic of a nation forcing its
regal head into the clouds, throwing no downward glances; in the
sublimity of its aspirations ignoring the wretches who may
flounder at its feet. The roar of the city in his ear was to him the
confusion of strange tongues, babbling heedlessly; it was the
clink of coin, the voice of the city's hopes, which were to him no
hopes.

He confessed himself an outcast, and his eyes from under the
lowered rim of his hat began to glance guiltily, wearing the crimi-
nal expression that comes with certain convictions. (Pp. 37–38)

The new social condition of the initiate is made manifest by the
temporal loss of structure and meaning, the invisibility of inferior
status, and the immense social distance between culture and subculture which leads to the calculated indifference of urban life. These final
passages summarily document the findings of the experiment's descent and discovery: reidentification exists as an alienated state of
perpetuity. Homelessness, as a type of social death, seeks its own
grave level beneath the vertical rise of the city. The aggressive crush
of those grinding wheels, necessary to break the spirit, is now followed by its natural consequence, the passive and impersonal specter
of urban forms, which render the spirit naught. As nonentities, the
Bowery homeless fulfill their role at the bottom of a nation's social
hierarchy, that of outcasts. Entrapped in this position of structural
inferiority, they find the conditions of their social being amplified in
consciousness. In the confession of guilt and criminality, social existence breeds its germs into psychological reality, predetermining the
latter's convictions.

The conclusion of the sketch isolates a quiet irony, for the experiment, undertaken to overcome distance, ends in distance. But the latter form is distinctly *outré*, an inversion which stands the perspective of social distance and mystification on its head. To the initiate, entrenched in the vision of subculture, it is now culture, enmeshed in its cash nexus, that appears strangely indecipherable and abstracted. When the distance is reversed, culture appears less hidden or concealed than simply remote, inaccessible, alien in its matter. The social distance emanating from subculture is not, as with culture, one of mystifying auras and inevitable insubstantialities, a category of reified interpretation, but, rather, the felt consequence of a pattern of descent within the social order. It is a perception which results from the experience of inferiority, aimed to commit the reader to an act of empathy with the internal perspective of subculture.

The young man who commits himself to the experiment extends his own sense of reidentification to the vicarious experience of his reader. He is presented as a model for the readjustment of social perception, a sort of case study in the abandonment of self to the subcultural processes of descent and discovery. As the closing frame of the originally published sketch propels the seasoned youth's disengagement and recovery from the experiment, he asserts a generalized program of action that exists beyond the perimeter of the text. In summing up his message, Crane indicates the value placed upon direct experience and encounter as a source of knowledge and mode for personal as well as cultural change:

"Well," said the friend, "did you discover his point of view?"

"I don't know that I did," replied the young man; "but at any rate I think my own has undergone a considerable alteration."[26]

It is a message which seeks to educate culture rather than subculture, a message to those who are truly in need of elevation.

Crane's companion piece, "An Experiment in Luxury," has the effect of bringing both sketches into a dialectical relationship. When taken together, the two sketches show how the contextual position of one's social being varies in shaping consciousness and class attitudes. Though grounded in the experiential form, Crane's narrative strategy in "An Experiment in Luxury" is simply that of conscious reflection, a strategy allied to test the popular opinion that the wealthy share equally in the immiserization of the lower half. In this sketch, Crane does not resort to a rite of passage, a method more suited to depth experience, but, rather, to a stream of thought and commentary which glides gracefully along the polished surfaces of his direct encounter with an ascendant social plane.

In contrast to the hard realities of the lodging house, the interior of wealth fills the youth with an illusory sense of wonderment. "The splendor of the interior filled him with awe. He was a wanderer in a fairy land" (p. 45).[27] He eases into this luxurious state, lounging and smoking pipes in his friend's room, a domain that "expressed to the visitor that he could do supremely as he chose, for it said plainly that in it the owner did supremely as he chose" (p. 46). Here, as the youth becomes enclosed in comfort, an aura of containment begins to predominate with only the slightest suggestion of externality: "There was a glimpse of a side street" (p. 46). The youth struggles with this growing sense of containment and its reflective consequences, widening his imaginative vista of the street so that it might invade the contented atmosphere of the room.

> He was beginning to see a vast wonder in it that they two lay sleepily chatting with no more apparent responsibilities than rabbits, when certainly there were men, equally fine perhaps, who were being blackened and mashed in the churning life of the lower places. And all this had merely happened; the great secret hand had guided them here and had guided others there. The eternal mystery of social condition exasperated him at this time. He wondered if incomprehensible justice were the sister of open wrong. (Pp. 46–47)

But as the youth settles into his milieu of containment social distance reinstates itself, putting an end to his searching inquiries: "Presently he began to feel that he was a better man than many—entitled to a great pride. He stretched his legs like a man in a garden, and he thought that he belonged to the garden. Hues and forms had smothered certain of his comprehensions. . . . In this way and with this suddenness he arrived at a stage" (p. 47). The bourgeois construction of a world of chance and fate as moral justification for social inequity becomes, in time, less a critical point of contention than an insidious mode of being. The trappings of wealth take over, subduing the reality of the streets. Our youth thus arrives at the stage of philosophical speculation, the mental equivalent of his social condition. He is back, albeit in a highly exaggerated manner, to his point of departure in the companion sketch. Now, in his portal of luxury, "he indulged in monarchical reflections" (p. 47). Situated as he is, poverty becomes a remote prospect, "an idle, half-smothered babble on the

horizon edge" (p. 47). Assuming the rationalizing logic of his incorporation into the upper class, he continues: "It was necessary that it
should be so, too. There was the horizon, he said, and, of course,
there should be a babble of pain on it. Thus it was written; it was a law,
he thought" (p. 47).

Crane's intent here is to simultaneously express and parody the
vacuous reasoning of incorporation. Yet the caprice of such thought is
not entirely without its suasive qualities and, when it is mingled with
the fetishism of place, the insignia of privilege and exclusivity, the
young man succumbs to its governing law of power. "The splendor of
color and form swarmed upon him again. He bowed before the
strength of this interior; it said a word to him which he believed he
should despise, but instead he crouched" (p. 48).

While the interior of wealth is rendered in chromatic imagery, the
bloom of riches, the interior of poverty, as given in the companion
sketch, is overlaid with monochromatic shadings. The imagistic difference in style evokes the qualitative divergence in social existence. In
short, luxury is not misery and, of course, the rich are different. As
the youth recovers his critical faculties, he experiences a changed
perception of what he had been taught to see among the rich by those
apologists of the social order:

> Theologians had for a long time told the poor man that riches did
> not bring happiness, and they solemnly repeated this phrase until
> it had come to mean that misery was commensurate with dollars,
> that each wealthy man was inwardly a miserable wretch. And
> when a wail of despair of rage had come from the night of the
> slums they had stuffed this epigram down the throat of he who
> cried out and told him that he was a lucky man. They did this
> because they feared. (Pp. 50–51)

Crane thus dispels a popular myth. But the conclusion of the experiment is perhaps subordinate to the manner of its unfolding. For the
perceptual correlates of incorporation are displayed in a way that enables the reader to see the manifest destiny of mystification in both an
ironic and convincing light. Seen in the shadows of its companion
sketch, "An Experiment in Luxury" presents the missing link in a
totalizing effort to relate the spatial and conceptual aspects of the
social spectrum. Understood in their relational value, poverty and
affluence, alienation and incorporation are thus brought into dynamic
collision as if to refute that ethereal principle in which "all this had
merely happened."

Crane's entry into both the exploited and dominant classes contrasts the interiors of each in terms of condition as well as conceptual orientation. From his descent into the subculture of the Bowery homeless, Crane arrives at the nether side of alienation, while from his ascent into the abode of wealth, he conveys the opposing cultural attitude, that of incorporation. When both attitudes are paired we have, in summation, the critical response to the major social tension of Crane's era, poverty and affluence in the great metropolis. Crane fixes the social meaning of each attitude. His conclusion from "An Experiment in Luxury" is that "wealth in a certain sense is liberty" (p. 51), a proposition which suggests that incorporation into the upper class produces a condition of maximum choice and minimum constraint. In contradistinction, the alienation of poverty results in entrapment, reversing the formula to that of maximum constraint and minimum choice.

Crane arrives at these conclusions by virtue of his participant observations within the two opposing realms of social condition. On the surface, therefore, his method approximates an ethnographic approach. Yet, as fiction, his critical realism is liberated formally and imaginatively from the positivist restrictions inherent in the ethnographic representation. Crane's approach is attended by a radical subjectivity, for, in these "Experiments," the relation between self and social process is also under investigation. In both "Experiments," Crane cannot remain a detached participant observer but instead must undergo a personal transformation (wrought by an immersion in social experience) in order to render a provocative cultural critique. For Crane, social awareness is the result of an experiment in process; more than the sharing of life worlds, this requires the very merger between self and social condition so that, through his rhetoric of involvement, we can see that what begins in social distance collapses into a heightened state of social consciousness. The self, then, is affirmed as the medium for discovery and transition, thus magnifying the individual as a bridge between culture and subculture and as a model for social change.

Crane's two Bowery sketches, "An Experiment in Misery" and "The Men in the Storm," reveal the difference between liminality, a spatial sequence in a rite of passage, and *communitas*, a transfixed mode of relationship often stimulated by liminality but also apparent in other more permanent social arrangements, such as outsiderhood and structural inferiority. "The bonds of communitas," Victor Turner explains, "are anti-structural in that they are undifferentiated, equalitarian, direct, nonrational (though not irrational), I-Thou or Essential We Relationships, in Buber's sense."[28] Turner opposes the construct of *communitas* to social structure, or "all that holds people apart, defines their differences, and constrains their actions."[29] *Communitas*, as a form of antistructure, emerges as a spontaneous reaction to social structure; that is, to the formal network of economic and sociopolitical standards which regulate the nature of interaction within an institutionalized social system. Social structure is thus necessarily materialistic, bureaucratically mechanized, and hierarchically differentiated into roles and statuses. *Communitas*, on the other hand, is a corrective expression of solidarity which seeks the unity of man beneath the structural tensions of society, a reclamation of man in culture by man in a state of nature.

In "The Men in the Storm," Crane's concentration on the Bowery homeless, as a tension beneath the sustained tension of the social hierarchy, frees him to symbolically frame this underclass in accordance with the values of *communitas*.[30] In this sketch, Crane changes his role from participant to that of omniscient observer, blending consciousness with place. To connect narrative perspective with mood, he masterfully employs the trope of the blizzard to arrive at an intensification of experience commensurate with the condition of antistructure on the street, the supreme leveler of humanity at its lowermost region of existence. The blizzard, with its turbulent force of snow and wind, can be seen as a generative metaphor for the momentary disruption of structure and the evocation of *communitas*. As a rhetorical device, the blizzard resembles a type of counter-authority in which the practical is replaced by the aesthetic. Elevated as such, the symbolic vehicle of the blizzard is both disintegrative, in its attenuation of structure, and unifying, in the foregrounding of its counterpoise—the otherwise occluded realm of antistructure and *communitas*.

Crane's sketch, first published in 1894 in the *Arena*, appeared one year after Stieglitz's widely acclaimed and exhibited print of the early 1890s: *Winter on Fifth Avenue*.[31] Stieglitz's photograph, taken with an eight-by-ten-inch hand-held camera, marks the celebrated entry of the blizzard into the iconography of the American imagination. Since it is well known that Crane lived and maintained an exchange with artists and illustrators during his stay at the old Art Students League Building on East 23rd Street, it is more than likely that he knew of the print. But even if he did not, the photograph still works to thematically

Winter on Fifth Avenue, 1893, *1897 photogravure by Alfred Stieglitz.*
National Gallery of Art, Washington, D.C.

connect the visual presence of the blizzard, objectively depicted by
Stieglitz, with the narrative design of Crane's sketch.

Winter on Fifth Avenue captures the inextricable rhythm of man and
nature in the city. A stagecoach drawn by four almost inseparable
horses is moving through the severity of a storm. The driver, aloft in
his seat, is exposed to the cold and inexorable assault of snow and
wind. There is both tension and balance in the persistence of the
struggling coach, itself an indication of the endurability of the city, of its

habitual comings and goings. The photograph depicts the overall sense of urban hardship; the blizzard, though severe, does not paralyze the urban mechanism, for there is movement and a suggestion from the frame of a procession of coaches steadily and bitterly making their way—even the pedestrians are commingling with the elements.

But in the photograph the city is obscured by the blizzard; only the vague outline of a block of buildings conveys any semblance of structure to the city. They stand towering and erect in the midst of their decomposition, like stolid sentries maintaining the line of a crumbling order. The storm erases the background beyond the second stagecoach, which is already dissolving into the blizzard. This effect draws one into the foreground of the photograph, to that expanse of street which does not so much invite as it thrusts the observer into the spatial immediacy of the moment. The primary figure of the coach can, in fact, be considered as occupying the middle ground of the scene.

It is the foreground of the street, with its integument of furrowed slush, that claims our perception. All the tension in the photograph is centered here in a region which permits us to enter the storm. Within the street the urban image appears increasingly undifferentiated, temporarily stalled in the patterned swirl of blizzard. Men, animals, vehicles, and snow all seem to blend into an anonymous whole. There are forms but no distinct features in this agitated visualization of antistructure. The intensity of the blizzard and its all-over surface quality resemble impressionistic technique and are instrumental in achieving the dissolution of structure. It is, above all, the veil of the storm, snow diagonally superimposed over the photographic image, which obliterates all but the powerful drama of the street, a dramatic closure that is at once harmonious and metaphysical.

In "The Men in the Storm," Crane extends Stieglitz's presentation of the blizzard as an image of oppression as well as a means to display a sense of antistructure. For Crane, the dual role is, in fact, inseparable, coordinating the condition of structural inferiority with its contextual mode of relationship. *Communitas* among the homeless takes its form from the relentless beat of the storm—the precondition for its presence, thus symbolizing the social significance of antistructure within the broader social system. In terms of the scene-agent framework, the storm locates the moving principle on the outside, a determinate external force, establishing the design of the resulting activity. The blizzard thus sanctifies the condition of *communitas* in the very moment in which it asserts its domination over it. As such, the trope takes on two qualities: the authoritative power of the social situation

over the homeless (a symbol of social oppression) and the vehicle
which dissolves structure so as to transgress the opacity of the
storm—to step down into the exposed configuration of antistructure,
to the detritus of its sweep.

The focus of the sketch is on the spatiotemporal dimension of the
moment, a passing scene in the Bowery which is suspended and magnified before it recedes once again, as it must, into the great enduring
flux of the street. Crane's purpose and method permit readers to pass
through the barrier of the blizzard and into its core, where they can
then interact with the experience of homeless men who are gathered
in the storm, waiting for the doors of a charitable house to open. The
point of view, a "detached floating perspective,"[32] skillfully modulates
the tone and perceptual angles of the sketch. In ordering the evanescent fragments which compose the whole, Crane's perspective,
though shifting, ultimately encloses readers within the humanity of the
storm to its conquest of the street so that they might arrive at some
awareness of themselves and their society in the confines of an urban
space. This complicity with the blizzard, an agent for antistructure, is
also effective in dismissing the regimented and structured otherness
of the street as quickly as it is presented, thereby attending to the
inferior mass of homeless men, who, like the blizzard itself, have fallen
from structure.

In the opening line of the sketch we are given a time referent and
date, both speedily engulfed by the remainder of the sentence, which
introduces the blizzard's descent. It begins "to swirl great clouds of
snow along the streets, sweeping it down from the roofs and up from
the pavements."[33] It is here, in the ubiquitous scope of the storm, that
one is interposed into its immediacy, into the midst of departure and
uncertainty. The impressionistic perspective of the opening paragraphs evinces the scattering of the city's representative structure.
Among the shifting visual array of pedestrians, coach drivers, street
cars, laborers, and El trains, one can sense mobilization and a pres-
cience of destination in the dazzling rush of the street. The onset of
the storm conveys an implicit message to those who are able to
escape its distress, to those who animate the street only to abandon it
for shelter. To punctuate this desertion of the storm, "there was an
absolute expression of hot dinners in the pace of the people" (p. 92).
This provides a sharp contrast to the homeless men slowed and
trapped by the storm, "to whom these things were as if they were
not" (p. 92). Though an exclamation of radical negativity in light of its
affirmative complement, the blizzard also gives meaning to the home-

less, who, like the snow itself, are drawn in packs from the pavement, from the hidden recesses of structure. As the blizzard dispenses with structure, carrying it off from the street, it redirects its forceful sweep to the immobile drift of antistructure, to the homeless, who are coalesced by the storm, whose presence is, in fact, made manifest by the storm.

With this renewed focus, the precise time frame which had opened the events is now ambiguously referred to as a protracted moment: "It was an afternoon of incredible length" (p. 92). Both the calendar and clock are lost, thus fulfilling the temporal equivalent of *communitas*, a condition outside of time, an eternal now. Not only time but place as well is vaguely outlined, becoming a desolate remnant of the city's shattered presence:

> The little snow plains in the street began to assume a leaden hue from the shadows of evening. The buildings upreared gloomily save where various windows became brilliant figures of light that made shimmers and splashes of yellow on the snow. A street lamp on the curb struggled to illuminate, but it was reduced to impotent blindness by the swift gusts of sleet crusting its panes. (P. 93)

In the midst of this ghostly demarcation appear the homeless, rising suddenly and reminiscent of old Lazarus come back from the gray dream of dust. Throughout Crane's treatment of them the snow is unkind; the granite wheels of "An Experiment in Misery" have here given way to the more tenacious metaphor of the blizzard. It springs upon the men with peculiar cunning: "The snow, blowing in twisting clouds, sought out the men in their meagre hiding-places and skillfully beat in among them, drenching their persons with showers of fine, stinging flakes" (p. 92).

As the collectivity of homeless begin to settle in front of the lodging house, Crane, through a tight shot, attempts to distinguish among its elements, comparing ethnic composition as well as the difference between hesitant newcomers and veteran Bowery types. But the close angle cannot hold and soon fades into a long shot which, in an accommodation of perspective to mode of relationship, views the homeless congealed into a homogeneous entity.

> They were all mixed in one mass so thoroughly that one could not have discerned the different elements. . . . The sidewalk soon

became completely blocked by the bodies of the men. They
pressed close to one another like sheep in a winter's gale, keeping one another warm by the heat of their bodies. The snow came
down upon this compressed group of men until, directly from
above, it might have appeared like a heap of snow-covered merchandise, if it were not for the fact that the crowd swayed gently
with a unanimous, rhythmical motion. (P. 93)

The men are "pressed close," a "compressed group," seemingly concealed products, but their steady rhythm and oneness betray this
latter image and identify them with the undulations of nature in the
storm. These are images which relate the idea of *communitas* and its
felt presence in the sketch, realigning our perception of the homeless
from that of dehumanized cultural objects, "merchandise," an authoritative vision of structure, to that of purification, given by the
counter-authority of nature.

Through another tight shot, Crane sets his sights within the group,
exposing its divisions, its sense of conflict amid the cooperative form.
It is as if he wishes to remind the reader that this collectivity is no
blessed pilgrimage but, given its situation, one of survival. Yet the
conflict itself, unlike the divisiveness inherent in structure, retains an
underlying sense of unity, of shared struggle, of humor blackened by
the conditions of this catastrophic brotherhood.

The winds seemed to grow fiercer as time wore on. Some of the
gusts of snow that came down on the close collection of heads cut
like knives and needles, and the men huddled, and swore, not like
dark assassins, but in a sort of American fashion, grimly and
desperately, it is true, but yet with a wondrous under-effect,
indefinable and mystic, as if there was some kind of humor in this
catastrophe, in this situation in a night of snow-laden winds. (P.
95)

The homeless men who have surrendered to the street, however,
are seen to exert a kind of power and domination which issues from
their helplessness and inferiority. Near the end of the sketch, Crane
recalls the eclipsed social structure, manipulating it into a dialectical
standstill with antistructure so that the reader can closely examine
their dynamic correspondence. In a shop window across the street and
strategically above the homeless men "in a brilliantly lighted space
appeared the figure of a man" (p. 95). This interloper appears from

nowhere as if an apparition in the great white storm. "He was rather stout and very well clothed. His whiskers were fashioned charmingly after those of the Prince of Wales" (p. 95).

As the homeless men step out of structure, this man glides into it, looking down at the men "in an attitude of magnificent reflection" (p. 95). Erected as a sort of live model of the bourgeois class, he is presented as the exemplar of an insulated affluence—secure, contained, protected from the stormy venue of social strife. When a homeless man, "one of the mob," sees him, many others join in the sight and begin yelling up to him. "They addressed him in every manner, from familiar and cordial greetings to carefully-worded advice concerning changes in his personal appearance" (p. 95). It is here, by means of Crane's effective shift in perspective and rearrangement of the spatial aspects of social class, that the reader is brought to witness this classic confrontation. The masses in the street, by the threat and implication of their underclass, conquer the individualistic image of wealth looming down from its lofty height. The live model abdicates, physically as well as symbolically. "The man presently fled, and the mob chuckled ferociously like ogres who have just devoured something" (p. 95).

If the homeless gathered in the blizzard enjoy a brief respite of triumph, they owe it to the strength of their unity, to their symbolic merger with the street and storm. Through it they have intimidated the artifice of civilization, sent it on its heels, and they turn once again to the simplicity of nature and their own dispossessed condition, a state made holier by its degree of absence.

When the door of the lodging house finally permits entry to the group, a policeman, the representative figure of social authority, supervises its passage out of the storm. Here, the authority of culture and the counter-authority of nature stand balanced in a moment of transition. At the conclusion of the sketch, antistructure is on the very threshold of structure, and as it passes through the vestibule into another world the reader is given two archetypal metaphors for *communitas*, which is simultaneously at its zenith and on the verge of its decline: "When the door below was opened, a thick stream of men forced a way down the stairs, which were of an extraordinary narrowness and seemed only wide enough for one at a time. . . . It was a difficult and painful operation. The crowd was like a turbulent water forcing itself through one tiny outlet" (p. 96).

The metaphorical representation of the homeless men as a "thick stream" and "turbulent water" expresses the fluidity and pure organic

quality of *communitas* in its inevitable phase of transformation. In this
state of nature, there is no mechanistic segmentation of the collectivity, no sense of differentiated status which would assert their inequality in the urban setting. But already the banks begin to close in on
this vibrant form of *communitas*, reenacting the division of homelessness into discrete urban quantities. As the homeless find their enclosure within the charitable house, the blizzard remains visibly behind, seizing the men up until the last moment in a harsh consecration
of their sacrifice, the continuity of their social being despite its shifting
boundaries: "The tossing crowd on the sidewalk grew smaller and
smaller. The snow beat with merciless persistence upon those who
waited. The wind drove it up from the pavements in frantic forms of
winding white, and it seethed in circles about the huddled forms,
passing in one by one, three by three, out of the storm" (p. 96).

The sketch, which reads like a prose poem in its force, unleashes
the blizzard as a disintegrative social enzyme, liquefying those hardened strategies of containment which uphold the values of structure.
Crane's design works conversely to displace the reader from the petri-
faction of cultural presuppositions and into the enclosed social space of
subculture. The sense of containment is thus reversed in terms of
perspective, rendering yet another form of descent and discovery.
This type of containment, though primarily concerned with the homogeneous zone of the homeless, does not simply reverse its direction,
keeping social distance intact by merely relocating it in its obverse
sphere. Crane's method is relational rather than reified, one of inter-
relation rather than fixity. His use of double perspective and modu-
lated perceptual angles allows not only for sustained focus on the
condition of homelessness but also for a dynamic comparison of culture with subculture, affluence with poverty, and structure with antistructure. As such, the sense of containment is more existential than
rigidly conceptual, leading the reader to an act of confrontation rather
than confirmation, to an understanding of the blizzard as a symbolic
entity, one signifying the overwhelming power of a determinate situation in effecting the subcultural designs of human activity. Such an
awareness would surely mitigate social distance rather than magnify it.

Crane's evocation of *communitas*, an alternative mode of relationship, arises from the suffering caused by one's vulnerability to the
storm and the ability to prevail against it by descending into an unpre-
tentious and base humanity. The homeless men, huddled deep within
the blizzard, share a glimpse of solidarity in their common lot. Their
gathering is not mediated by structural considerations; that is, by the

economically patterned materialism of a norm-governed social system, intent on production, consumption, and collecting the proper change. Instead, as with Stieglitz's *Winter on Fifth Avenue*, the *communitas* that is shared is mediated solely by the blizzard, nature's effacing of structure and its driving adversity to man in his ceremonious collectivity.

It is clearly evident that Dreiser had both Stieglitz's *Winter on Fifth Avenue* in sight and Crane's "The Men in the Storm" in mind as paradigms for his resolution of Hurstwood's plight in the denouement of *Sister Carrie*.[34] For Dreiser, the essentially persuasive feature of Stieglitz's photograph was this: "It had the tone of reality."[35] In his first novel, Dreiser would capture that tone, would translate it from the still medium of photography to the highly developed patterns of literature, fleshing the quality out with plot, characterization, theme, and detailed descriptions of place and encounter. His treatment of Hurstwood's failure and Carrie's complementary success appears within the broader context of a realistic novel, a novel so expansive in its range as to encompass the inevitable drift of fate and the structured rise of fortune. The representation of these opposing social realities, the actualization of their destinies, expresses Dreiser's interest in exposing the directional grid beneath the realist's preoccupation with enumerating the thick surface of details, facts, events, the quotidian, and the like. For underneath this busy surface lies the shaping schematic structure of the novel's activity; that is, the binary division between Hurstwood's descent and Carrie's ascent. Both social patterns shape the kinetic world of the novel, giving to the narrative design a predictable physics of contradictory motion. The structure thus operates to efficiently compress the major thematic emphases of the novel and the period of its creation—the conflictual processes of poverty and affluence, the social gulf between the conditions of subculture and those of culture, and the ensuing states of alienation and incorporation which condense the meaning of both process and condition.

For Dreiser, the subtle, almost imperceptible gradations of Hurstwood's classic descent are more a study of the pathway to inferiority than they are a presentation of a rite of passage or an evocation of *communitas*. Though liminality is implicit in Hurstwood's processual degradation, it is not magnified nor mined for its symbolic import but, rather, simply given, hardened into a prosaic fact which prefaces the character's subsequent landings in his slippage through the social system. Dreiser seems more concerned with the antistructural conse-

quences of descent, with the degrees of status reversal in molding
character and remaking Hurstwood from a slick saloon manager into a
Bowery denizen. We are thus conscious of the various but related
results of such a retrogressive process and of the changing conditions
which are prompted by Hurstwood's social and psychic downfall. The
confluence of the character's sociality and individuality amplifies the enveloping scene-agent frame of reference in the novel; that is, the
unyielding force of a situation (tragic in scope) upon social position,
consciousness, and the latter's defining attitude. The fact that Hurstwood's own failure is set against the civic failure of a city during the
depression years of the 1890s works to concretize the vision of this
framework, leading us to see the agent as inseparable from the turmoil
of his society.

The blizzard's appearance in the novel might be likened to the
"snows of reduction";[36] that is, the erasure of human traces which we
witness in the progressively structured disappearance of Hurstwood's
social being. It is the blizzard that reinforces the transformation of his
character as he slides downward to an irreversible condition of structural inferiority. At several significant junctures, the blizzard marks his
declensional passage, and it is there in the terminus of the Bowery to
help finish Hurstwood off, thus completing the job in a final act: the
absolute reduction of his social being. As place and theme, the Bowery
exists as a receptacle for the social process of descent in its final
plunge. It is the supreme scene of suffering which entraps Hurstwood
as he reaches the very perfection of his descent, the logical fulfillment
of the novel's tragic slope. The Bowery (terminal in terms of the
novel's chronological development as well as in the thrust of its thematic message) is pregnant with fate in that it becomes a complete
symbolic merger of all the tragic propensities and consequences converging in the text. The scene of the Bowery, fortified by blizzard
imagery, adequately collapses the agent (Hurstwood's final presence
as a chronic Bowery bum); the fundamental act (descent to the lowermost rung); the overriding attitude (one of finitude); the agency for
this final condition (a pattern of deepening disaffiliation and alienation);
and the purpose (loss of personality and social belongingness, and
reidentification of character into a distinct yet anonymous subculture).
In effecting this conflation of formal textual elements, the Bowery is
thus represented as a compact form of antistructure that ominously
awaits in its own definitive certainty the unraveling of fate implicit in
the novel's tragic design. For Dreiser, the cultural significance of the
Bowery rests in the fact that, by the fin de siècle, this distinct urban

enclave had become entrenched in its association with a place of endings, the final destination of social deprivation, despair, failure, and
death, both real and symbolic. Dreiser knew well what lay ahead for
those who had fallen into oblivion: "Beyond them is the Bowery, the
hospital, and the river—the last . . . the most merciful of all."[37] There
is no doubt that the Bowery had stilled Hurstwood's pathetic drift,
entombed it even before the river could make its claim, thereby cer-
tifying its social meaning as an epitaph to the painful processes of his
descent.

For the full impact of the novel's heightened pattern of descent,
Hurstwood's final state must be seen in contrast to his original social
position and his initial role in the overall design of the story. Our first
glimpse of Mr. G. W. Hurstwood does not occur until the fifth chapter
of the novel. His appearance is preceded by Carrie's arrival in Chicago,
the encounter with Drouet, her search for work, and the "hard contract" she briefly endures as an employee of a shoe factory. Hurstwood's introduction into the novel thus completes the triangulation of
principal characters whose inner involvements deepen the complica-
tion of the plot and the unfolding of destinies.

He is initially presented as a successful manager of Hannah and
Hogg's Adams Street saloon, a respectable establishment catering to
the celebrities about town. His posture displays the altitude of his
position and his social standing as a member of the affluent American
middle class. With an air of opulent confidence he stands before us,
"his coat open, his thumbs in his pockets, the light on his jewels and
rings relieving them with agreeable distinctness. He was the picture of
fastidious comfort."[38] In this holding pattern, Hurstwood's resplendent status and structural affiliations come to light: he is a man of
property and wealth, the head of a household, a sporting soul with
horses, and a member of an eminent circle of society—masculine,
mildly venturesome, amiable, jocular in nature. In short, Hurstwood
figures as an esteemed American type, a good fellow worthy of acquaintanceship: "He was acknowledged, fawned upon, in a way
lionized. Through it all, one could see the standing of the man. It was
greatness in a way, small as it was" (p. 180).

But this holding pattern is soon vanquished by the subsequent
events of the novel. The fundamental act which precipitates Hurstwood's descent is the affair over the stolen money. He steals the
money away from Hannah and Hogg's safe, accidentally left open, after
a torturous inner dialogue between conscience and desire. His desire
takes the money from the safe, conscience puts it back; back and

forth, back and forth, the conflict plays itself out in a rhythm of indecision. Finally the lock on the safe springs; the money is without. Did he do it? No, it merely seems to have happened, an inscrutable force in a moment of interdiction. Nevertheless, a crime has been committed.

Behind the agonizing over this fatal act are the anterior circumstances: domestic turmoil, threat of divorce, and his liaison with Carrie. The act speeds the action of the novel, displacing it from the sedate sphere of his Chicago to the frenzied movement of a train which "swept on frantically through the shadow to a newer world" (p. 281). Suddenly placed in the role of fugitive, Hurstwood schemes, elopes with Carrie under a false pretext, and takes flight. He wins Carrie over while aboard the train, thereby undermining his rival, Drouet, by persuasively mollifying Carrie about his earlier deceptions: the concealment of his marriage and his immediate lie regarding Drouet being sick in the hospital. The final deception, the stolen money, remains secretive.

But as Hurstwood beholds the prize of his seduction, his loss becomes apparent. Moved on by the train, another tempestuous force, he becomes a passenger, relinquishing his control and self-determination to the power of this medium. His feet are not securely fastened; his substance is shadowy and uncertain. With Hurstwood propelled by the train, a truly liminal zone in itself, a passage between spatial locations, we witness his deepened sense of separation, the disassembling of his past, and the premonition of his reduced state. The significance of the act, by which "he had severed himself from the past as by a sword" (p. 300), jolts Hurstwood into comparative reflection.

His condition was bitter in the extreme, for he did not want the miserable sum he had stolen. He did not want to be a thief. That sum, or any other, could never compensate for the state which he had thus foolishly doffed. It could not give him back his host of friends, his name, his house and family, nor Carrie as he had meant to have her. He was shut out from Chicago, from his easy and comfortable state. (P. 287)

The ruminations over his loss of structure, "that dread yearning for the fixed, the stable, the accustomed" (p. 288), are contrasted to his foreboding sense of the future, a glower of antistructure "which lay before him—dark, friendless, exiled" (p. 287). This juxtaposition of structure with antistructure, of the known with the unknown, is followed by a mock change of identity in which Hurstwood momentarily assumes the name on a sign shooting past the train window. In three successive paragraphs Dreiser has both linked and condensed the reoccurring pattern throughout Hurstwood's descent: a graduated deflation of character and social being in which he drops lower and lower from his original position within structure. The ensuing series of precarious landings (or stops along his descent) in turn reshape identity and so function to preface the next step in a series of status reductions. Here, on the train, the downward spiral is suspended in an elegant statement of summary. It is not until Hurstwood arrives in New York, via Montreal, that the descent begins to activate its mode of operation, spiraling down to its eventual flop in the Bowery.

Upon his arrival, New York signified to Hurstwood the hardened contrast between the scale of the city's own established wealth, the conspicuous show of its luxury, and his own distressed condition, made more obscure by virtue of its imperious surroundings. Without his fortune (forfeited to his wife) and with only the paltry sum left from the stolen money (the rest he had returned), Hurstwood shrank before the realm he most aspired to—"wealth, place and fame" (p. 306). It was made plain to Hurstwood that here he was nothing, his possibilities limited, his condition markedly diminished. New York spoke to him in terms of struggle and hardship, of beginning life anew on a dire plan of necessity.

After three years of life in New York City, Hurstwood was neutralized. He "had been moving along in a path which might have been called even. There was no apparent slope downward and distinctly none upward" (p. 337). He and Carrie were situated in an uptown apartment on Amsterdam Avenue, a factor not without its spatial significance in light of successive physical locations. Hurstwood, acting quickly, had invested his money in a partnership in a Warren Street saloon and gained a modest income from the venture. In all, Hurstwood had succeeded in constructing a cheaper, far less imposing facsimile of his former state, only an approximation of his life-style in Chicago. He was given to frugality and restraint, a stinging reminder of his dispossession. His managerial position did not bring him into eminence or esteem. He merely plodded along uneventfully in a distinctly lower-caliber establishment frequented by the common run of clientele. The existential difference which resulted from this subtraction sent Hurstwood into fits of depression, brooding over his present and diminished status. He likened his own situation to "a city with a wall about it. Men were posted at the gates. You could not get in. Those within did not care to come out to see who you were. They were so merry inside there that all those outside were forgotten, and

he was on the outside" (p. 339). The difference expresses itself as an
acknowledgment of exile, a precondition for further descent.

Under a ruse to live more economically and save for another investment, Hurstwood convinces Carrie to take a smaller flat downtown, on
13th Street just off Sixth Avenue. The first signs of a growing poverty
attend this change of address, a spatial descent which precedes Hurstwood's slide into unemployment prompted by the dissolution of the
Warren Street partnership. A real estate deal by the owner of the
building and his partner's shady maneuverings bring an end to Hurstwood's even pace. The business transaction means the loss of his
investment when the lease expires, and as that time passes he is left
with only $700 from his share of the sale of fixtures. During this time,
Hurstwood begins to hunt for other opportunities, but he lacks the
resources to strike a suitable business connection. Even before the
Warren Street arrangement comes to a close, he has mentally undergone the transition from a member of the dominant managerial class to
the déclassé rank of the wage earner. The change in consciousness,
induced by the condition of this lower status, attests to the importance
of one's class position in shaping social attitude. For now Hurstwood
reads with absorbing interest the pathos of city life writ large by the
dailies. During the winter of 1893–94, the worst of the depression
years, Hurstwood takes empathic notice of the headlines in the
"World": "80,000 people out of employment in New York this winter."
The fact "struck as a knife at his heart" (p. 346). This is hardly the
attitude of the old robust manager who had once passed, with an air of
indifference, a bum in Chicago asking the price of a bed.

The loss of employment is perhaps the most crucial factor in accel-
erating Hurstwood's descent, attenuating his structural affiliation to
society and inciting his drift through the counter-realm of antistructure. The physical and emotional coldness of his search for work lead
Hurstwood to an increased state of idleness. In the Broadway Central,
as in other notable hotels, Hurstwood becomes a chairwarmer, a
lounger in lobbies, reading and passing the time away. "Taking a chair
. . . was a painful thing to him. To think he should come to this. . . . It
had always seemed a cheap, miserable thing to do. But here he was"
(p. 353). The act of becoming a chairwarmer signifies both his movement away from accustomed cultural affiliations and his inward objec-
tions, which still show the continued hold that culture retains on him.
We must remember that both culture and subculture become divisions
within the man at this point, before the latter gradually engulfs him and
such residual admonishments. Hurstwood's immersion in the dailies,

both in hotel lobbies and at his flat, augments the passivity of his new spectator role, revealing his rising apathy and deepening physical as well as psychic withdrawal. It is the onset of a three-day blizzard which underscores these developments, blanketing Hurstwood's transformation from a temporary member to a permanent fixture of the unemployed.[39] His own deteriorating situation is set against the general social strife of a city caught amid the blustering crush of the storm.

Hurstwood's appearance soon reveals the torpidity of this profound status reversal. He takes to hanging about in old clothes and forgoes shaving until the end of each week. His physicality becomes an emphatic expression of his degenerating social and psychological condition, signaling a total integration of his descent. As the money dwindles, the descent becomes increasingly empowered, insidiously nurtured by a steady state of nothingness. Hurstwood's estrangement from Carrie also intensifies the processes which redirect his social being: the faltering alliance paves the way for the lonely vigils of Hurstwood's acutely delimited world. In a moment of recrudescence, Hurstwood dons his old suit for a night on the town. "I'm not so bad—I'm not down yet," he tells himself (p. 373). Thus propped, he sallies forth into the night, a nostalgic figure retracing the dubious contours of outline, for "it was not the old Hurstwood—only a man arguing with a divided conscience and lured by a phantom" (p. 374).

As Hurstwood's money runs out, he becomes wholly dependent upon Carrie's earnings as a small but budding actress in the city's low comedy theater. In a last-ditch effort to seek work, he applies as a motorman during the heightened conflict of the Brooklyn Trolley Strike. His determination is undercut by his gloomy countenance, showing "a dark, silent man" (p. 412), and by the severe wintry cold which attends his employ as scab. The storm and stress of the overall situation and the barrenness of the streetcar barn in which Hurstwood is holed up reflect the turmoil and privations of his own inner dwelling. In manning the streetcar, Hurstwood is assailed by the projectiles hurled by the striking crowd, by their threatening epithets, and by their violent kicks and punches. The sound of a bullet ring brings a resounding finish to Hurstwood's adventure. It proves too much for him and he sneaks away in retreat. But his escape is not without its lasting effects. As he makes his way home by foot and by ferry, his passage is accompanied once again by the onslaught of a blizzard, an accomplice to the furious blows of his transformation. To Hurstwood, the ultimate meaning of his experience as scab was the fact that "he had tried and failed" (p. 430). And now there was nothing left to do but invest in the latter.

Carrie gracefully exits the enveloping scene of pathos to pursue her own fortune in the theater. After she departs, Hurstwood rocks in his chair, contemplating the floor. His sights are turned downward, and his body soon follows his vision. He does what must be done, selling the furniture as a momentary stay against destitution. Then "the ex-manager turned his face toward the lower portion of the city. He knew where the cheap hotels were" (p. 441). It is as if he holds a cognitive map which correlates social status with urban locality. The importance of Hurstwood's spatial dislocation becomes apparent here. Naturally establishing himself uptown upon arrival in the city, a simulation of his former standing, he then moves to the middle vicinity of Greenwich Village, neither up nor down but moderately even. But from here it is but a short walk to his next residence, a third-rate Bleecker Street hotel, making the destination of his final habitat—a Bowery lodging house—a mere tumble. The ontological value of Hurstwood's descent is thus neatly capsulized by the segregated geographical pattern of the city and his movement from the top to the near bottom of the island's socially resonant districts.

As Hurstwood secures the urban embodiment of his flagging condition, Carrie becomes instated within the walled city, commanding a salary of $150 per week, a harbinger of her increasing value as capital. Their relationship is now solely mediated by whatever bits and pieces Hurstwood reads in the papers covering her success or from the image of her person on billboards. For Hurstwood, the sign registers distance, and as she recedes from him he ceases to be distressed, at least temporarily, about his own present condition. His personal store of history, activated by his last remaining resource, memory, begins to fill in those immeasurable gaps of his current lifeless condition. While in a fifteen-cent lodging house in the Bowery, "his preference was to close his eyes and dream of other days. . . . It was not sleep at first, but a mental harking back to scenes and incidents in his Chicago life" (p. 459). In this temporal exchange of being, the annihilation of Hurstwood's present is thus chastened by the golden aura of his past.

It is not long before Hurstwood is scraping bottom. Down to his last twenty cents, he finds temporary work as a scrub man and errand boy at the Broadway Central, the hotel where he formerly whittled away the hours as a chairwarmer. Now the lobby becomes an inaccessible luxury; he is relegated to the back room, so to speak, where even porters, cooks, and clerks are all above him in rank. Sickness fore-shortens his period of menial labor, and he is sent to Bellevue. When he returns to the streets, Dreiser gives us this picture of the man:

> No more weak-looking object ever strolled out into the spring sunshine than the once hale, lusty manager. All his old corpulency had fled. His face was thin and pale, his hands white, his body flabby. Clothes and all, he weighed but one hundred and thirty-five pounds. Some old garment had been given him—a cheap brown coat, and a misfit pair of trousers. Also some change and advice. He was told to apply to the charities. (P. 463)

From Bellevue, it is back to the Bowery and to a new mode of sub-sistence, beggary. The parasitic means of Hurstwood's production, feeding off the crumbs of surplus, amounts to a transvaluation of the verities which inhere in the economic structure of society. Yet it is precisely in this manner that he is integrated into the Bowery subcul-ture of homelessness, into its principles of economic life.

Hurstwood's initiation into subculture is strengthened by his en-counter with the benevolent ex-soldier who secures beds for the homeless near Madison Square Park. It is here that Hurstwood finds his class, recognizable by virtue of its physical and social attributes of deformity. The ex-soldier is no mountebank. The paramilitary design of his charity, reminiscent of Coxey's tramp army of 1894, makes him out to be a sincerely efficient barker for the homeless, a magnet that attracts them in their collective need. His presentation of the men to the public in order to solicit money for their lodgings is a dramatic enactment of their dependency, a sort of desperate sideshow to the teeming activity of the theater district. The wandering Hurstwood stumbles upon the scene: "In the glare of the neighboring electric light, he recognized a type—his own kind, the figures whom he saw about the streets and in the lodging houses, drifting in mind and body like himself" (p. 469). Jaded and needy, Hurstwood lines up with the homeless crowd to be thus counted and identified among them. He takes his turn, and, as the "Captain" pleads for him in this trans-ference of authority, Hurstwood is duly emasculated. When the last bed is secured, the "Captain" assembles the men, 137 in all, and upon his command they march downward, one body in spiritless parade.

Hurstwood soon emerges as a chronic bum and beggar of the Bow-ery subculture. His descent can go no further and so folds into a permanent condition of structural inferiority. It is down on the Bowery where Hurstwood is finally flattened, where the plasticity of process hardens into the petrified form of fatality. He becomes a habitué, patronizing such charities as the convent mission house of the Sisters of Mercy on 15th Street and Fleischmann's midnight bread line on the corner of Broadway and 9th Street. His disaffiliation from culture is now complete and, as Hurstwood seeks its compensation within the brackets of subculture, he becomes firmly implanted in the subsoil of antistructure. He becomes but one member in an overall typology of homelessness.

> A study of these men in broad light proved them to be nearly all of a type. They belonged to the class that sits on the park benches during the endurable days and sleeps upon them during the summer nights. They frequent the Bowery and those down-at-the heels East Side streets where poor clothes and shrunken features are not singled out as curious. . . . Miserable food, ill-timed and greedily eaten, had played havoc with bone and muscle. They were all pale, flabby, sunken-eyed, hollow-chested, with eyes that glinted and shone, and lips that were a sickly red by contrast. Their hair was but half attended to, their ears anaemic in hue, and their shoes broken in leather and run down at heel and toe. They were of a class which simply floats and drifts. (P. 489)

The identification of this underclass with a sense of place brings subculture into harmony with its relegated urban domain. Thus superimposed, social form and segregated space relax into a homogeneous zone of dilapidation where neither is "singled out as curious." This cultural arrangement, a category of the inconspicuous, fosters social distance by rendering subculture invisible. Yet it also coheres the homeless through their attachment to setting, making their state highly visible to each other. Dreiser's group portrait of the homeless works to disclose their prominent exposure, to detail the haunting visage of antistructure with its ghoulish cosmetics naturally applied. While structure is taut, erect, integrated, substantively ruddy, antistructure by contrast is here portrayed as lax, emaciated, bagged-out, and at sea, floundering.

As a point of light in this broad portraiture, Hurstwood plays his part, a discernible element enlarging the significance of the whole. His profound attachment to the Bowery circumscribes his degenerating existence. The essence of the place not only brands Hurstwood with its stigmata but also, through a centripetal force of gravity, fastens him into its geography of imagination. At one point near his finale, after a series of rejections from passersby while seeking alms, Hurstwood decides to give up the ghost. "'I'm no good now. I was all right. I had money. I'm going to quit this,' and with death in his heart he started down toward the Bowery" (p. 492). Money is equated with worth and the Bowery with defeat in its most definitive posture. Though the intention is real, the act itself is ironically precluded by Hurstwood's receipt of a quarter, which he spends to procure food and lodging. On another occasion, in the middle of a winter snowstorm, Hurstwood's wanderings have left him at the Boulevard and 67th Street, "where he finally turned his face Bowery-ward" (p. 493). The sense of place becomes so intertwined with the pattern of his descent as to encapsulate it. From uptown to downtown he drifts, gimplike, in this unidirectional course of endings. As destination, the Bowery tirelessly awaits his return, his coming home. At 42nd Street, the contrast between the affluence of the surroundings and his own destitution overwhelms him. "'What's the use,' he thought. 'It's all up with me. I'll quit this'" (p. 493). He shuffles on toward the Bowery to a fate that binds him, turning his incoherent determination into an act of clarity.

The novel's sense of finality is energized by the presence of a blizzard, which brings Hurstwood to his knees.

> It was a truly wintry evening a few days later when his one distinguished mental decision was reached. Already at four o'clock the sombre hue of night was thickening the air. A heavy snow was falling—a fine, picking, whipping snow, borne forward by a swift wind in long, thin lines. . . . Along Broadway, men picked their way in ulsters and umbrellas. Along the Bowery, men slouched through it with collars up and hats pulled over their ears. In the former thoroughfare, business men and travellers were making for comfortable hotels. In the latter, crowds on cold errands shifted past dingy stores, in the deep recesses of which lights were already gleaming. (Pp. 494–495)

The storm creates a symbolic web, setting the poverty of the Bowery thoroughfare against the affluence of Broadway. Having thematically evoked an image of the whole, the storm then recasts the interrelationship of destinies among the principal characters in the novel's conclusion. The social structure of the novel is thus reinstated, placed into the foreground of the storm, in order to examine the connection among its divergent attitudes and social contexts. In the elasticity of the blizzard, Hurstwood's final reduction is set against the other characters' relationship to the storm, to its symbolic quality of social strife.

The consequences for each represent the various but related maneuverings of his or her social position through the vortex of the storm.

Installed in her comfortable chambers at the Waldorf, Carrie is insulated from the blizzard. While reading Balzac's *Père Goriot* (a distinct elevation in her literary education), she pauses to look out from her window onto the storm below. She is overcome by sympathy, largely engendered by the contents of the novel. "'Isn't it just awful'" (p. 495), she remarks as she views the wintry scene. Driven by insatiable dreams and vaguely glimpsed ideals, Carrie is protected from the harsh realities of the blizzard. It is not the clarity of life but the figures of artifice that concern her as she offers her gesture of generalized pity, revealing the immense distance that marks Carrie's relation to Hurstwood's condition. In light of Hurstwood's social posture down on the Bowery, Carrie's attitude is lent a tragic irony by her roommate's remark: "'How sheepish men look when they fall, don't they?'" (p. 495). Carrie's response to the storm underscores her sense of mystification rather than her awakening. As Dreiser had put it in his article "Curious Shifts of the Poor," written just previous to *Sister Carrie* and later reworked into the ending of the novel, "the attitude of pity which the world thinks proper to hold toward poverty is misplaced—a result of the failure to see and realize . . . for society is not better than its poorest type."[40] The slumbrous incantation of pitiful bourgeois sentiments, as with Carrie at this very moment, seals the storm from any further encroachment upon the boundaries of social distance and containment. For Carrie, contained in mind and body, the Waldorf provides the symbolic enclosure for both, a social entity within the walled city that adjusts the consciousness of mystification to its related coordinate of an ascendant affluence.

The storm is no impediment to Drouet, who ducks out of it and into the Imperial Hotel, shaking the snow from his garments, a gesture of its innocuous effects. He is already preparing an antidote to the inclement weather, an evening of entertainment and comfort. "Bad weather had driven him home early and stirred his desires for those pleasures which shut out the snow and the gloom of life. . . . The old butterfly was as light on the wing as ever" (p. 496). Drouet is actually leavened by the storm, one of its lightsome flakes that flutters on the span of the city's dandified trivialities.

In the meantime, Hurstwood's ex-wife and estranged family make their formidable appearance "on an incoming vestibuled Pullman, speeding at forty miles an hour through the snow of the evening" (p.

496). The powerful machine, the most sophisticated means of overland travel at the time, defies the blizzard as it carries the Hurstwoods unhindered toward their destination, New York City, and then a passage to Italy. The free movement of the train, indifferent to the elements at play, embodies the supercilious attitude among its select travelers. Their contemptuous superiority, afforded by wealth and position, is also given unrestrained movement. The storm is merely a passing point of conversation, an incident in the condescending wink of an eyelash, a scene no more or less important than cards, dinner, and the moody restlessness of anticipated leisure.

"The last of this small and once partially united company, however, was elsewhere, having reached a distinguished decision" (p. 497). Hurstwood is here emphatically detached from structure, wholly within the storm and part of that growing body that is left down and out: "Before a dirty four-story building in a side street quite near the Bowery, whose one-time coat of buff had been changed to soot and rain, he mingled with a significant crowd of men—a crowd which had been and was still gathering by degrees" (p. 497). This disassociation recalls Crane's dramatic juxtaposition; that is, the fluid pace of structure countered by the abrupt positioning of antistructure. Dreiser too accentuates this sense of being elsewhere, waiting before the doors of a lodging house to open, and thus halts all of the structured action which precedes Hurstwood's emergence in the storm. As the numbers of the men increase, Dreiser seems more intent on a detailed description of their inferior condition, the desperate nature of their underclass. Compared to Crane, his treatment of the scene is prosaic yet forceful, plodding along brick by brick in a style that persuades by its sheer cumulative weight.

> In the drive of the wind and sleet they pushed in on one another. There were wrists, unprotected by coat or pocket, which were red with cold. There were ears, half-covered by every conceivable semblance of a hat, which still looked stiff and bitten. In the snow they shifted, now one foot, now another, almost rocking in unison. . . .
>
> Now a sharper lash of wind cut down and they huddled closer. It was an edging, shifting, pushing throng. There was no anger, no pleading, no threatening words. It was all sudden endurance, unlightened by either wit or good fellowship.
>
> A carriage went jingling by with some reclining figure in it. (P. 498)

The rocking movement of the men is similar in design to Crane's rhythm of nature, but the intended results are quite different. For Dreiser's interest remains at the level of social oppression, highlighting a sense of anonymity which reinforces the structural inferiority of the collectivity. He does not, as with Crane, tandemly evoke the bond of *communitas*, for the novel seeks a more complicated resolution of character and thematic development. The reclining figure in the carriage is again analogous to Crane's interloper, though without the punch. The potential of the contrast goes undeveloped; it is merely given, a passing sign in the rush to the novel's terminal designation.

Dreiser is more bluntly naturalistic in his design of the blizzard scene, picturing the men's endurance of the storm's steady punishment with a passive sense of stupefaction, as in their face-to-face encounter with the closed doors of the lodging house. "They looked at it as dumb brutes look, as dogs paw and whine and study the knob. They shifted and blinked and muttered. . . . Still they waited and still the snow whirled and cut them with biting flakes" (p. 498). When the doors open, Dreiser presents more of the same primitive animalistic imagery but with one significant difference, for the sense of character is here pronounced in Hurstwood's further detachment from subculture, from the boundaries of both structure and antistructure: "It was push and jam for a minute, with grim, beast silence to prove its quality, and then it melted inward, like logs floating, and disappeared. . . . It was just six o'clock and there was supper in every hurrying pedestrian's face. And yet no supper was provided here— nothing but beds. Of these, Hurstwood was claiming one" (p. 499).[41]

Contemplative and yet a man of action, Hurstwood takes his own room with a small gas jet. Though he separates himself from the subculture of homelessness, he retains its indelible characteristics. He remains invisible in his cell, "hidden from view" (p. 499), after he turns the gas off, and the nature of his suicide is itself passive in nature, reflecting the defeatism of his subculture. Furthermore, the feigned dignity in which Hurstwood faces his doom is an attitude that quickly reveals itself to him as inauthentic, a grandiose posture inconsistent with his general condition. He drops it and retreats to a more suitable posture of complete anonymity and finitude, again consistent with the demands of his inferior class. Dreiser's depiction of subculture and characterization here combines in a conclusive act of abandonment.

After a few moments in which he reviewed nothing, but merely hesitated, he turned the gas on again, but applying no match.

Even then he stood there, hidden wholly in that kindness which is
night, while the uprising fumes filled the room. When the odor
reached his nostrils he quit his attitude and fumbled for the bed.

"What's the use," he said wearily, as he stretched himself to
rest. (P. 499)

The resolution of the novel is dramatically enacted by the symbolic
vehicle of the blizzard, the means for the novelistic convergence of
scene, agent, act, agency, attitude, and purpose. All of these primary
textual facets are swept into the concentrated force of the blizzard, a
single compressed entity of determinant value. Hurstwood's suicide,
the final event of the novel, is but a swan song to the reduction of this
merger, the completion of its tragic inevitability. In its integration of
this finalized reduction, the blizzard produces an intensification of experience, heightening our awareness of the Bowery. As the ultimate
scene of suffering, the Bowery collapses the entire superimposed
range of textual elements into its abyss, much like the perceptual
quality of black in absorbing the combined spectrum of light into its
own monochromatic depth. It is an exercise in the one and the many,
though black, as the absence of color, never reveals itself as anything
other, despite the breadth of its constitutive elements. Extending this
analogy, we may safely presume, in light of the overall pattern and
synthetic culmination of the novel, that the real magnet which attracts
is none other than the Bowery, the culturally laden and alluring grave
of the novel's thematic as well as spatial destination.

Though the first chapter of Dreiser's originally published novel—
"The Magnet Attracting: A Waif amid Forces"—leads us to believe
that it is Carrie who is the primary character and the presence of
Chicago that exerts the centripetal force, Dreiser's intention (as revealed in the Pennsylvania edition) appears to have been just the
opposite. All the real depth, movement, and purpose in the novel
derive from Hurstwood and his fall, that spiraling trajectory of social
being drawn increasingly downward into the whorling nucleus of New
York City, the Bowery, the essential terminus of social descent, and
the inevitable vacuum of a languishing destitution. The text of *Sister
Carrie* is thus circumscribed by the forceful suction of its ending and
by the overriding novelistic pattern curving toward that conclusive
realization, rather than by the flirtatious beginnings of the novel when,
filled with suspense and uncertainty, we are momentarily fixed on the
plane of another necessary though insufficient departure.

The thrust of Dreiser's naturalistic vision, his adaptation of a Spencerian determinist philosophy, places the moving principle of the novel within an amoral framework, that of scene-agent. This vision sees Hurstwood as shaped by forces beyond the control of his will, be they fate, or the inscrutable powers of chance, or chemisms. Such a determinant situation, when placed within the tragic form of the novel, finds its summarizing attitude in a statement of fatalism, the agent quitting the scene of his discontent.[42] The formal design of the novel is in itself a category of critical realism, particularly in its exchange of pessimism for optimism, in its assertion of situation over agent, and in its gradual replacement of structure with antistructure. Moreover, the entire pattern of reversal and descent signifies the demystification and rupture of the strategies of containment. With the emphasis on process as a predetermining principle, embodied in Hurstwood's descent, we can chart the course of its finely complex gradations, which span the entire social spectrum from the heights of culture to the depths of subculture. Hurstwood's descent provides those connecting links within the social system, proving that culture and subculture are not immutable entities but, rather, transferable. Consider, for instance, Hurstwood's suicide in the lodging house room. Whereas Riis's reportage would view the room as the isolated cause and encompassing condition of Hurstwood's plight (the room would, in effect, captivate Hurstwood's meaning), Dreiser's fiction reveals the room as the final embodiment of a descending series of social processes which ultimately lead Hurstwood there. Thus, distance is surmounted, and the fragmentation and fixity of the standard bifurcation between classes, which inadvertently helped people to conceive of them in terms of nonrelationship, is thereby upset. The processual pattern of Hurstwood's descent concretely defies the simplicity of such reified thought, premised as it is upon the condition of social distance. The social and ideological purpose of Dreiser's strategy is to represent the whole of society, its cross-currents of ascent and descent, its dual processes of affluence and poverty, its values of cultural incorporation and subcultural alienation, all in a realistic style that seeks to intimately relate the disparate emphases as they traverse the weblike interior of a specific historical period.

Together, Crane's and Dreiser's representations disinterred the Bowery from its state of concealment. In disclosing the essence of its contents and themes, both writers worked to reintroduce the Bowery into the critical realism of American literature and social existence. With Crane's interest in ritual passage and *communitas* and Dreiser's preoccupation with character and thematic development (actualized in the status of structural inferiority), we have both the antistructural context and condition of social being among the Bowery homeless along with the traces of its long stretch, its processes of descent. When the concerns of both writers are taken together, they not only present the results but tell the story of the process as well.

4 / BOWERY TALES

I saw a man pursuing the horizon;
Round and round they sped.
I was disturbed at this;
I accosted the man.
"It is futile," I said,
"You can never—"

"You lie," he cried,
And ran on.

—*Stephen Crane*
  The Black Riders and Other Lines

his chapter continues the discussion of critical realism by examining Crane's extension of it. The concern here shifts somewhat from the Bowery *per se* to its role in revealing Crane's idea of society. In both of his Bowery tales, *Maggie: A Girl of the Streets* and *George's Mother,* Crane broadens the conceptual boundaries of the Bowery in order to ironically treat the urban social structure in its entirety. This inclusiveness is fundamental to Crane's critical perspective on American urban life and values in the 1890s. His comprehensive outlook on the dialectic between culture and subculture extends the range of social content he is able to manipulate in the above works as it extends the literary form, style, and tone in which such material is expressed. In conjunction with his inimitable ironic technique, Crane's selective choice of narrative strategies for *Maggie* and *George's Mother* clearly enables him to expose and transcend the guiding assumption inherent in mystification. In doing so, Crane reveals the complexity of critical realism as both literary form and social meaning.

The underlying dynamic in mystification, contained in all its myriad styles, is the distortion of urban poverty which results from a misrecognition of social realities. In short, mystification distorts (or makes strange) our perception of poverty and homelessness so as to conceal the involvement of culture with subculture and thus hide the process while presenting and condemning condition. Obviously, the effectiveness of the strategy rests in its reification of the Bowery and the exclusion of social, historical, political, and economic forces, all of

which, when considered, would intricately connect culture with subculture in accounting for the prominent skeins of urban social structure
and the expansive web of ideology.

In *Maggie*, Crane formulates and employs the antithesis of the
dynamic of mystification. Through his strategy, a strategy naturally
aligned with the tenets of critical realism, Crane makes the old, familiar social world strange not to hide but to magnify the involvement
between culture and subculture. I call this strategy *defamiliarization*.
By defamiliarized (a Russian Formalist concept) I mean the ability,
which Crane masterfully achieves, "to dislocate our habitual perceptions of the real world so as to make it the object of renewed attentiveness."[1] In sum, to defamiliarize means to make strange, not for the
facile omission of the dialectic, but for its pronounced inclusiveness.
Thus, I mean to extend the term *defamiliarization* from its traditional
association with formal technique and poetry in general (all fiction and
poetry imply this aspect of making ordinary language strange and,
hence, altered) to a more critical social and ideological purpose which
Crane undoubtedly advances—the challenge to the established codes
culture employs to perceive and interpret the social phenomenon of
urban poverty.

In order to reveal this intimate and interconnected dialectic, Crane
tells a story of subculture while simultaneously engaging in a critique
of cultural values and systems of belief. By superimposing the ideological content of culture onto the grotesque realism of Bowery subculture, Crane is able to defamiliarize the cherished codes of a genteel
culture and make them the object of heightened scrutiny and reevaluation. The social distance between culture and subculture is thus undermined so that the disfigured middle-class moral standards, appropri-
ated by and embodied primarily in the Bowery mission and Bowery
theater, become the false, idealized values foregrounded in the text.
From this dislodged perspective, victimization is perceived as imposed
on subculture by the attitudes and systems of belief resident in culture. In *Maggie*, then, Crane's strategy of defamiliarization successfully exposes and inverts the dialectic so that subculture becomes
the empowered point of reference for a fundamental critique of the
values and patterns inherent in American culture and their insidious
influence upon subculture. While Maggie's demise is seen as the failure of an ideal imposed by culture and internalized by subculture, the
conclusion of the novella also suggests an open textual system. At the
banks of the East River, Crane leaves us with the hope and possibility
of a new realignment between culture and subculture. Crane's vision

looks to the future of critical realism for authentic social inquiry and
literary representation that will continue to address the epidemic of
false consciousness and demystify the channels through which it is
disseminated. Though critical, Crane's aim here is also positive in that
he promotes a self-critical awareness of culture's ideological "givens"
and their influence upon interpretation and action. Maggie's sacrifice is
then not without its compensating humanistic values, for her end
brings a new beginning to fruition.

The narrative strategy of defamiliarization in *Maggie* sustains the
dialectic throughout and, in the flickerings of that requisite oscillation
between the two antipodes, focuses the reader's attention on the
workings of culture. In contrast, *George's Mother* goes beyond defamiliarization to incorporate a more altered social outlook; in Crane's
later novella Bowery subculture annihilates the ordered system of
meanings and beliefs that cohere a dominant culture. Whereas defamiliarization entails the progression of the dialectic, implying a corrective program of action beyond the narrative design (and thus affirm-
ing the potential viability of culture), annihilation signals the
degeneration of the dialectic and the utter illusion of "program." As
with *Maggie*, Crane's treatment of descent and disillusionment in
George's Mother fulfills, in part, the same aim of reflective judgment on
the injurious ideological "givens" of culture. But Crane's later novella,
more darkly conceived, assumes a more radical critical position than
the former. By choosing the strategy of annihilation and the withering
away of the dialectic, Crane projects a nihilistic attitude into the
thematic scene of the Bowery. Through Crane's analogic method, this
projection naturally extends to the remains of culture itself as it erodes
into subculture's encompassing abyss. The descent and dissipation are
thus much broader than the character of George Kelcy, for they comment on a similar process undergone by culture.

In the conclusion of *George's Mother*, culture, associated with the
old, anachronistic order, is no longer seen as potentially viable (in
contrast to Crane's position in *Maggie*); instead the whole architec-
tonic design fades away, thus leaving Bowery subculture as the new
paradigm for a transformed social reality—the secular age of urban
industrialism. Crane's shift in perspective from *Maggie* to *George's
Mother* is premised upon the notion that a culture whose viability is
dependent upon illusion and deception is a culture not worth the affirmation. The result is a sort of devolutionary payment—the distended
presence of subculture, which, in this closed textual system, reiterates the sense of ritualistic entrapment, which amounts to a grim

program of inevitability. It is as if Crane puts into question the whole idea of culture and thus the credibility of the human enterprise, man in society. As such, recreating culture from its illusive "givens" is, for Crane, tantamount to the futility exercised in that wondrous activity— the pursuit of a horizon. Crane evidently grew weary of the "lie" and found critical resolve in some extreme though tangible Bowery truths.

Crane's first Bowery novella was originally entitled *Maggie: A Girl of the Streets (A Story of New York)*.[2] That last tag of the first edition—*A Story of New York*—seems to be a clue, lost in subsequent publications, regarding Crane's purpose: the inclusion of both culture and subculture in a story of Bowery tenement life. The ironic structure of Crane's novella swerves between two points of reference: the explicit presentation of subculture and the implicit deflection of surface content to the dominant ideological code of middle-class culture. With Crane, the word moves inward and outward, to the withinness of subculture and to the withoutness of culture. It is the oscillation of the ironist, yet in *Maggie* Crane creates a fusion of both spheres so that we see the cultural/subcultural monster in its full symbolic raiment, bloated "like a fat monk in a picture."[3]

If we ignore the implicit dimension of "withoutness" in the novella, we are left with a truncated account of *Maggie*, wholly contained on the single level of subculture. In the words of one critic, reading the novella as a foreshortened treatment of subculture, the reader is thus placed within "the moral void of these slums."[4] Such a restricted focus leads us to view victimization, embodied in Maggie, as coming wholly from within the subculture: enacted by her mother, the players in the tenement building, the Bowery theater and mission, her brother, and, of course, Pete, her seducer. Seen from within, the design appears to be Crane's indictment of subculture, for subculture according to this version is disconnected from culture, from the entire urban social structure and its great influence.

This reading of the novella, which folds its depth into a flat surface, is not entirely without justification. Crane's ironic style, narrative structure, impressionist method, and symbolization reinforce his parodic intent, which again appears directed at the distended presence of Bowery subculture. Plot and characterization are derived from standard melodramatic formulation. By appropriating this cultural form, Crane shows how the values of subculture, drawn mainly from the mission and theater, are false to experience. Both setting and characters are swollen in their physical and emotional expansion: the tene-

ment district is bursting its boundaries, an implosive image of the
modern industrial city in teeming and frenetic energy; the theater
audience swells with the values of sentimental melodrama; Maggie's
heart is swollen with romantic ideals; Pete's head is overripe with the
prowess of a Bowery Boy; Jimmie's double standard and "sublime
license" of slum warrior inflate his stature; and Mary Johnson, Maggie's mother, is just plain bloated, swollen with righteous indignation
and indiscriminant vengeance. Abstract and virtuous notions, such as
honor, heroism, purity, sentimental piety, respectability, and social
approval, pervade the perceptions of the Bowery players so that moral
appearances clash loudly with slum realities. Although the moral pos-
ings ultimately lead to Maggie's fall and denunciation, subculture expi-
ates itself of its collective guilt by making her the scapegoat. Crane's
irony, however, exposes this as condemnation without the social reckoning.

Yet in this reading the social purpose of Crane's ironic technique is
sealed, incapable of transcending his literal meaning. The object of
attack thus reverberates within the homogeneous zone of the Bowery
so that the summarizing attitude appears to be ridicule of inappropriate
values and derision of absurd conduct. Such a constricted interpretation of the novella's import leads critics to conclude by reason of
omission. "Crane makes no judgments about the sources of the slum
mud puddle," writes one critic.[5] Another critic assumes the following:
"*Maggie* holds no polemic; Crane did not think much about social
questions, and nobody has suggested that he read much about them."[6]
These statements underrate the full gist of Crane's parody and neglect
the complexity of the novella's design and cultural meaning. Crane was
no social reformer nor crusader, but this fact does not preclude his
deep involvement in social criticism at the levels of both subculture
and culture. His selection of material, method, and strategy in creating
Maggie reveals the intimate dialectic between culture and subculture,
the correspondence between paradigm and ersatz, source and enactment, which completes the configuration of American society in the
1890s.

Even if we take *Maggie* at face value, we cannot escape the moral
reference that permeates subculture. Place and character are swollen,
suggesting not a scrawny moral void but an environment suffused with
ideals, attitudes, and systems of value. An examination of the moral
standards which inform the perceptions and behavior of subculture
indicates that they do not emanate from within but are imposed from
without. The ideology which inscribes itself in the novella is none

other than those conventional categories of middle-class culture displaced to the "toif" of subculture. The Bowery thus presents itself as an environment crafted by the superimposition of cultural modes of belief onto tenement existence. In keeping with this view, environment becomes a determinant condition, a "tremendous thing," in Crane's words, but the determinism is less a consequence of material factors and much more a result of false consciousness produced by culture and consumed by subculture. As Donald Pizer writes, "Maggie is . . . destroyed not so much by the physical reality of slum life as by a middle-class morality imposed on the slums by the missions and the melodrama, a morality which allows its users both to judge and to divorce themselves from responsibility from those they judge."[7]

But why should the Bowery subculture be the mouthpiece for mystification in the form of muddled sentimentality, delusion of self and other, quixotic quest, self-justification, evasion of social responsibility, and individualized interpretations of social evil? There is no doubt that these distorted values of culture are operative in the lives of subcultural members. But to what end? Is the agency of victimization simply transferred to a lower social plane? To move beyond appearances, Crane's novella is not only a story of subculture but also, and more essentially, a criticism of culture. The full intent of his ironic method is consummated by presenting subculture as a looking glass which reflects the ideological presuppositions and exertions of culture. Such a design demands the incorporation of culture into textual analysis in order to fulfill Crane's ironic inclusiveness.

Crane's technique affects the recontextualization of this cultural ideology into the lower social plane of subculture. In rendering this descent, Crane gives the ideology of culture its hideous cast—the parody. Yet it is a parody with a purpose in mind. As Eric Solomon asserts, Crane parodies critically and not conventionally. His aim is positive, not absurdist. His parody maneuvers by way of dislocation and incongruity. The attribution of middle-class morality to subculture disfigures cherished cultural concepts of good order and propriety, and the result is that, exuding from the bosom of Mary Johnson, the ideological content becomes defamiliarized and, hence, subverted.

In *Maggie*, Crane works on those entrenched terms of seeing prescribed by middle-class ideology in order to expose, invert, and parody them. By placing the categories of dominant ideology within the setting and conduct of the Bowery, within an exploited subculture whose own terms, conditions, and way of life are completely *outré*, Crane effectively degrades the investiture of the ideal. The strategy of

Crane's critical realism, a criticism aimed at the level of superstructure (culture and ideology), is to display before readers the distorted anatomy of their encultured beliefs in order to force a reevaluation of the content itself, a content dangling out of context, defamiliarized and deadened. The complacent posture of social distance is here challenged by an attempt to remove readers from their class position and from the familiarity of its inherently tendentious perspective. Dislodging the ideological content and implanting it within the grotesque realism of the Bowery might just also dislodge readers' programmatic social reflexes of apprehension and understanding.

The inversion of melodramatic formula, the appropriation of the theater and mission as cultural forms of ideological expression, and the expressionistic symbolism of Maggie and her mother reveal Crane's enveloping social purpose, his artful craft, his stealth in concealment and exposure. Can there really exist a Mary Johnson? The parody of her characterization suggests the grotesque realism which Crane employs as if to goad culture into inquiry: "Why, but what an ugly caricature you are, madam." And the response: "Oh, all the better to see yourself, my dear." By keeping the ideological content intact and simply rearranging its social ground, Crane provides the necessary condition for this ideology to effect its own ruin by virtue of its free expression. The real tragedy of the novella is not the code's deconstruction, for that is welcome, but its influence in determining who lives and who dies. On the level of fable, the symbolic message of the novella exhorts culture to reexamine itself, to reevaluate ideology not only in the estranged terrain of subculture but at its very source. Such self-critical reflection might produce greater clarity, honesty, and social recognition through the greatest leap of all—from mystification to critical realism.

Crane's narrative helps to frame the ironic structure of *Maggie*. The plot, loose and episodic, does not merely appropriate the melodrama but inverts it as well. The heroine is not rescued in the end, as the standard formula would have it. Maggie perishes in the streets, and her suicidal act is an unregenerative one for her community. Her mother, a pathetic bestial creature, survives her. The villain, Pete, is himself degraded rather than uplifted by a stroke of salvation. And a happy ending is replaced by suffering and sanctimonious drivel. The whole structure of the melodrama, informed by a perversely adapted Christian ethos, is thus ruptured from within. In light of these altered features, the concluding gesture toward an affirmation of a benevolent moral order appears ludicrously misconceived. The underlying ironic intent is to reject the form and its values through the posture of acceptance. When we consider the character of Mary Johnson as espousing the virtuous pose of the melodramatic convention, her righteous proclamations of forgiveness amount to an affirmation of the pernicious. Moreover, the patterned melodrama that unfolds in the novella stands in sharp contrast to the idealized version displayed in the Bowery theater with its message of "transcendental realism." Crane's realism thus undermines social myth. Rather than transcendent realism, Crane gives us blasphemous realism.

Crane's subversion of the conventional melodrama heightens his sense of humor and focuses his object of attack. The social purpose of this method is summarized well by Northrop Frye's observation on the general significance of irony and satire: "One pole of ironic comedy is the recognition of the absurdity of naive melodrama, or, at least, of the absurdity of its attempt to define the enemy of society as a person outside that society. From there it develops toward the opposite pole, which is true comic irony or satire, and which defines the enemy of society as a spirit within that society."[8]

Crane's irony, which slides into satire, recreates the issue of victimization. For Crane, the enemy of society is seen as dwelling within its own body, a spirit made incarnate by the host of idealized values overlaying the reality they purport to explain. The incongruity between idealized and unidealized existence (where irony pivots) signals discontinuity, an inappropriate fit between cultural code, or stock moral categories, and Bowery life. The result is ridicule, a parody unto the end, and not the merger of ideology and context into tragic catharsis. The real issue, sustained throughout, is the malevolence of the conceptual code itself as the social enemy. Crane makes it plain that to the extent that dominant middle-class systems of value are projected onto and internalized by subculture, the sense of victimage will be seen as staged from without; that is, as propelled by the agency of culture, the spirit animating society.

Crane's object of attack is particularized by his criticism of the thematic armature of melodramatic convention. His deidealized representation of melodrama (as both a category of popular literature and an expression of cultural ideology) extends to the major social configurations, or spheres of mystification, in the novella. The thematic armature is housed in the following forms: domesticity (or tenement family life), the Bowery mission, the Bowery theater, and the street. These configurations comprise the established channels through which the

moral ideal is at once assimilated and converted by Bowery subculture. The cultural themes of feminine purity, the sanctity of motherhood and the hearth, familial harmony, heroic virtue, and righteous
social justice swell the subcultural forms in which they germinate. The
forms themselves are continuous rather than discrete expressions of
ideological content, overlapping into an organized and interrelated pattern of espousal, impersonation, and derangement.

An analysis of these configurations and a study of the linguistic
styles of the novella—dialect mixed with idealized and virtuous epithets, verbal and nonverbal posturings, as well as overstated attitudes
drawn from the moral realm of culture—reveal the subculture's consumption of an ideology undoubtedly alien to its experience. The ideology, with its emphasis on romantic sentiment, moral hypocrisy, and
emulation of bourgeois respectability, is not only false to experience
but devastating in its ramifications; that is, in its wholesale misrecognition of social reality. Writing of the melodramatic dimension "of womanhood pure and undefiled," Jacob Riis adequately expresses one
central aspect of this misrecognition:

> That it should blossom in such an atmosphere [of Bowery tene-
> ment districts] is one of the unfathomable mysteries of life. And
> yet it is not an uncommon thing to find sweet and innocent girls,
> singularly untouched by the evil around them, true wives and
> faithful mothers, literally "like jewels in a swine's snout," in the
> worst of the infamous barracks. It is the experience of all who
> have intelligently observed this side of life in a great city, not to be
> explained—unless on the theory of my friend, the priest in the
> Mulberry Street Bend, that inherent purity revolts instinctively
> from the naked brutality of vice as seen in the slums—but to be
> thankfully accepted as the one gleam of hope in an otherwise
> hopeless desert.[9]

Crane's ironic method is the antidote to this melodramatic vision. As
Frye comments, "one notes a recurring tendency on the part of ironic
comedy to ridicule and scold an audience assumed to be hankering
after sentiment, solemnity, and the triumph of fidelity and approved
moral standards."[10] Crane's purpose is to attack the conventions
themselves, to break through the entrenched stereotypes of such
sentimental attitudes which uphold virtue as a form of redemption
rising out of the chaos.

Although Crane's Maggie "blossomed in a mud-puddle," defying the
odds, her beauty is a quality which does not sustain its transcendence.

Riis sets the image for Maggie's rare presence, but Crane recreates the formula for her symbolization. Rather than having his heroine proceed untouched by her environment, as Riis would have it, Crane presents the symbol of inherent purity in its fall from innocence. If Maggie blossoms in a mud puddle, she also withers there amidst an environment that plunders, contaminates, and seduces. And for Crane the degradation of feminine purity is wrought not by the "naked brutality of vice as seen in the slums" but, as Pizer rightfully puts it, "by the very moral codes established to safeguard it."[11] Maggie is less a realistic product of her environment than an expression of its inherent principle of victimization. As victim, she does not instinctively revolt; rather, she is forced to succumb in futile sacrifice to a specious moral order. In the contention between the purity of democratic individualism and the defilement of social domination, Crane sees the latter as primary, the thief in the night. Maggie may come to us "as a pearl dropped unstained into Rum Alley from Heaven," but she exits as one of the "painted cohorts of the city," a jewel that has lost its natural luster (pp. 82, 96). Herein lies all the difference between Riis's mystification of "the one gleam of hope in an otherwise hopeless desert" and Crane's critical realism. It is as if the latter was conceived as a direct literary and cultural argument against the former position; for Crane, that "gleam of hope" is suffocated by the "otherwise hopeless desert," a desert which he views as much less "otherwise" than omnipresent.

The ironic tone of the novella is set in the very first line: "A very little boy stood upon a heap of gravel for the honour of Rum Alley" (p. 39). Here, in the public realm of the street, the denizens of Devil's Row and Rum Alley are deeply engaged in heroic battle (Crane's tone is mock heroic), reminiscent of those mid-century bouts between the Dead Rabbits and Bowery Boys. The conflict which erupts on the street flows into this realm's natural extension of disruption, the tenement. Around the Johnsons' hearth, a "panther's den," the quiet felicities of domestic life give way to frantic disorder. The Johnson home is less a sanctuary than a battlefield, where even the furniture is wielded as weapons. The effect is a thorough disorganization of family solidity and harmony, a powerful blow to the complacency of middle-class culture.

The fragmentation of the idealized familial unit is represented primarily through the sensual key of sound. Though we are initially introduced to Mary Johnson through sight ("they entered a lighted room in which a large woman was rampant" [p. 44]), the dominant impression of the flat is rendered in grating notes which test the reader's natural inclination toward the melodious cohesiveness of the harmonic. [12] Jimmie screams, the father bellows, and the mother puffs, snorts, and howls like a runaway freight train that frightens her son, "shrieking like a monk in an earthquake" (p. 46), into the halls. Crane complements the auditory with the visual only after the ear has had its fill. The sounds of debris become a sort of prelude to the sight of the demoniac, an image embodied in the fierce, pulsating muscle of motherhood:

> His mother's great chest was heaving painfully. Jimmie paused and looked down at her. Her face was inflamed and swollen from drinking. Her yellow brows shaded eyelids that had grown blue. Her tangled hair tossed in waves over her forehead. Her mouth was set in the same lines of vindictive hatred that it had, perhaps, borne during the fight. Her bare red arms were thrown out above her head in an attitude of exhaustion, something, mayhap, like that of a sated villain.
>
> The urchin bent over his mother. He was fearful lest she should open her eyes, and the dread within him was so strong that he could not forbear to stare, but hung as if fascinated over the woman's grim face. Suddenly her eyes opened. The urchin found himself looking straight into an expression which, it would seem, had the power to change his blood to salt. He howled piercingly and fell backward. (P. 49)

Crane's image of motherhood is a far cry from Riis's notion of "true wives and faithful mothers." Mary Johnson's influence is not one of nurturance but of fear and destruction. As the real head of the Johnson family, she personifies the debased qualities of culture and subculture and is an agent of turbulent force who vacillates between "muddled sentiment" and "drunken heat" (p. 46). She would be much less harmful if left to her own devices, but the ideology of the mission (which she incorporates) extends her sphere of influence, turning her otherwise barbarous character into a demoniac one and making her the cause of Maggie's seduction by Pete.

The Bowery mission as the source of this attitudinizing not only interposes its standards onto subculture but exists at cross purposes with it. The dialogue between culture and subculture is summarized in the following exchange:

> While they got warm at the stove he [the preacher] told his hearers just where he calculated they stood with the Lord. Many of the sinners were impatient over the pictured depths of their

degradation. They were waiting for soup-tickets. A reader of the words of wind-demons might have been able to see the portions of a dialogue pass to and fro between the exhorter and his hearers. "You are damned," said the preacher. And the reader of sounds might have seen the reply go forth from the ragged people: "Where's our soup?" (Pp. 50–51)

This is a fine statement of the misrecognition of social class; religion prefaces its charitable act by pointing down its righteous finger of condemnation, and the malevolent supplicants respond, not from their contemptible souls, but from their empty guts. Ideology and reality fire far above the heads of each other in this misdirected liturgy. Perhaps misrecognition should be qualified, reduced to its lowest common denominator—blind ignorance. "Once a philosopher asked this man [the preacher] why he did not say 'we' instead of 'you.' The man replied, 'What?'" (p. 50).

The Bowery mission evades social guilt by projecting it onto subculture, transforming collective responsibility into punitive religious categories in the process. As such, the genuine model of Christianity is perverted by the hypocritical attribution of good and evil along class lines. Goodness, in fact, becomes entirely publicized and asserted solely by its renunciation of evil, which resides in subculture. Condemnation of evil as a standard for goodness not only deflects social guilt but dismisses the glorification of the good itself. It cannot stand alone upon its own criteria but instead must be buttressed by that which it speaks against—evil. This is the hypocrisy of the mission's dogma, a message that invariably resounds in the unreflective style of righteous indignation by assuming a congregation of sinners as a necessary precondition for the election of goodness, respectability, and virtue.

Jimmie's dispossession is abetted by the mission's distorted theology, though Crane makes it plain that he had "confused the speaker with Christ," an admonishment of his own deviance and misrecognition. Jimmie begins with naught, a socialization into the negative in which disappointment is merely a way of life. He "studied human nature in the gutter, and found it no worse than he thought he had reason to believe it" (p. 50). Yet his dispossession retains the double standard of the Bowery mission and its strained efforts to appear respectable. Though Jimmie has ruined several women throughout the city and is repeatedly annoyed by their accusations of paternity, he cannot recognize his act in Pete's betrayal of Maggie. Even though he wonders for a time if the women he has seduced have brothers like

himself, he cannot bring himself to equate the two parallel situations.
Like the Bowery missionaries, he exonerates his guilt by transferring
the blame to others and becoming preoccupied in the evil that exists
outside the self. His rejection of Maggie and his brawl with Pete lend
his denial the necessary diversion it requires to avoid culpability.

It is Maggie's mother, however, who best exemplifies the mystifying vocation of the mission ideology. When not engaged in her sancti-
fied vocation, she is absorbed in her ritual avocation—drinking, being
blasphemous, and delighting in floundering amidst the wreckage of the
flat. While Maggie frequently attempts to create a semblance of
cleanliness and order in their home, her mother, a constant agent of
degradation, tears it apart. The lambrequin that Maggie hangs on the
mantel, a symbolic extension of her aspirations to maidenhood, becomes part of the general squalor left in the wake of her mother's most
recent rampage. Even before Maggie is seduced by Pete, she is
defiled by her mother's chaotic scourings. The bedraggled lambrequin
and the general despoliation of the place not only prefigure Maggie's
fall but prompt it as well.

> When Pete arrived, Maggie, in a worn black dress, was waiting for
> him in the midst of a floor strewn with wreckage. The curtain at the
> window had been pulled by a heavy hand and hung by one tack,
> dangling to and fro in the draught through the cracks at the sash.
> The knots of blue ribbons appeared like violated flowers. The fire
> in the stove had gone out. The displaced lids and open doors
> showed heaps of sullen grey ashes. The remnants of a meal,
> ghastly, lay in a corner. Maggie's mother, stretched on the floor,
> blasphemed and gave her daughter a bad name. (P. 60)

On this, Maggie's first date with Pete, her mother utters her standard refrain: "'Yeh've gone t' d' devil, Mag Johnson'" (p. 71). The
prophecy fulfills itself eventually, not through any fault of Maggie's but
by the actions of the spokeswoman whose rhetoric is her intent. The
phrase is particularly unwarranted on the first date when Maggie
refuses Pete a goodnight kiss, an uncommon occurrence for Pete
which leads him to think out loud that he has "'been played for a
duffer'" (p. 64). Before Pete and Maggie meet again, the mother's
refrain reaches such a level of intensity that it succeeds in driving
Maggie out of the home: "'Yeh've gone t' d' devil, Mag Johnson, yehs
knows yehs have gone t' d' devil. Yer a disgrace t' yer people. An' now,
git out an' go ahn wid dat doe-faced jude of yours. Go wid him, curse
yeh, an' a good riddance. Go, an' see how yeh likes it'" (p. 71).

When news of Maggie's intimate liaison with Pete arrives, Jimmie is the bearer: "'Well, Maggie's gone teh d' devil!'" (p. 73). But now the expectation is received by her mother with incredulity. Assuming the stature of an impassioned preacher, "her blotched arms raised high in imprecation" (p. 73), she reels off her denunciation in a mimetic travesty of mission oratory.

> "May she be cursed for ever!" she shrieked. "May she eat nothing but stones and deh dirt in deh street. May she sleep in deh gutter an' never see deh sun shine again." . . . The mother raised lamenting eyes to the ceiling. "She's d' devils own chil', . . . Ah, who would t'ink such a bad girl could grow up in our fambly. . . . An' after all her bringin'-up an' what I tol' her and talked wid her, she goes teh d' bad, like a duck teh water." (P. 73)

The false, idealized values of the mission are further played out by mother and son in a hypocritical litany which revolves about that requisite core of evil. "'She had a bad heart, dat girl did, Jimmie. She was wicked t' d' heart.'" Jimmie affirms, silently. "'We lived in d' same house wid her an' I brought her up, an' we never knowed how bad she was.'" Once again, Jimmie affirms. "'Wid a home like dis an' a mudder like me, she went teh d' bad'" (pp. 82–83).

Such righteous lamentations place the evil in the heart of Maggie, much in the tradition of those individualized and moralistic interpretations of poverty, vice, and social deviance. But the utter sham of it is revealed by the dialect in which the mission ideology is couched and by the sordid background of the Johnson family thus far presented. Ideals and slang express the contradiction between model and actuality so that their integration effects the defamiliarization of the cultural code. Ultimately, throughout Mary Johnson's tirades and mournful befuddlements, it is the code itself that appears ill-conceived, grossly constituted, and absurdly adapted. More than Mrs. Johnson, it is the dominant cultural ideology that is really on trial here. By making the content appear strange, Crane redirects the pointed finger of condemnation away from the evil heart of Maggie and the evil-minded obsessions of her attackers to the warped perceptual apparatus of culture itself. Even Jimmie momentarily apprehends the dissemblance he and his mother are engaged in. It is expressed best in his own words spoken to his mother: "'Well, look-a-here, dis t'ing queers us! See? We're queered'" (p. 83). It is at once a fleeting admission of shared guilt or uncertainty and a hesitant step toward reconciliation. But his interest in bringing Maggie back home is cut short by his mother's pretense to their chaste surroundings. "'What! Let 'er come an' sleep under deh same roof wid her mudder agin? Oh, yes, I will, won't I! Sure! Shame on yehs, Jimmie Johnson, fer sayin' such a t'ing to yer own mudder!'" (p. 83). As attitudes take on tabloid qualities, her anger shifts to sentimental babbling. The interaction between mother and son soon fades into ludicrous biblical analogies in which they argue the resemblance, if any, between a "prod'gal daughter" and a "prod'gal son." They find themselves over their heads, and Jimmie puts an end to the mockery: "'Well, I didn't mean none of dis prod'gal bus'ness anyway'" (p. 83). The moral reference of the mission explodes in their faces, leaving both the content and the adherents trudging blindly through ideological debris.

After Maggie is forsaken by Pete, she returns home only to be freakishly exhibited before her family and a tenement audience. She is branded, a descendant of Hester Prynne, and becomes a specimen for examination and purgation. In this change of scene, Maggie's mother exchanges the pulpit for the stage. Though the design of the props has changed, the essence of the message remains the same. "Maggie's mother paced to and fro, addressing the doorful of eyes. . . . Her voice rang through the building. 'Dere she stands,' she cried, wheeling suddenly and pointing with dramatic finger. 'Dere she stands! Look at her! Ain' she a dandy? An' she was so good as to come home teh her mudder, she was! Ain' she a beaut'? Ain' she a dandy?'" (p. 92).

Once again, that crooked finger jabs, Bowerylike, at the heart of darkness. The mother exhorts the spectators to look at Maggie with derisive contempt, to empty their blemished vision into the scapegoat for their own sense of social approval. The collective gaze toward the other on this public stage of condemnation might be interpreted by the sermon from the pulpit: "You are damned." The concealed pronoun "we" remains repressed along with a whole level of social discourse that would impugn the mystification of evil. Maggie takes the blame, a defiled figure laden with the maleficent secrets of her society. A final appeal to her brother is received with crafted scorn: "Radiant virtue sat upon his brow, and his repelling hands expressed horror of con-tamination" (p. 92).

It is the performance of an attitude, perfervidly adapted yet slavishly enacted, that drives Maggie out into the streets, homeless. Her descent is at the crossroads, so to speak, and in a last-ditch effort to escape the enacted prophecy of her mother she approaches a clergyman, "a picture of benevolence and kindheartedness." But this servant of God remains a distant image, a mobile icon who though on the street is certainly not of it: "As the girl accosted him he made a convulsive movement and saved his respectability by a vigorous side-step. He did not risk it to save a soul. For how was he to know that there was a soul before him that needed saving?" (pp. 95–96). The clergyman misses a golden opportunity to intervene and do good, to turn the prophecy around, precisely because charity, the essence of Christianity, is mutilated by his ideological code. Clearly, he is not accustomed to the praxis of amelioration. His arms have been trained to lift reflexively in entreaty or to point in imprecation rather than to embrace or enfold in shelter. Without the calamity of evil parading before him, his justification for existence perishes. Moreover, his theological dogma, an idealism nurtured in the limited enclosure of pew and pulpit, disassembles in the encounter with social reality. Petrified and meaningless, it simply cannot see the reality that is, a reality that those of his ilk have artificially studied, discoursed upon, revolted over, spasmodically imagined, and vigorously avoided. In short, the clergyman cannot make a difference because he does not know how; he cannot even recognize the chance to do so, for his pictured respectability and idealized misconceptions assure social distance. In this sense, respectability unifies the clergyman with the unctuous assumptions of Maggie's mother, her brother, and Pete.

That last sentence of the aforementioned quote—"For how was he to know that there was a soul before him that needed saving?"—elevates Crane's critical irony, for it is thrown back at the clergyman and his church in their very own conception; that is, through the rhetorical language of the pulpit. The passage is effective because of this covert irony, a criticism which blends in perfectly with the stylistics and highly mannered appearances of the mission representatives.

The fraudulent impact of the Bowery mission upon the attitude and conduct of subculture culminates in the final chapter of the novella. Maggie's forced alienation from both culture and subculture had led to her prostitution and suicide, the fulfillment of her rejection. When news of her death reaches the Johnson flat, Maggie's mother begins to weep, donning the role of a wronged mother only after she has finished her meal, as if to say, "the body calleth before the heart." Her mournful lament, "that sounded like a dirge on some forlorn pipe" (p. 103), attracts the tenement residents, who enter the flat as spectators but, taking their cue, become transfigured into a funereal chorus, sounding the antiphonies of grief and consolation. The other principal actress, aside from Mary Johnson, is one Miss Smith, who bursts onto

> "Ah, poor Mary!" she cried, and tenderly embraced the moaning
> one. "Ah, what ter'ble affliction is dis!" continued she. Her vo-
> cabulary was derived from mission churches. "Me poor Mary,
> how I feel for yehs! Ah, what a ter'ble affliction is a disobed'ent
> chile. . . . Yer poor misguided chil' is gone now, Mary, an' let us
> hope it's fer deh bes'. Yeh'll fergive her now, Mary, wont yehs,
> dear, all her disobed'ence? All her t'ankless behaviour to her
> mudder an' all her badness? She's gone where her ter'ble sins will
> be judged." (P. 103)

The woman continues to beseech Maggie's mother with her odious
refrain: "'Yeh'll fergive her, Mary! Yeh'll fergive yer bad chil'! . . .
She's gone where her sins will be judged'" (p. 104). Portions of this
exhortation are echoed by the chorus along with some other pat liturgical responses, such as "'deh Lord gives and deh Lord takes away.'"
Finally, Mary Johnson submits in a convulsive offering of her
magnanimous absolution: "'Oh, yes, I'll fergive her! I'll fergive her!'"
(p. 104). Maggie's rejection from both culture and subculture, which
leads to her prostitution and death, results in this ironic absolution,
thus rendering her alienation complete.

In this final scene, Crane's irony is stridently overt in outlining the
sonorous and misdirected march of a cultural attitude into the dwelling
of subculture. The ideology of the mission churches is not merely an
influence but a dramatic presence or, more accurately, a presence of
dramaturgy. It invades the tenement household, making it over from a
blasphemous hellhole into a shrine of humility and forgiveness. The
effect is to turn the bathetic qualities of melodrama and the absurd
slipperiness of mission righteousness into a burlesque, a form more
suitable to the misrecognition of social reality, which guides the perceptions of culture and subculture alike. In this final scene, the farcical
attitudes of the mission and melodrama take command, uniting
through the medium of the Bowery players and, in particular, through
the appropriately grotesque personage of Mary Johnson, whose moralistic play at forgiveness signals the utter lunacy of form and content.
The result is a fusion of character and ideology that betrays itself as
the true haunt of social evil, a fusion that demystifies the ways in
which a cultural system of beliefs engenders false consciousness. One
critic, who objects to this scene, cites "its false church-like setting, its

hideous antiphonies, its dreadful absolution" and refers to the writing as "one of the weak things about the novelette, for it is contrived and stagey and exists as Crane's outstanding indulgence in melodrama."[13] But it is precisely for these reasons that Crane's last chapter succeeds, becoming the strongest part of his novella when viewed in light of his overriding ironic purpose—the defamiliarization of the ideal, the parody of cultural ideology and subcultural mimicry. Crane's parodic style may have confused critics from Howells on down to our own time, but his message seems unmistakable if one listens not so much to what is said as to the tone of what is said and its deflection from enactment to source, from ersatz to paradigm.

The Bowery theater duplicates the insidious machinations of the mission in an alternative form. As previously mentioned, we see their intimate partnership merge in the final chapter of the novella, a complete identification of pulpit and stage performed in accordance with liturgical dramatization. Crane's handling of the Bowery theater reveals not only its meretricious qualities but, more significantly, its powerful influence in manipulating the emotions of its audience into an enraptured deception of self and other.[14] The Bowery theater is the supreme diversion from self-critical thought, parading a circus of popular cultural forms which appear, disappear, and reappear as if driven by frenetic desperation to present the appropriate stimulus and receive a confirmatory response. The ritual between actor and audience thus preserves the contortions of social perspective.

The Bowery variety show and melodrama feed Maggie's incipient delusions and direct her attention, and that of the subculture in general, to the realm of romantic fantasy. Even before her deepening involvement with the various forms of Bowery leisure and entertainment, she appears before us as an ingenue. The false consciousness which informs her naiveté is the result of her contained environment, her limited exposure, her ignorance immanently manifested in the cognitive restrictions of her surrounding models. Maggie's romantic quest is one born of necessity, an affective solution to the stifling problems of labor (her toil at the collar-and-cuff factory), a hostile home life, and the "yellow discontent" which may be generalized to encompass her tenement environment. When Maggie initially samples Pete's strutting style, portrayed to the reader in ironic shadings of strained yet amusing prowess (the performative antics of a typical Bowery Boy lingering in faded glory), she transforms the comical, plebeian features of his posturings into aristocratic idealization. Here was her gallant "knight," her "ideal man" (pp. 57, 58). "Her dim

thoughts were often searching for far-away lands where the little hills
sing together in the morning. Under the trees of her dream-gardens
there had always walked a lover" (p. 57). Here Crane's heavy-handed
irony underscores the translation of the real into the escapist yearn-
ings of the ideal. But it also makes it plain to the reader that Maggie's
perceptions are not *tabula rasa*; instead, she comes to us as a pre-
coded template, a product as well as victim of her surroundings. Yet
she is a template underwritten by culture and, in the course of her
development, overwritten by subculture, completed in the image of its
popular forms.

Pete, a virtual product of the Bowery theater and other places of
amusement, initiates Maggie into its tawdry artifice. She is first exposed to a variety show, becoming a member of a somewhat respectable audience comprised of laborers, sailors, and immigrant families.
The various acts which appear before her include dancers, singers,
ventriloquists, black melodies, and sorrowful lays. They follow each
other without any sensible sense of tradition, an ensemble of forms
erupting from the wings in frantic, jerky motion as if spliced haphaz-
ardly in the style of early cinematic features. Yet there is no one theme
which connects the acts. Rather, their multiplicity of expression is akin
to the pronounced dance or wiggle of an attitude which draws the
audience toward it in momentary complicity. Once satisfied, the attitude dons another costume, entertains another gig, and wins the
audience over in collective espousal. The overdone medley of acts is
symbolically represented in the encapsulating finale. Here the summation of maniacal tempo and grotesque attitudinizing—the rapid and
careless shift from the patriotic, to the risqué, to the comic, to the
tragic, and the like—is given appropriate display. It is not the content
of these attitudes but the absurd form in which they are packaged and
publicized that is of interest in this romping finale:

> After a few moments' rest, the orchestra played noisily, and a
> small fat man burst out upon the stage. He began to roar a song
> and to stamp back and forth before the footlights, wildly waving a
> silk hat and throwing leers broadcast. He made his face into
> fantastic grimaces until he looked like a devil on a Japanese kite.
> . . . His short, fat legs were never still a moment. He shouted
> and roared and bobbed his shock of red wig until the audience
> broke out in excited applause. (P. 63)

There are no lapses in the Bowery variety show, only a disconnected series of inflamed social appearances, "fantastic grimaces,"

each batting a wink of collusion between culture and subculture. But in *Maggie* the whole effect reinforces her naiveté, her puppylike dependence upon external forms of accepted conduct. Her response is one of awe at the splendor of the thing, a wonderment which incites her imitative fancies so that she begins to envy "elegance and soft palms" (p. 64), mistaking the meretricious for the genuine. Her consciousness is further skewed toward illusion and fantasy through her encounter with the melodramatic fare of the Bowery theater. Though the form is standardized, the content is altered to feature the downtrodden conditions of subculture in its Algeresque rise from rags to riches. The message of the Bowery melodrama reflects Maggie's own plight and her private wish fulfillment. Her psychic script, which substitutes Pete as heroic savior, is legitimized in the subcultural copy of the popular structure, "in which the dazzling heroine was rescued from the palatial home of her treacherous guardian by the hero with the beautiful sentiments." "The latter," Crane ironically comments, "spent most of his time out at soak in pale-green snow storms, busy with a nickel-plated revolver rescuing aged strangers from villains." But the irony is set in contradistinction to Maggie's duped sense of engagement:

> Maggie lost herself in sympathy with the wanderers swooning in snow-storms beneath happy-hued church windows, while a choir within sang "Joy to the world." To Maggie and the rest of the audience this was transcendental realism. Joy always within, and they, like the actor, inevitably without. Viewing it, they hugged themselves in ecstatic pity of their imagined or real condition. (P. 66)

Though Maggie and the audience might inadvertently stumble upon the potentially realistic construct of social exclusion, its critical meaning is entirely submerged in the emotion which transcends the real. Alienation is here received and interpreted by the effusion of sentiment, the squeezing out of the social by the private. Realistic factors, such as class, social structure, spatial segregation, and subcultural exploitation, are thus manipulated by the melodramatic formula into an etherealized gush of mystification. As the idealized plot unfolds, Maggie joins the audience in hissing vice and applauding virtue, proving her susceptability in learning an appropriate response, conditioned by culture and evoked by subculture. In this perfectly inverted melodrama, poverty subdues affluence and assumes its stance at the top of the heap in a picture of didactic triumph. The import of this popular pedagogy is the certification of distortion. For Maggie, "the theatre made her think" (p. 67). Crane's understatement places delusion as the major ingredient in Maggie's conceptual and affective development, a development premised upon misrecognition and fed by the overstate- ment of the transcendental: "Maggie always departed with raised spirits from these melodramas. . . . She wondered if the culture and refinement she had seen imitated, perhaps grotesquely, by the hero- ine on the stage, could be acquired by a girl who lived in a tenement house and worked in a shirt factory" (p. 67).

The malformation of Maggie's social perceptions, which replicate those of her subculture, is objectified by her excursions to dime museums, zoos, and concert halls. The latter places of entertainment become more disreputable and thus parallel Maggie's pattern of de- scent. The first of these, the "hall of irregular shape" (p. 80), is anomalous because of the presence of two prostitutes at one of the tables, a harbinger of Maggie's degraded future. The other, a "hi- larious hall" (p. 85), includes a woman at each of its tables, signifying an acceleration of the process as well as a growing sense of en- trapment.

Yet both halls are also significant for their degree of smoke-filled cloudiness, a density which opposes its opacity to the transparent glow of Maggie's miscolored vision of events. In the "hilarious hall," "the usual smoke-cloud was present, but so dense that heads and arms seemed entangled in it. . . . The smoke eddied and swirled like a shadowy river toward some unseen falls" (p. 85). This infernal imagery steeps subculture in the disembodied atmosphere of misperception, transforming the solidity of place into a seemingly gaseous meandering of the insubstantial. The thick smokescreen is complemented by the furious pace of the hall's ongoing revelry. Racy music, booming conver- sation, and the free flow of drink all bubble over like the rushing rapids of the "shadowy river," an expression of the wild, reckless abandon before the river's abysmal fall—the crash of illusion into the patient, absorbing waters of endings. Like the river, Maggie too seeks her own level. After Pete deserts her in the "hilarious hall" for Nell, the "woman of brilliance and audacity" (p. 86), and after his subsequent repudiation of her, Maggie descends to the streets, the realization of her ideal.

But as a streetwalker, Maggie is less disreputable than her melo- dramatic ideal. Cultural script and subcultural adaptation again emerge as the primary objects of Crane's critical attack. The infinite distance between Maggie's clouded vision and her naked reality (a reality that in its final act is entirely stripped of cultural artifacts—a skeleton without even a sheen) shows Crane's interest in sabotaging the mass production and consumption of an injurious ideological form. Maggie's initiation into subculture and vicariously into culture turns her into an ardent consumer of cheap goods laden with symbolic meaning. The ideological nature of these goods and the cultural forms in which they are presented play an overwhelming influence in communicating the very structure and processes of the subculture's attitudes, beliefs, systems of value, sense of the future, and perceptions of society as a whole. In short, the cultural salesmanship of the melodrama in particular works its way, through a sort of contagion, under the skin, into the hearts, and through the minds of its subcultural market, cornering it and, ultimately, merging with it.

The result is an enhanced prosperity relative to the commodity of false consciousness. But Crane's rupture from within the formulaic designs of melodrama bankrupts the entire system. The collision between social myth and social reality, "transcendent realism" versus blasphemous realism, denotes Crane's own critical manipulation of a dominant expression of cultural ideology so as to defamiliarize it, turn it on its bald head, and thus spin the revered into a circus stunt.

Yet the final result of Crane's parodic thrust is more than a comical subversion. Maggie's final presence in the novella evokes the inclusion of the urban social structure that is otherwise implicitly developed throughout. Her stroll away from the structure of society, the "glittering avenues" (p. 96), and down through the gathering night of side streets, dumping like tributaries into the East River, reinstates Crane's total perspective—his story of New York. Maggie's sultry death walk condenses the "story" so that its symbolism is contained within the scene. Her solicitations function to telescope the social spectrum, from high to low, from pretensious civility to an abased primitivism. The spirit of society thus emerges from its hidden ground to its focused figural presentation. Faces loom before the reader like those in a dime museum, stylized, increasingly freakish in design and portent. The cosmopolitan man "with a sublime air" executes a double take, the man with "pompous and philanthropic whiskers" steadily makes his way, the businessman flashes by in characteristic haste, hardy laborers remark in passing, a young lad takes a careless rain check, a drunken man vents his pathos, and the image of a man with blotched features ushers Maggie to her terminus—a hardly noticeable splash into the "deathly black hue of the river."

> She went into the blackness of the final block. The shutters of the
> tall buildings were closed like grim lips. . . . Afar off the lights of

the avenue glittered as if from an impossible distance. Streetcar bells jingled with the sound of merriment. . . . The varied sounds of life, made joyous by distance and seeming unapproachableness, came faintly and died away to a silence. (Pp. 97–98)

Maggie's suicide (if appropriately futile in terms of formal melodramatic criteria) does harbor possibility for a renewed commitment to realism. Her ending, the drowning of a disfigured ideal, speaks to the redeemable future of American literature and social thought and not to its unredemptive past. Though the nature of her development looks backward, the pattern of her descent looks forward toward the potential renewal of cultural forms, belief systems, and literary styles—an offering made on behalf of modernism.

Crane's second Bowery novella, *George's Mother*, may have been inspired by Howells's passing remark that the novel should explore new thematic terrain, such as a mother's relationship to her son.[15] The fleeting suggestion must have stuck with Crane, for shortly after his 1894 interview with Howells such a filial topic materialized. *George's Mother* is essentially a more realistic novella than *Maggie*. Though it extends and deepens some of the familiar themes of its forerunner, such as the interest in descent, delusion, and entrapment, *George's Mother* is much less referential in the oscillation between culture and subculture. To be sure, the dialectic between culture and subculture is forcefully presented in *George's Mother* but, during the course of the novella, the dialectic erodes until by the end the referential point of view is canceled, so that the two formerly distinct yet interrelated entities have been collapsed into the single static dimension of subculture. Crane's social and ideological purpose in effecting this outcome (the retrogression of the dialectic) does not narrow his perspective but instead works to enlarge it so that, by eroding the antipode of culture, dispossession and homelessness become not simply the condition of an underclass within society but an analogue for the spiritual condition of society itself.

Crane's strategy of annihilation in *George's Mother* is enhanced by his assimilation of a historical perspective into the framework of the novella. In particular, his concern with historical transition—with the movement of American society from a rural to an urban-centered civilization—aligns subculture with the new urban-centered order and culture with the old rural form of social life. To further the associations, Crane situates subculture within a secular paradigm while viewing culture as embedded in the remnants of a sacred system. In this sense, the novella is more broadly conceived than *Maggie*, as it is framed by a context of temporality. The opposition between the cultural and subcultural equations in *George's Mother* also activates the sense of the historic by bringing the two modalities into dynamic contention and transition.

Through the techniques of irony and parody and through more individualized characterization, Crane makes the historical concrete in both its social and psychological ramifications. Eric Solomon, in fact, has viewed the novella in light of its manifold layers of social and literary parody aimed at some of the primary cultural ideals and norms of the age. In the novella, Crane takes on and artfully debunks the then rampant Horatio Alger myth, the staid temperance tract, explosive war imagery, and the sentimental qualities of the popular romance. Of the initial two subjects in the list of targets, Solomon concludes: "If we consider the novel from its success-story source, it is a parodic reversal; from its temperance source, it is a burlesque parallel. The two traditions provide a double perspective, and Crane plays them off against each other in order to make the character of George psychologically valid."[16] Crane's parodic treatment of these traditions also validates the broader social and ideological purpose inscribed in the novella, for in combination they reveal a society whose cultural "givens" are put into question, rendered illusive, and thus invalidated. In the setting of the Bowery slum, the formulaic constructs of middle-class morality and progress are ostensibly refuted in both word and deed so that subculture rejects all the distinctions and comes to stand for the whole of the present age. Through a more finely developed and controlled use of irony and parody, Crane achieves his higher purpose, an object of attack that is integrated with his concern for the opposing modalities of social control, competing forms of affiliation, and the social and psychic fallout that consummates the collision between an unusable American past (the dissolution of culture) and a misdirected American present (the looming prospect of subculture).

George's Mother begins with neither George nor his mother but with the ubiquitous presence of the city. Crane's evocation of the modern industrial city is mingled with medieval imagery, in which "the buildings loomed with a new and tremendous massiveness, like castles and fortresses. There were endless processions of people, mighty hosts, with umbrellas waving, banner-like, over them."[17] This conflation of new and old achieves a sense of the historic by commingling the structures of the modern city with those of a past, preindustrial age. Moreover, Crane's juxtaposition of the modern cityscape with his ref-

erences to the ceremonious forms of this former medieval period
("processions," "hosts," "banner-like") raises the specter of the
Church as a once formidable agent of social control. Yet having united
the two forms of human civilization, perhaps simply to imprint upon
the modern that other looming association, the Dark Ages, Crane
pulls them apart through his descent to the street, to the delimited
signs and structure of a new depersonalized modernity: "Horse-cars,
aglitter with new paint, rumbled in steady array between the pillars
that supported the elevated railroad. The whole street resounded with
the tinkle of bells, the roar of iron-shod wheels on the cobbles, the
ceaseless trample of the hundreds of feet" (p. 105). To round out this
impressionistic introduction to the novella, rows of shops and electric
lights give further presence to the achievement of commerce and
industrialization. The merger and disengagement between modes of
existence signal a nascent opposition, one between the illimitable expanse of the street and the contained boundaries of castles and fortresses. This opposition is soon refined in the ensuing events of the
novella, in which the saloon supplements the influence of the street
and the Church supplants the finely circumscribed boundaries of medieval structures.

This central opposition is given human form as George Kelcy, the
last heir of a family raised on the rural landscape of an American past,
emerges out of the "eternal procession of people" in the modern city
as a young wage earner. His movements within the mysterious complexities of the urban-industrial setting are simplified by his growing
allegiance to two worldly locales—the street and the saloon. Both
ceremonious entities menace his romantic inheritance of Emersonian
self-reliance and free will and initiate instead a process of dispossession in concert with Bowery realism.

While George begins his slide into the secular arena, to knowledge
qualified by the bar and street corner, his mother holds fast to her
sacred inheritance. Confined to her tenement dwelling, she recreates
the conflict between a cornered old order and an encroaching disorder
and confusion. George's mother wages a continuous battle in order to
preserve a purified room of her own amidst the pollution and defilement of the slums. To a large extent, and as a custodian of culture, she
is fighting for control and influence from her delimited stronghold. The
domestic maneuvers of the old woman are so furious as to be comical:

> In her arms she bore pots and pans, and sometimes a broom and
> dust pan. She wielded them like weapons. . . . There was a flurry

of battle in this room. Through the clouded dust of steam one could see the thin figure dealing mighty blows. Always her way seemed beset. Her broom was continually poised, lancewise, at dust demons. There came clashings and clangings as she strove with her tireless foes. It was a picture of indomitable courage. . . . The little intent warrior never hesitated nor faltered. She fought with a strong and relentless will. (Pp. 109–110)

The attack of this "little intent warrior" appears primarily defensive in nature, holding off the city at large, which deposits its flecks of contamination into the *cordon sanitaire* of her room. Equally significant is the fact that she fights with a "strong and relentless will," the repository of her faith, thus linking religion, domesticity, and the feminine ideal. She is up in arms with the vernacular armaments of pots and pans, wielded against the tenement jungle and the brewery across the way.

The relationship between George Kelcy and his mother transcends the comical and critical irony, lending an objective viewpoint and setting characters in motion. It is ultimately a tragic association that symbolically represents an insoluble moral dilemma. The distance between mother and son, which culminates in the death of the old woman, poignantly illustrates Crane's thematic concern with the failure of culture's guiding and coherent myth and with the absence of any unified supplanting ethos offered by the prospect of subculture. George's painful survival suggests the irreversible estrangement between the sacred domain of culture and the secular realm of subculture as well as the futility of each in addressing the realism of a rapidly changing society. Each defines its substance as a self-contained illusion; the reality between them has been breached.

The conflict between an ascendant subculture and an obsolescent culture is represented by the divergent movements of George and his mother. While he lights out for the saloon, she makes her way toward an evening prayer meeting. Force and counterforce go their separate ways and store up ammunition for an eventual confrontation. Though each sanctuary claims its ceremonious paradigm of affiliation and control, it is clear which is on the wane and which is on the rise. The old sacred order of culture is clearly viewed as impotent in its influence and funereal in appearance, while the new secular form of subculture is imbued with virility, an evanescent though misdirected energy. Crane presents the reader with a picture of the old woman, aligning femininity with the corroded conduit of culture, after George rejects

her offer to attend the prayer meeting: "She breathed a huge sigh, the
counterpart of ones he had heard upon like occasions. She put a tiny
black bonnet on her head, and wrapped her figure in an old shawl. She
cast a martyr-like glance upon her son and went mournfully away. She
resembled a limited funeral procession" (p. 114).

This pathetic image is complemented by a vigorous yet wayward
masculinity. In the back room of a saloon, a cultivated space of "isolation and safety" (p. 117), George finds his sequestered fraternal order.
As a newcomer, he feels his way around the jovial tribe. He is soon
accepted as an eternal friend by the mere fact that he is present and
accounted for. Infected by this amiable retreat, "he began to believe
that he was a most remarkably fine fellow, who had at last found his
place in a crowd of most remarkably fine fellows" (p. 116). The redun-
dancy reveals not only the simple thought of a simple man but the
mode of affiliation itself, which operates by way of reflection. In this
context, one for all and all for one becomes an existential motto, a
perceptual device which views the self as manifest in the other, the
other as a reiteration of the self. Rather than a submission to the
other, which marks George's role as wage earner, this forum allows
his self to merge and reemerge in the group. Hand shaking, back
slapping, mutual aggrandizement, and reassurance become ritualistic
efforts to reestablish a symmetry which is absent in the realities of the
world at large. The conversation that ensues in the back room is
entirely phatic in nature, fulfilling needs for relatedness, self-esteem,
and affirmation—social qualities negated on the outside and, ironically,
delusionary on the inside. This fraternal association that captures
George is suspect primarily because of its overweening sense of
soothing grandeur. Withdrawal from reality is the *modus operandi* of
its happy society, a society which regulates its mirthful expansiveness
through an appropriation of the irrational. Crane gives atmospheric
credence to the collective distortion through his familiar reliance on
cloudiness. "The tobacco smoke eddied about the forms of the men in
ropes and wreaths. Near the ceiling there was a thick grey cloud" (p.
118). Once again, Crane employs the image of smoke to put out the
fire of fatuous posturings. The fact that it is arranged in wreaths and
ropes suggests the dual rhythm of enchantment and death. The spell-
binding fog of drink and unchallenged fraternity is lifted as the crew
exits the saloon for the street. Outside, George's contact with reality,
his reawakening, is somewhat jolting. The formidable presence of the
city returns to him in slow yet steady sequence and, in the face of its
gathering momentum, George unwittingly touches ground.

The cold air of the street filled Kelcy with vague surprise. It made his head feel hot. As for his legs, they were willow-twigs.

A few lights blinked. In front of an all-night restaurant a huge red electric lamp hung and sputtered. Horsecar bells jingled far down the street. Overhead a train thundered on the elevated road. (P. 119)

The delusions reverberating within George's social circle are paralleled in his own psychic fantasies. His private deceit is heroic in stature, preoccupied with the attainment of power and an aura of mystification. Fantasies of the future formulate his being into a man "with a cloak of coldness concealing his gentleness and his faults, of whom the men, and more particularly the women, would think with reverence" (p. 124). The ambitious royalty of George's future is modified somewhat by his dreams much closer at hand. Subdued by his ignorance of the city's entangled plan, George longs to simplify the swirling intricacies in which he is caught. The irony of George's urban dreams is in the myopic focus of his dispossessed vision and in the emulation of his worldly model.

He had begun to look at the great world revolving near his nose. He had a vast curiosity concerning this city in whose complexities he was buried. It was an impenetrable mystery, this city. It was a blend of many enticing colours. He longed to comprehend it completely, that he might walk understandingly in its greatest marvels, its mightiest march of life, sin. He dreamed of a comprehension whose pay was the admirable attitude of a man of knowledge. He remembered Jones. He could not but admire a man who knew so many bartenders. (P. 125)

These aspirations are further complicated by George's private romance, gleaned mainly from the purplish lore of popular culture and its sentimental fiction. The vision of his romantic preoccupations transforms the commonplace into a world of dignity, dominance, and self-possession. The mechanism for this transport from the slum to the castle is none other than his belief in the benign conjurings of fate: "A chariot of pink clouds was coming for him. His faith was his reason for existence" (p. 126). George's faith in his heroic nature becomes, in fact, his tenuous allegiance to illusive cultural prescriptions. His dream emanates from his inheritance: "The world was obliged to turn gold in time. His life was to be fine and heroic, else he would not have been born" (p. 126). Thus it was writ in the lore of popular romances. As a

receptive agent of culture, George assimilates the fantastic vision,
completing his own improbable plot with an anachronistic code of manners. The configuration of his dream is whipped together with such
virtuous ingredients as nobility, grandeur, courage, and chivalry. Both
George and his mother intersect here along the plane of culture, for
she too harbors a similar heroic vision centered around her rescue of
George from "many wondrous influences that were swooping like
green dragons at him" (p. 122). In displacing George (and the rightful
namesake) as the conqueror of these dragons, his mother assumes
the saintly countenance of goodness over evil, thus ensuring his salvation and subsequent fate as a "white and looming king among men" (p.
124). Though the mother's dream is more benign in intent, preoccupied with qualities of goodness and knowledge in contrast to
George's yearning for power, both incorporate the distorted yet
motivating "givens" of culture. While the specious, melodramatic attributes of this mutually held "faith" reinforce the mother's convictions
in her role as caretaker of culture, they eject George from his ethereal
chariot to much more familiar surroundings.

George's major vision is complemented by a minor one in which he
focuses his romantic fantasy on a dream-girl closer to home. The irony
of the contrast rests in the fact that she is Maggie Johnson with a "pail
of beer in one hand and a brown-paper parcel under her arm" (p. 126).
Both Maggie and George inhabit the same tenement building, the
same illusory territory of social distortion and psychic withdrawal. The
melodrama is performed in the consciousnesses of its two principal
characters. Though George focuses his dreams of power and wonder
upon Maggie, he remains hidden from her, entirely contained within
his own force of imaginative grandeur. He cannot bring his own peculiar melodrama to coincide with Maggie's script. Communication is
thus impossible from the start, overcome by the enormity of the
unsaid and the inability of fantasy to accommodate itself to the coura-
geous simplicity of a greeting, an inquiry, a mild statement of genuine
contact within the plain stagecraft of everyday reality. George's flight
of heroic rescue in which Maggie accompanies him in that chariot of
pink clouds is grounded by the unfolding of events known to readers
from their familiarity with the conclusion of Maggie. The pattern of the
previous novella thus predetermines the irony of the succeeding one.
George "reflected that if he could only get a chance to rescue her from
something, the whole tragedy would speedily unwind" (p. 127).
George misses his own opportunity to make a difference because of
his impenetrable romantic encasement. His dream is emasculated

abruptly by his projection of guilt and shame, which causes him to misperceive his cowardice as Maggie's assumed indifference toward him, and by his presumed inferiority in comparison to Pete, whom George views as a virtual prince in armor. His perception of Pete reveals the extent of George's gross miscalculation of reality: "He had felt a sudden quiver of his heart. The grandeur of the clothes, the fine worldly air, the experience, the self-reliance, the courage that shone in the countenance of this other young man made him suddenly sink to the depths of woe" (p. 127). The self-deceit and erroneous perception of reality leave one tragedy to unwind its predictable course while commencing the dispossession of another: "Kelcy sank down in a chair with his legs thrust out straight and his hands deep in his trouser pockets. His chin was forward upon his breast, and his eyes stared before him. There swept over him all the self-pity that comes when the soul is turned back from a road" (p. 128).

George is thwarted from his path because of his disregard for the plain sense of things. His devout belief in a culturally determined romantic myth assures his resounding crash from the heights of Olympus to the depths of the Bowery. By transferring the culmination of those fine Algeresque qualities to Pete, the duffer we know him to be from his role in *Maggie*, Crane brings the parody of the success story to fruition. In doing so, Crane effects the deconstruction of the ordered system of meanings and beliefs which cohere a dominant culture. Such cherished qualities as sobriety, upward mobility, the work ethic, romantic individualism, and a noble code of manners are not only rendered illusive but, considering the embodiment, inconceivable. George's uncertain grip on the heroic mode of culture gives way completely, and his disappointment precipitates an accelerated process of descent and disillusionment. In keeping with this process, George slides into the opposite mode of the antihero, thus completing the transition from an adherence to the illusive givens of culture to an acceptance of the disenchanted realities of subculture. Subculture not only absorbs the illusions of culture but transforms them as well, reversing each affirmative quality to its negative value.

George's initiation into the antiheroic is hastened by his quest for a "partial self-destruction" (p. 129). This requisite subcultural process of descent is fulfilled at Bleecker's party, another fraternal gathering which recaptures the feigned social status of the Bowery denizens. Old Bleecker, attired in high collar and sitting about "like a fat, jolly god" (p. 133), plays host to this bacchic revelry. A pagan pitch among its participants lends the rite its ceremonious import, and the home-made bar and accoutrements to this feast create a kind of altar for the enthusiasts as if they were "at a festival of a religion" (p. 133). In all, the symbolic features of the setting, particularly the keg, dominate the room with the aura of George's longing—that mighty wavering of evil—which is set in contradistinction to his mother's stern yet tidy little Calvinistic world: "The row of bottles made quaint shadows upon the table, and upon a sidewall the keg of beer created a portentous black figure that reared toward the ceiling, hovering over the room and its inmates with spectral stature. Tobacco smoke lay in lazy cloud-banks overhead" (pp. 130–131). George's depressing vision of his mother's church, "of dreary blackness arranged in solemn rows" (p. 114), is obliterated by the heathenish qualities of Bleecker's party, lifting subculture right out of the moral frame of reference operative in culture. Symbolically, the blatant show of disbelief and complete lack of solemnity among the enthusiasts create for subculture its own endemic form of worship in which the rational forms of religious obligation and faith are not only refuted but overwhelmed. Subculture assumes the inverse, transforming sobriety into inebriety, rational dogma into nonsense, and stern belief in goodness and salvation into an overjoyed descent into reckless abandon. It is in such a manner that the cherished material of culture dissolves.

For all of its pretentious play toward the appearance of aristocracy, the scene and substance of Bleecker's party are distinctly lowbrow, regressing frantically from civilized posturings to a primitive horde (recitations of "Patrick Clancey's Pig," replete with grunts and snorts, suggest the level of "cultured" entertainment aspired to). It is as if Crane were picturing the hedonism and crudity of a people severed from the normative grip of culture and its associated realm of civility. Warming up to the feast, George takes comfort in the isolation, the safe company, the sentimental brotherhood that, as with the laughter, "arose like incense" (p. 133), enveloping him in the consecrated drift of mighty heroisms. The barbaric skid of the party is imagistically cast by the keg being tilted back and forth to speed the circulation of the potion. The effect "caused the black shadow on the wall to retreat and advance, sinking mystically to loom forward again with sudden menace, a huge dark figure controlled as by some unknown emotion" (p. 132). The menace, the vice of drink and delusion, is manipulated by an inarticulate desire, by a sensuality grounded in expressive sociality and devoted to a celebration of the irrational. Like his fellow enthusiasts, George moves within the expanse of this portentous shadow. "A valour, barbaric and wild, began to show in their poses and in their faces, red and glistening from perspiration" (p. 132). George's fervent participation culminates in a "yellow crash" to the floor, from which he quickly rises as if to defy the law of gravity or any semblance of the real. He regains his fantastic heights, turning the pain in his head into a pleasurable sensation, retaining illusion as a basic mode of experience. Subdued to the floor once more, buried under chairs and tables, he is forced into the reality of his drunken stupor. His complete loss of social balance is an offense which his fellows cannot endure. Here even barbarism has its limits, its restraints on unmanly dissipation.

The morning after reveals a slant of clarity to the debauchery: "mellow streams of sunshine poured in, undraping the shadows to disclose the putrefaction. . . . The grim truthfulness of the day showed disaster and death. After the tumult of the previous night the interior of this room resembled a decaying battlefield" (p. 136). Confronting the remnants in his field of vision as well as within his pained head, George rejects the "gold portals of vice." The rehabilitative force of an aching sobriety leads him to perceive "the futility of a red existence" and the somatic wholesomeness of a "white life" (p. 137). From gold to red to white: the hues which attend George's experience signify the chromatic path of the wayward son—that rocky yet brilliant trail of enticement, descent, and reform.

But George's resolution is short-lived. He is not suited for a "white life," and his momentary procession down that road of redemption turns abruptly. Yet his way is not new. The course has already been set, and George simply steps in line to follow the crowd. George's yearning for purification begins in accommodation and ends in rebellion. Finally conceding to his mother's request, he accompanies her to an evening prayer meeting. But for George, as well as for the city in general, this shift in allegiances exerts its own sense of futility, yielding its form to the surrounding urban structure.

> In a dark street the little chapel sat humbly between two towering apartment-houses. A red street-lamp stood in front. It threw a marvellous reflection upon the wet pavements. It was like the death-stain of a spirit. Farther up, the brilliant lights of an avenue made a span of gold across the black street. A roar of wheels and a clangour of bells came from this point, interwoven into a sound emblematic of the life of the city. (P. 142)

Crane's depiction of the scene works not only to bring the two paradigms of culture and subculture into contention but to show the effects of historical transition, the results of a battle once waged and now relinquished. The little chapel and its evocation of village life are overshadowed by the dominant cityscape. It is also significant that the Bowery has broadened its conceptual boundaries and become interchangeable here with the social form of the city that captures the visual space, squeezing out the old way of life and the bucolic beatitudes of humility, faith, and devotion. Surrounded on all sides by subculture, which comes to represent the city at large, the religious paradigm of culture appears as a flattened smear upon the pavement, something trampled over *en route* to the glitter of the avenue. Sound and sight combine here to assert the supremacy of an already established secular paradigm. If urban structure frames the chapel's submission and bleeds it of its vitality, then representative urban sounds complement the conquest by the sheer force of a new materialism. The design of a more sedate and coherent American past is not delicately ushered out of existence; its angelic voice is rendered mute, drowned by the endless cacophony of city life. Doubtless, the clangor of bells is not the melodious offerings from the belfry. The periodicity of churchly decorum has given way to those "eternal processions" of urban mechanisms and their Babellike rumblings of regimented disorder that "seemed somehow to affront this solemn and austere little edifice. It suggested an approaching barbaric invasion" (p. 142).

George's evanescent feelings of guilt, which temporarily led him to acquiesce to his mother, are all that remain alive in him of the religious outlook and thus reflect the resulting vacuum of this paradigm shift. Forsaking the guiding beliefs of the sacred model, his psychic equipment substitutes an essentially secular construct for a religious one. Yet the adjustment is further complicated through Crane's ironic displacement, for George's sense of sin is operative only in the secular domain—the world of saloons and street corners. The notion of sin is thus upended; it becomes something to be achieved rather than repented, a mark of distinction and initiation into the key institutions of urban civilization:

> He understood that drink was an essential to joy, to the coveted position of a man of the world and of the streets. The saloons contained the mystery of a street for him. When he knew the saloons he comprehended the street. Drink and its surroundings were the eyes of a superb green dragon to him. He followed a fascinating glitter, and the glitter required no explanation. (P. 144)

In taking this path, George merely states his affiliation with the contemporary; after all, "youths . . . were superior to mothers." And to be sure, "his mother was not modern" (p. 150). The generational theme which transcends the familial conflict of mother and son comments on the broader process of history itself, the temporal reality of change and abandonment.

In choosing the glitter of the avenue, George deepens his own process of descent and disillusionment. Begun in the rear rooms of a saloon and ritually enacted at Bleecker's party, this process gathers momentum in George's commitment to the street and in his subsequent actualization of this belief. In fact, all of George's purple heroisms empty into the prowess of the street, where he reaches the aspiring nadir of the antiheroic. His dispossession is finalized here, much like the fate of Maggie's melodramatic ideal. George's membership in a common street gang signals his ultimate repudiation of the orthodox values inherent in culture. His acceptance of futility and idleness, of "social safety and ease" (p. 149), provides for entry into the collective band which enables him to transcend his sense of guilt. The guiding beliefs of subculture, embodied in the street gang, usurp those of culture and, in doing so, represent the very antithesis of the latter's shared values. It is here, on the very ground of urban civilization, that the erect and affirmative posture of culture slumps into the negative specter of subculture. The ethos ingrained in the members of this emblematic street gang lends its own brand of substance to the shadowy form:

> They were all too clever to work. . . . Their feeling for contemporaneous life was one of contempt. Their philosophy taught that in a large part the whole thing was idle and a great bore. . . . The vast machinery of the popular law indicated to them that there were people in the world who wished to remain quiet. They awaited the moment when they could prove to them that a riotous upheaval, a cloudburst of destruction, would be a delicious thing. They thought of their fingers buried in the lives of these people. They longed dimly for a time when they could run through decorous streets with crash and roar of war, an army of revenge for pleasures long possessed by others, a wild, sweeping compensation for their years without crystal and gilt, women and wine. This thought slumbered in them, as the image of Rome might have lain small in the hearts of the barbarians. (P. 149)

George's opening appearance of self-reliance in the novella is given renewed meaning in light of his newly founded affiliation. The romantic attribute becomes radically negativized, imbued with contempt for the values of both past and present civilizations. It is not the republi-

can virtues of productive work and economic freedom which define the
gang but, rather, an expression of sabotage by the underdog, of individuality antagonistic to any moving target. Not only self-reliance, but
George's overblown romantic heroisms as well are converted from
positive (though outlandish) idealisms to realistic brawn, a descent to a
means of control circumscribed by bodily equipment—the defiant
sneer and the direct fist.

Crane's devolutionary perspective on subculture in the novella is
projected outward from its final state, the street gang. Annihilation,
either real or fervently imagined, is the gang's preferred mode of
perception and core value. Whether manifested as a physical presence, "a cloudburst of destruction," or as an object lesson in the
possibility of terror, the street gang incarnates that "approaching barbaric invasion" so menacing to the institutions of culture. But the gang
does not act in isolation, a mere subgroup within the context of subculture, for it represents the negative valence of subculture itself severed from the illusive though affirmative givens of culture. It is
through a symbolic reduction, the abysmal nucleus of the gang, that
Crane is able to realize his enlarged thematic vision, which extends
the void that envelops both subculture and culture.

Projecting from the abyss, the Bowery street gang and subculture
declaim the magnitude of their void by inverting the virtues inherent in
the guiding beliefs of culture and made manifest in the morality of
industrial capitalism. The descent to the street represents the deifica-
tion of failure in which the qualities of success (upward mobility, progress, and perfectibility) are rendered naught. This in turn transforms
the beatitudes of the Protestant work ethic (honesty, chastity, ini-
tiative, delayed gratification, thrift, etc.) into idle contempt and aggressive longings. The gang's sheer idleness reveals its lax sense of
time, at best an abiding metronome for eventual upheaval and ruin
rather than an efficient mechanism to be harnessed for the procure-
ment of capital. And the family, that fundamental social unit which
transmits the cultural ethos, is conspicuously absent, a tangential
thought or begrudging obligation. The pattern outlined above is in
itself a form of upheaval which delineates the guiding beliefs that
constitute the nihilism of Bowery subculture. Like the barbarous
street gang, so emblematic of the encroaching urban structure in
general, the project of subculture is to spread the engulfing boundaries
of its resident abyss to the utmost and absorb the illusive givens of an
effete culture into it. For Crane, it is from this vantage point that
subculture comes to stand for the whole of the present age.

Though the degree of influence that culture exerts has declined steadily throughout the novella, the dramatization of its degeneration and eventual erosion into subculture is enacted in the conclusion. In the final chapters of the novella an ineffectual culture is subdued and laid to rest, thus completing the process of engagement, conflict, and nullification. This is represented in part by George's confrontation with his mother, a culmination of his deepened sense of futility and his moral collapse. In her vestigial role as the caretaker of culture, she is still the scheduler of George's life and prompts him to rise each morning in order to fulfill his duty. George, however, feels that "it was an injustice to compel him to arise morning after morning with bitter regularity, before the sleep-gods had at all loosened their grasp. He hated the unknown force which directed his life" (p. 152). His mother, as the messenger of this dreaded force, bears the brunt of George's ill will. She "saw that the momentous occasion had come. It was the time of the critical battle. She turned upon him valorously" (p. 152). But her righteous insistence is met with the artillery of modernity, and George's profane litany of oaths shreds her virtuous line of attack. In the ensuing escalation of assaults, the religiously informed cultural paradigm proves powerless: "She threw out her hands in the gesture of an impotent one. He was the acknowledged victor. He took his hat and slowly left her" (p. 152). While the departure advances a state of further dispossession, the past is left ensconced in the faded glory of submission and defeat: "A pale flood of sunlight, imperturbable at its vocation, streamed upon the little old woman, bowed with pain, forlorn in her chair" (p. 153). This portrait is both a tragedy and a mockery, for she evokes an overriding sense of pity, existing as a faint outline of something to be disparaged and forsaken. In contrast to a revered icon, the old woman does not inspire awe or respect. From her ignoble posture she does not even transmit; instead she simply crumbles under the weight of an unmanageable counterforce.

When George is fired from his job, it is a mere *fait accompli* in light of his direction and pursuit. As a full-time hanger-on in the street gang, his opportunities are limitless. The street is his shrine, his epistemology, his measure of worth. He is only temporarily jolted out of his existence by a messenger who brings word of his mother's flagging health. When the two meet there is a genuine moment of communion, of filial devotion, and a touch of the endearing past. However, the reparation is fleeting, and her rapid recovery brings George back to his senses and to the street, raw and comprehensible. The second message, however, is dark with both intent and accuracy: "A little boy,

wild of eye and puffing, came down the slope as from an explosion. He
burst out in a rapid treble: 'Is dat Kelcy feller here? Say, yeh ol'
woman's sick again. Dey want yeh! Yehs better run! She's awful sick!
. . . She was hollerin'!'" (p. 159). George flees his gang for his mother's deathbed. At her side, in the midst of her mystic visions of finality,
origin and ending meet:

> Kelcy called to her as to a distant place. . . . [He] felt himself
> being choked. When her voice pealed forth in a scream he saw
> crimson curtains moving before his eyes. "Mother—oh,
> mother—there's nothin'—there's nothin'—"
> She was at a kitchen door with a dish-cloth in her hand. Within
> there had just been a clatter of crockery. Down through the trees
> of the orchard she could see a man in a field ploughing. "Bill—o-
> o-oh, Bill—have yeh seen Georgie? Is he out there with you?
> Georgie! Georgie! Come right here this minnet! Right—this—
> minnet!" (P. 161)

The distant dialogue between mother and son, past and present, is
mediated by feverish hallucination. Yet the past, insistent unto the
end, manages to break through, reeling out like a disjunctive frame of
reference. This disjunctive form of communication, disorganized and
desperate, is appropriate not only to the death scene but also to the
final retrogression of the dialectic between culture and subculture; for
the rhetoric of that "mystic being upon the bed" (p. 160) sounds more
like the utterances of the undertaker of culture than like those of its
caretaker. With the death of George's mother comes the domination of
the city's new image, the distended presence of subculture; the past,
embalmed with all its illusions, is laid to rest in an inconsequent grave.

The message in the novella's conclusion is that a culture sustained
by its illusive "givens" is a culture that cannot be sustained at all.
Crane renders these givens, contained in the mother's obsolete religion with its temperance crusade, in the sentimental heroisms of the
popular romance, and in the morality of industrial capitalism, null and
void. The removal of culture from the dialectic is curative from a
critical viewpoint, for it expresses a radical position necessary to
counter the legerdemain of culture. It satisfies an aesthetic proposition: dispossession and homelessness exist as remainders and come
to represent the spiritual predicament of society itself.

Yet the resulting condition is rendered as a sort of payment made in
punitive retribution for culture's ideological offenses. As such, the
condition itself is wholly other than curative. It is, at best, the nihilistic

drift of subculture. George's mother becomes the isolated martyr of an archaic cultural era who, worn down from numerous collisions, finally quits the battle: at the head of her deathbed stood a glass, on which "reflected lights made a silver star" (p. 161). But there is no redemption in her Christlike offering, and a painful though authentic understanding develops because of this. Her myth, which is the myth of culture, is impotent and must die. One is then dropped into the encompassing abyss of subculture, of a wholly secularized society that is poorly equipped to resolve the modern existential crisis. Severed from the past, George is left to an urban cycle of spiritual and material impoverishment, compensated for by a new industrial breed of barbarism. Compelled by his own heightened sense of guilt and mortality, George stares at the wallpaper pattern of brown roses, which felt "like hideous crabs crawling upon his brain" (p. 161). All of the fantastic grandeur is refocused in the faded image of those roses, a *memento mori* of his own false and misdirected heroisms, the mighty march of folly and the minuscule yield of such fancy footwork. Crane's narrative eye slides beyond George's individual psyche, gliding past the play of sunlight on the tablecloth and out the window to the cityscape. The pattern of this movement shifts quickly from internal to external states, passing over any substantial mediation between self and society which would normally reside in the domestic setting of home and family. The sequence of this final imagery gives credence to the direction of the novella and the symbolic merger of Bowery subculture with the transformed social reality of the city at large. George succumbs to the cityscape, which reasserts itself, framing the introduction and conclusion of the novella in an exertion of presence and totality: "The window disclosed a fair, soft sky, like blue enamel, and a fringe of chimneys and roofs, resplendent here and there. An endless roar, the eternal trampling of the marching city, came mingled with vague cries" (p. 162).

The image of the city reveals itself once again in terms of absence and presence. A "fringe of chimneys and roofs" defines the visual meaning of its appearance. Significantly, there are no steeples to be espied, no tapering spires in this scene. Such religious mediation between man and the heavens has been buried by a new, much bolder skyline. George recedes from view as well, yet all that he and his subculture represent is embodied in the "endless roar," "the eternal trampling," and those "vague cries," as if the street gang had finally realized their wish and ravished the city, toppling over its vertical structure to gambol in the ruins. The view outside the window is not one of escape and possibility, a sort of safety valve to the pervading sense of nihilism which Crane projects throughout. The feeling of entrapment is unrelieved by the ending as the repetitive cycle, given in the familiar conflict of another mother and son in a neighboring tenement flat, is set in motion. The ritual, signifying the persistence of Crane's nihilistic attitude, is a program of inevitability, a recapitulation of the conflict which returns to the closed system of the text rather than a program of action that exists in the open spaces beyond it. Over the transom, the entire story begins anew, a tale of the city, its slums and inhabitants, all advancing in a high-stepping parade to some unknown territory, blind to the corpses left in its wake and deaf to the sounds of its own multitudes.

So, for Crane, as the illusions of culture vanish, so does its viability. Like a *trompe l'oeil* painting, the perception of culture appears intact until subjected to scrutiny. It is only then that the eye, staring close up, recovers its senses. Yet once the trickery has been discovered, the vision loses its grip. Crane forces such an irony in his treatment of culture, for his perspective reacts to seeing the typical viewer regaining his ground, preferring to accept culture as an illusory whole rather than to discover the illusoriness through a critical examination of its realistic parts. In the end, the reasonable man would rather be fooled. This suggests an inherent human propensity for mystification as opposed to critical realism; in other words, if mystification is our cultural inheritance, then critical realism must exist as anomaly.

Crane's disruption of the dialectic appears to reflect his sense of disillusionment regarding this proposition; that is, the persistent inability or unwillingness of culture to grow and develop from an awareness of critical realism and how it plays against mystification. Perceived as anomaly, critical realism would be, like subculture itself, petrified and thus placed at an immeasurable social and cultural distance. This is why Crane's novella terminates with the wholesale obliteration of culture, as any program of action initiated to rearrange its distorted elements would surely seem futile and meet with an incredulous stare. Crane minimizes the risk of choice by making the decision for the viewer. The portrait of culture, whole yet deceptive, viable though mistaken, undergoes a curative treatment commensurate with its qualities and given by the author's hand—it simply vanishes.

Yet there is something Crane leaves us with that is viable; that is, the notion of mystification as a universal structuring principle in human society. But although this was the position that Crane reached, his treatment of it resulted in its annihilation. Thus, without the coexistence of the contradictory sign systems inherent in the dialectic between culture and subculture, human society drops into the abyss of the latter. For Crane, as well as for Dreiser, this too was the endpoint for Bowery critical realism. Both writers, in responding to the profoundly fluid process of their social and historical situation, tracked the dialectic downward to its ultimate tragic result. In pursuing the inevitable consequences of this path, they ended by severing the underlying annihilative impetus of the tragic pattern from the creative power of the continuing dialectic between culture and subculture. Therefore, as it reached its fulfillment, Crane's and Dreiser's critical realism became fixated on the death drive, which, though implicit in the nature of the dialectic, obscured an awareness of a counter-impetus that completes the total pattern—the life force emanating from within subculture, one dependent upon the retention and continued flickerings of the dialectic. As we shall witness in the conclusion, it is precisely the need for this tension, or misalignment between culture and subculture (mystification and critical realism), that keeps Bowery subculture elevated above the abyss in a wondrous whirl of symbolic action.

Crane's and Dreiser's endpoint is intricately connected to their late nineteenth-century conception of culture and so, from a modern viewpoint, can be seen to harbor some inescapable qualities of mystification. This mystification, however, should not be confused with the cultural ideology Crane and Dreiser had so effectively undermined during their era. It is of an entirely different cast, one attributed to them from the hindsight of a modern perspective on the notion of culture, a notion which, as both producers and products of their age, they could not have possibly entertained.

The impact, however, of Crane's insight into mystification as cultural inheritance touches on a much larger issue which underlies the present study. My view on the persistency of the dialectic between culture and subculture into our own time, and of the culture-making process of the latter treated in the conclusion, reinstates the conflictual nature of both symbolic systems in dynamic interaction. The persistency of this dialectic speaks for the fact that the dominant culture, as Fredric Jameson notes, tends to view history as an "absent cause."[18] It is precisely this perceived absence of the historical process (the interworkings of those shaping spheres of social existence, be they cultural, ideological, political, juridical, or economic) that makes for the present state of mystification. The symbolic system of mystification reaches beyond a commodity fetishism, in which the processes of work and production are hidden, and into the very spheres of social activity outlined above. In this fashion, mystification not only works unconsciously to conceal the economic organization of industrial capitalism, but also to keep the interrelated spheres and the social and aesthetic processes hidden as well. Thus the dynamic played out in the late nineteenth century among economic and urban segregation, social distance (which produced an enticing sense of mystery), the symbolic system of mystification, and the countering sign system of critical realism remained buried beneath the surface of that era's ahistorical outlook.

From a contemporary perspective, it is difficult to point to the class struggle or, in our present context, to the patterning of descent by a member of culture into the subculture of the Bowery. A reasonable man, looking out from his suburban front porch, our current center of American civilization, cannot possibly see his counterpart, a bum looking out from Rivington Street and the Bowery. If the social and physical distances keep the extremity of condition alone worlds apart, then access to the determinant processes which make for such a contrast in life-styles becomes even more remote. Of course, the journalistic media may keep a member of culture abreast of subculture, but the information is likely to be both rendered and received in the light of static condition rather than an understanding of process. With a subject such as the Bowery, as with any social phenomenon, one's primary access to historical process will be largely achieved by searching out its prior textualization. Yet this activity requires both motive and direction on the part of our reasonable man. Who is to say that, beginning in the tunnel of mystification, he will emerge in the light of critical realism? But even if he does end up intellectually on the other side, his affiliations within the established networks of culture and social structure will effect his reclamation and hence exert the symbolic system of mystification upon his social perception.

To the extent that human society is organized into complex, fragmented, hierarchical, and modern arrangements (into the structure of "incorporation"), mystification necessarily will be a natural component of a culture's world view. Yet, as Crane and Dreiser so well demonstrated, the release from such a taut hold is not only granted by stepping out from culture but also, in the light of Bowery subculture, by stepping down and thus attaining a felt awareness of the hidden processes. This sense of liminality, of descending to the realm of antistructure, is a method by which to fully appreciate an overall vision of the whole. For, as one traverses between the affiliations of culture and the affiliations of subculture, one begins to see the process as paramount and the conditions as consequent manifestations. One also sees the inseparable nature of culture and subculture and the visibility of the underlying assumptions which guide each realm into dynamic unity. For instance, after I had originally embarked on my ethnographic study of the Bowery, the common refrain I received from my fellow members of culture was the following: that is "a little too real" for me. Did this necessarily mean that culture was therefore unreal? Looking back, that refrain seems to have been a spontaneous expression of mystification, for the evocative power of the Bowery as taboo was a perceived threat to the basic assumption of cultural order. Herein lies the fascination of culture with subculture, yet herein also lies the calculated distance. But subculture also has an understanding of as well as a stake in culture's predilection for mystification. As one Bowery man I came to know half-jokingly put it to me: "When you finish that book you're writing, put it up your arse and call it *The Hidden Mystery.*" Evidently, I had incited the notion of taboo on both sides of the dialectic, for, in both instances, I had expressed an interest in making each social domain known to the other. Bowery subculture too has its own developed sense of integrity and its members know very keenly that, in their present condition, the existence of culture provides for their *raison d'être*, as much as the haunting presence of the Bowery stimulates the impetus for one's attachment to the structural bond of culture.

CONCLUSION

Without men, no culture, certainly;
but equally, and more significantly, without culture,
no men.
—Clifford Geertz
The Interpretation of Cultures

rane's ending to *George's Mother*, and his endpoint for Bowery critical realism in general, is a fitting point of departure for looking out from the inside of the contemporary
Bowery. In fact, both Crane and Dreiser encapsulate the late
nineteenth-century conception of culture, even when the dialectic between culture and subculture is pushed to the ultimate limit of that
historical period. Both writers achieved more than any other literary
figures during this era relative to the discovery of urban poverty in the
Bowery, the nature of the social processes of descent, and the more
inclusive, relational view surrounding the dialectic between culture
and subculture. And yet, from a contemporary perspective, even
though Crane and Dreiser elevated the level of social and aesthetic
discourse which informed critical realism, the fulfillment of their radical perspective was ultimately bound by their participation in history.
Living in history, as we all must, whether we approve or not, Crane's
and Dreiser's perspective on the dialectic between culture and subculture was incomplete in the sense that, even though they had reached
the farther shore of the dialectic, they were, like troubled fugitives,
looking backward over their shoulders at culture.

The basic assumption resident in the late nineteenth century, an
assumption which both Crane and Dreiser could not outdistance in
their flight from the traditional values of the genteel tradition, was the
dominant evolutionary thought of the period which placed culture at
the apex of human development. As viewed in that era, culture (with a
k) was conceived more as the imaginary, literary, and social artifacts
and codes of conduct which upheld a fixed morality and social structure
rather than as a "way of life," which summarizes the contemporary
definition. What strengthened this normative construct of "kulture"
was the universalist understanding of man gleaned from the Enlightenment's view of his innate capabilities for development. This develop-   *171*

ment was seen as occurring in concert with the constancy of nature. Thus the absolutism of the Enlightenment and the evolutionary emphases inherent in Darwinian thought produced a curious amalgamation which deeply embedded the tenets of metaphysical idealism (teleology, progress, and perfectibility) in the symbolic ground of this historical moment. And though critical realism, embodied in Crane and Dreiser, fought hard to expand the framework of this conceptual position, these figures were still going the rounds within the public arena—pushing out its boundaries yet always engaged within.

This late nineteenth-century conception looked on culture, in its final development, as the finest flower of civilization. Thus any divergence from the summit was viewed as a descent into anticulture. In putting into question the viability of culture, as Crane did in *George's Mother*, the result was a devolutionary perspective, a degenerative slide into the abyss of subculture. Such a view, though critical of culture (in fact, rendering its despoliation), framed subculture as the opposing nadir, a nongenerative form of dispossession. Crane fortified this idea of Bowery subculture as null and void by his reliance on barbarism to highlight the result when culture withers from the stem of civilization. Dreiser too reiterates this inert conception of the Bowery by perceiving it as a passive receptacle for the social process of Hurstwood's descent in its final hour. Recall that, for Dreiser, the Bowery also functions in that abysmal capacity by absorbing the conflation of textual elements and social categories (scene, agent, act, agency, attitude, and purpose). So though, for both writers, the descent resulted in the incisive discovery of previously unexamined social processes and led to the rupture of middle-class strategies of containment, once there they were at a loss—for though the descent beckoned, the ascent did not. What was lost in the Bowery was the normative grip of culture, and if that standard frame of reference represented the finest, then subculture manifested the worst. From such an evolutionary/devolutionary dichotomy, subculture can only be seen as wholly negative, a nihilistic condition of social death without any compensating humanistic value that might continue, albeit in an altered form, the culture-making process. Entrapment takes on a much larger meaning in this context, for if we cannot return to the pinnacle of culture, due to the specious qualities of its "illusive givens," and if we are abandoned deep within the walls of a subcultural abyss, then there is no possibility for recovery. Thus the entire conception of the nature of man is also put into question, for without the generative sphere of culture his prospects are naught as well.

Crane's and Dreiser's position on the construct of culture presents a formidable challenge when confronted from within the parameters of their historical age. Yet, when viewed from a contemporary perspective, the conception of these critical realists is simply untenable and, ironically, the return to a renewed conception of culture is granted from a foundation in modern evolutionary theory. From an anthropological definition, culture is inherent in the very nature of man. As Clifford Geertz neatly summarizes it, "we are . . . incomplete or unfinished animals who complete or finish ourselves through culture— and not through culture in general but through highly particular forms of it."[1] When the ethical and moralistic assumptions of an absolutist conception are undermined, a relative view of the culture-making process takes hold which is generative of symbolic forms and meanings despite a group's social position, physical location, or stage of historical development. Culture, as Geertz defines it, "denotes an historically transmitted pattern of meanings embodied in symbols, a system of inherited conceptions expressed in symbolic forms by means of which men communicate, perpetuate, and develop their knowledge about and attitudes toward life."[2] In light of such an adaptive definition, no group or individual person could possibly exist outside this framework. From an evolutionary point of view, biology and culture become inseparable processes in formulating and completing man, his limits as well as possibilities. Language, as the essential and generative vehicle for symbolic systems, catapults man to a fundamental duality: symbolic action and nonsymbolic motion. Kenneth Burke distinguishes man as the "symbol-using animal" for whom language functions as the creative act of expression and communication. Once the word comes into being man begins his ascent from the "infinite wordless universe" (nature) into the "countless universes of discourse that story can make of it" (culture).[3]

In contrast to the late nineteenth-century viewpoint, this more encompassing discourse on the construct of culture comprises an open system which rests upon less fixed and mechanistic principles of man and his habitat. In this contemporary outlook on culture, the constituting attributes include variability, relativity, symbolic action, historical transmission, social change, contextual and determining realities of time and place, and a search for the complexities which define a people's ethos and world view. Operating within this broad and inclusive conception, Bowery subculture emerges from its inert status, as given in the late nineteenth-century paradigm, to one generative of a way of life which completes its members' social being and individuality. The ability to endlessly engage in the uniquely human enterprise of symbolic action continues rather than retards the evolutionary culture-making process. Symbolic systems are thus ingredient to the reality of man in society, as opposed to tangential accretions:

> They are extrinsic [and extrasomatic] sources of information in terms of which human life can be patterned—extrapersonal mechanisms for the perception, understanding, judgment, and manipulation of the world. Culture patterns—religious, philosophical, aesthetic, scientific, ideological—are "programs"; they provide a template or blueprint for the organization of social and psychological processes, much as genetic systems provide such a template for the organization of organic processes.[4]

As we shall see, Bowery subculture invents and perpetuates such "programs" commensurate with its unique experience, thus attesting to the fact that it too can have "blossomed in a mud-puddle," and not despite but precisely because of its fertile bed.

Although Crane's and Dreiser's late nineteenth-century conception of the culture-making process was incomplete, the value of their critical realism reveals an alignment with the broad purposes given in modern ethnography. In its concern with evoking a social and cultural totality relative to the "other" both at home and abroad, in its thrust toward offering substantive critiques of our own society, and in its provocative challenge to the basic assumptions through which we function and grasp other cultures and subcultures, ethnography can, in fact, be viewed as a distinct category of critical realism. The notion and practice of defamiliarization, for example, bring together the narrative design of Crane's fiction and the critical strategies of modern ethnography. Of course, as a unique subfield of cultural anthropology, ethnography ultimately diverges from the fictive designs of Crane and Dreiser in terms of form, style of representation, analytical concepts, social science methods, and the level and inclusiveness of cultural analysis attained. Yet, despite these generic differences, the correspondence between fictive and ethnographic categories of apprehension and knowledge underscores the continuity of symbolic action when formulated in the particular demystifying strategies of critical realism. The correspondence also illuminates the valuable contribution both categories make in revealing the deep structure of meaning resident in culture and society.

Some consideration of the contemporary Bowery works to complete and round out Crane's and Dreiser's critical perspective on the dialectic between culture and subculture. From the modern perspective on the culture-making process, the dialectic is somewhat complicated by the fact that we are dealing with two generative, culture-making processes which overlap, at least from the perspective of a Bowery man. Bowery subculture operates under the same general dynamics as outlined by Geertz and Burke, as does the dominant American middle-class culture to which it is symbiotically related. We must keep in mind, however, that subculture, as a particular outgrowth of the dominant culture, is as much shaped and defined by the latter's persistent influence as well as by its own immanent processes. Bowery subculture is not a discrete entity—this is not the Bororo tribe resident in urban America, but rather a distinct yet discontinuous subgroup of the dominant culture, differentiated by such significant socioeconomic and political factors as income, class, housing, employment, patterns of consumption, affiliations, structurally inferior status, ecological base, social organization, dispossession, deprivation, and transiency. These, and related factors, as well as the symbolic systems of meaning, belief, and value which give them cognitive and expressive awareness, function to unify Bowery subculture and act collectively on its members. Yet they do so because of the symbiotic relationship between culture and subculture; both are separate yet interdependent entities whose opportunities for collision and conflict are generative of both cultural ideology and social distance as well as the subcultural way of life (its ethos, world view, belief system, social relations, institutional supports, adaptive strategies, etc.). The interdependency should not, however, signify free access (mobility) between subculture and culture. In general, Bowery men do not have the privilege to cross those boundaries (modes of social being) at will, at least physically, socially, politically, and economically. Culture is largely retained through proximity, internalization, and symbolic action. Yet the social distance is fundamentally generative to one of the Bowery subculture's chief offices: the contravention of a dominant system of value and order, precisely that reflected in culture.

My own descent into the contemporary Bowery was just that, a self-conscious drop into the lowlands of the urban terrain, where I spent three years, from the fall of 1977 to the fall of 1980. (For the sake of clarity and convenience in the narrative, I am using the pronouns "I" and "my" even though the following field accounts speak to the presence of my fieldwork collaborator, Mr. Jeffrey Grunberg.) Although drawing on the interpretive constructs of such symbolic anthropologists as Clifford Geertz, Mary Douglas, and Victor Turner, the actual design, process, and social context of my ethnographic study more closely resembled the work represented in Elliot Liebow's *Tally's Corner* (1967) and Carol Stack's *All Our Kin* (1974), participant observation studies of black street corner men and kinship networks in a poor black community, respectively. In addition, Samuel Wallace's notion of skid row as a distinct way of life and James Spradley's *You Owe Yourself a Drunk* (1970), an ethnography of urban nomads on the Seattle skid row, helped to pave the way for my understanding of the highly complex dimensions, differentiated strategies, and profound social processes operative within skid row subculture.

In pursuing an ethnographic approach to Bowery life, I assumed the role of a participant observer. As such, I exercised both integrated functions of that role and soon found myself accepted by my Bowery associates and collaborators. "Societies, like lives," Geertz writes, "contain their own interpretations. One has only to learn how to gain access to them."[5] Evidently I had learned, mostly through persistence, good faith, and authentic encounter, for I became a sort of fixture for a time, a known entity, a friend, researcher, confidant, and curio to the men who drew me into their subculture. Once I gained access and in keeping with my own approach (an eerie process of discovery), I let the experts guide my passage. The men themselves proved valid epistemological scouts, leading me to structures and processes inherent in their lives as well as to the interplay of social and cultural dynamics which outlined the totality of their condition. Had I not heeded the descriptive, interpretive, and particularistic trail of experience created for me by the men (real men with names such as Jack and Jerry, Pee Wee King, Jimmy, Moe, Thorazine Al, Fred, Harry, Chief, Hewey, Frank, Bobby, Donny, Sugar Hart, Richie, Nicky Star, and the like), I would have soon been caught in the net of cultural assertions, which would have focused my attention strategically elsewhere. The intensity of experience I enjoyed with the men is attributable to the fact that I followed their lead, their illuminating drift through homelessness, thus letting subculture begin the departure for meaning.

The Bowery men involved me not only in clues to their condition but in dramatic events spontaneously rendered by the harsh pressures on their existence. Early on, there were conversations (social discourses, if you will) which incited the men to highlight the essence of their condition. This was often done with a genuine performative intensity which enabled me to focus not only on the ensuing definitions, comments, stories, etc. but also on the style and attitude in which

such content was being expressed. I soon came to appreciate that, in
the Bowery, words were imbued with the value of deeds which attested to the importance Bowery men placed on the struggle for
meaning, knowledge, and expression. At times, these conversations
produced metaphoric complexities that took days to disentangle. At
other times, however, the meaning was crisp and elemental, as when I
inquired of one man as to the absence of women on the Bowery: "This
is skid row, brother!" he replied. "There ain't no room for women. A
man's gotta have a shelter, some food, if he can get it, and his wine.
Women don't fit in down here." In pursuing one line of inquiry, a host of
others surfaced upon this man's response. Though I learned little
about the dearth of women on the Bowery from this response, I was
quickly drawn into the projection of his life world which viewed "wom-
en" from a perspective of masculine pleasure, romance, and sexuality.
But more importantly, "this is skid row, brother!" worked to forcefully
halt any speculation on the prevalence of heterosexual relationships on
the Bowery, to make that thought, in fact, preposterous. Instead, the
reality of condition became foregrounded: the stripped-down necessi-
ties of being homeless (shelter, food, and alcohol) and the priorities
within a spatial location perceived as distinctly below ("down here")
relative to the structure of social hierarchy. It was in countless similar
situations to the above that I was able to discover, identify, describe,
and interpret the significant constructs, processes, and phenome-
nological issues of my collaborators and their locale.

There were also revealing and witty one liners, such as "remember,
you can't spell bum without *u* in it," which, when reinforced by others,
helped me again during the initial stage of the encounter to acquire a
firm grasp of the broad cultural context by which the Bowery men
were inextricably bound and bordered. If subculture was the victim,
then culture became the fugitive accomplice. The total vision, culture
in its relationship to subculture, was more fully developed in the multitude of incidents I shared with the men in bars, bottlegang groups, flophouses, mission services and dinners, and the ocean of time spent in
aimless retreat on the street. In all these places, the phenomenology
of their lives became apparent—in the form of whole stories, fables,
myths, protracted trials by jury, exhibitions of prowess and remorse,
imagistic fantasies, street scenes, and humor, as well as in the realistic
dimensions of survival, disillusionment, and death.

As we shall see, the root paradigm of the Bowery subculture is
tragedy, and the men's haunting expressions did justice to their
adopted mythoi. Yet this condition of finitude, a result of their disaffilia-

tion, has repeatedly been seen as the *fons et origo* of their state. The Bowery men facilitated my understanding of their condition by reconstructing the processes of their descent. To define the Bowery man as disaffiliated, a habitual categorical reduction among social scientists, is to establish the reification of the Bowery. Studies that have focused on the Bowery, or skid row homeless men in general, are often replete with middle-class bias and pejorative descriptions. In its entry on homelessness, the *International Encyclopedia of the Social Sciences* defines homeless men in respect to the normative standards of culture and the social structure of the larger society: "Homelessness is a condition of detachment from society characterized by the absence or attenuation of the affiliative bonds that link settled persons to a network of interconnected social structures."[6] Based on implicit established criteria (family, school, community, state, production group, occupational union, church, and recreational associations), the article, which distills much of the research on disaffiliation into a format that by its very nature certifies "knowledge," draws its conclusions and cultural assertions:

> At the extreme point of the scale, the modern skid row man demonstrates the possibility of nearly total detachment from society. . . . Homeless persons are poor, anomic, inert, and non-responsible. They command no resources, enjoy no esteem, and assume no burdens of reciprocal obligations. Social action, in the usual sense, is almost impossible for them. Lacking organizational statuses and roles, their sphere of activity extends no further than the provision of personal necessities on a meager scale. Their decisions have no implications for others. . . . A certain apathy regarding self preservation often develops in addition to the collective helplessness. The homeless in great cities . . . stand and watch their companions assaulted by strangers without offering to interfere and without taking any measure to protect themselves.[7]

There is little doubt that the Bowery man is disaffiliated from society and culture, but to leave it at that is to commit an ideological error of omission. Such an argument, which is premised upon the methodological practice of social distance (structured interviews, questionnaires, and codified surveys) and the strategy of mystification, obscures the fact that there is a compensatory social process of affiliation within the subculture which assures safe landing and commonality even while it ironically accelerates the tragic pattern. Aside from demonstrating those rather persistent cultural devices (social distance, mystification, and the corroboration of preconceived hypotheses), the above passage is strikingly reminiscent of the language of condemnation found in the sensationalistic genre of the late nineteenth century, here reformulated into the language of a positivist discipline. A myopic perspective has caused these and similar researchers to neglect to examine the affiliative ties between homeless men and the social organizations and structures endemic to their ecological base. I have found that, within the context of the Bowery, the men are deeply enculturated into their subculture. They are integrated within their community and have daily attachments to bars, restaurants, flops, liquor stores, social agencies, missions, used clothing stores, and bottlegang groups. In a manner that parallels this internal integration, the men have direct public contact with the domain beyond their own community through passersby and sojourns out of the Bowery and indirect contact via the electronic media.

Within their own network of social relations, I have witnessed Bowery men to be responsive in extending mutual obligations. The interactions between the men do create shifting roles, at times differentiated, which grant measures of esteem to the men. I have seen their activities extend beyond fulfilling basic physiological needs to survive. Also, an underlying "code of honor" is at times operative in providing collective assistance in times of peril. And some men are motivated, perhaps not to attend church services weekly or sustain gainful employment, but to spend long hours begging in often unbearable conditions to meet both personal and collective wants. In sum, what I have witnessed from my participations and observations in a time-depth study does not lend generalized support to purely external perspectives, which lack inclusiveness and the sharing of lives prescribed by an ethnographic approach.

The proponents of the restrictive ideology of disaffiliation find a degree of security and order in the opposition between incorporation into the social structure of culture and the alienation, or loss of incorporation, of the Bowery man. This becomes a facile conceptualization in which the transgressions from the dominant culture and social structure are necessarily categorized and understood. It is all condensed in the label of "bum," which provides both culture and subculture with a convenient picture of condition and social relationship. The label issues from the conception of disaffiliation, a sort of layman's tag for the more formalized argument, and works to the culture's advantage by preserving order through the classification and regulation of disorder. In violating cherished cultural norms and relations, the Bowery resembles the disorder associated with pollution and taboo. "Last week a manicure, this week a bum," is the point of view resident in subculture, a view that articulates the significance of each social antipode as a pronounced demarcation of difference, not to mention the suggestion of distance covered—the descent. But this man's succinct commentary also highlights the oscillation between culture and subculture and hints at the purpose of the latter, which is the disruption of a dominant and regulated system of order. Subculture is to culture, much like bum is to a manicure, if we take bum in the context of pollution and taboo to mean something out of order, something broken. In concert, disaffiliation and its tag, bum, work to maintain a stringent sense of social distance and mystification; due to the fact that the internal complexity of the Bowery's generative potential is not even acknowledged, the model minimizes the ambiguity and challenge emanating from subculture. Thus, culture does not see subcultural affiliation as the compensatory drive, which emerges from beneath the condition of alienation, and does not recognize the consequences which result from this dynamic.

What is systematically denied among researchers who rest their case upon the ideology of disaffiliation and its etiological forms of mental illness, substance abuse, and unemployment is the recognition of Bowery homelessness as a condition *sui generis*. This style of deflection is keenly embodied in the following passage commenting on the Keener Report, a passage which undermines the rather fine discussion preceding it on the heterogeneous nature of the contemporary homeless in New York City and on the consideration of some "New Arrivals" data:

> The clients in the Keener study classified as "psychiatric only" are homeless, but this is because they are severely mentally ill. The "alcoholic only" and "drug only" cases are another issue: these people are homeless, but again, their dominant problem is not homelessness but alcoholism or drug addiction. Finally we have the "economic only" cases. It turns out that in many instances, these people are not simply homeless before they come to the shelters at all. Many do, in fact, have other housing options available to them.[8]

The effect of this representative "finding" is to turn our attention away from the constitutive nature of homelessness as a dynamic social process. In such instances homelessness, in fact, does not exist; it is

merely the static consequence of other anterior pathologies. Somewhat reminiscent of Riis and his tenement argument, these antecedents are then assumed to be both the root cause of homelessness and *Conclusion*
the major problems at hand. Yet they are themselves symptomatic of
much deeper socioeconomic, administrative, public welfare, housing,
familial, and personal configurations whose utter complexity and interrelationship defy this kind of analytical laxity and mystification.[9]

The notion of the Bowery man as disaffiliated is often bolstered by
his use of alcohol. Once again, subculture and its mode of affiliation are
concealed factors in this phenomenon. On the Bowery, affiliation flows
through the use of alcohol. Among Bowery men, the chronic or moderate use of alcohol takes on symbolic importance. In a sense, it
functions to mediate the immense distance between one's disaffiliation
from the paramount structures of authority and one's complementary,
and compensatory, affiliation within a well-defined counterculture.
This opposition between alienation and affiliation implies the significance of a gradual process of descent, a loss of identity, and the
resocialization into a community of protest and defeat. The fact that
alcohol has been used in part to clinch this rite of passage has been
well documented by many observers of skid row life.[10]

Alcohol consumption in the Bowery not only cements one's reas-
sembly of self and selfhood but also expresses the antithesis to the
ultrarational as a guiding mode of being. Steeped in the "irrational,"
the very appearance of a Bowery man offers an implicit critique regarding the prevailing pattern of social order (with its host of structural forms and relations), which aims toward efficiency, productivity,
bureaucratization, and incorporation. In fleeing from the contemporary network, the Bowery man has retreated into a more basic, albeit
submerged, style of existence. This style of existence does not characteristically incorporate a struggle for economic gain or political
power; those prospects are rather hopeless. Instead, what is at stake
is a struggle for definition, integration, and survival—a means of cop-
ing with the adversity of condition and the ambiguity of meaning and
dignity relative to the ideals and norms that define both culture and
subculture. In short, it is a struggle for completion, a regeneration of
that which has been severed.

As the Bowery men conform more and more to the rigorous requirements of their subculture they also become increasingly attached
to it and to each other. Upon this enculturation, the men have discovered that they share a similar humanity; they are an underclass united
in a condition of incalculable poverty. They have left an indifferent

culture and have reappeared in an aggressively destructive subculture. In meeting the requirements for self-preservation they rely upon each other, developing solidarity for physical, psychological, and social survival. This affiliation is tantamount to the invention of their new reality. It allows the men to experiment with their former and present lives. It demands that they adhere to and manifest a certain subcultural lifestyle and express its values and attitudes in an attempt to instill their lives with meaning and purpose. These networks of friendship and attachments in the Bowery, though particularly significant during moments of intense stress and distress, are not limited to the utilitarian compulsion toward biological survival. As the deep structure of the subculture's culture-making process, they function to formulate, communicate, and manifest the ethos and world view of this collectivity. The critical importance of affiliation was often described to me by the men: "One hand washes the other down here, it's like what Ford did for Nixon"; or "Friendship is like a watchful eye"; or, as William said with his hands clenched into a tight circle, "Friendship is like a core."

As one fluid embodiment of affiliation, the bottlegang group is a spontaneous and tenuous structure. The formation of the group permits the men to pool their resources and thereby drink communally as well as cheaply. Though all the men, usually three to six in a group, may not contribute an equal share of money into the kitty, or "frisco circle," the bottle is passed without regard to how much each has spent among them. These groups, which spread in pockets along Bowery streets, can be viewed as adaptive strategies to the problems of limited subcultural resources and the cohesive organization of social relations. They provide the public arena for the fulfillment of interpersonal and primary group relations (a reestablishment of surrogate kinship ties) which convey the meanings the men introduce to friendship in the Bowery. The interactions that occur render the men's subcultural existence more transparent. Humor, edifying remarks, news (the latest robbery caper at the One Mile House, a Bowery bar, for example), helpful information, mutual aggrandizement, reminiscences, sense, and nonsense (the high-strung sounds of the alphabet spoken backwards) characterize the range of content which fills the inner circle of such groups. All of this, but, in particular, the supportive behavior, directly appeals to the men's thwarted quest for security, belongingness, and self-esteem. Whether the supportive act is an impromptu collection for an associate whose father recently passed away, or finding and returning a lost article, or brainstorming a gimmick (such as the use of bar coasters for makeshift yarmulkes on Yom

Kippur in order to better sway the Jewish public), or bandaging the
wounds from the previous night, the men reveal to each other that
they are indeed alive, noticed, and appreciated. Even conflictual interactions, which occur at times and primarily in the form of arguments
and verbal abuse, reinforce a man's realization that another individual
is preoccupied with him in some way. While affiliation flows through
the use of alcohol and the men know they are together to drink economically, they also know that drinking is a pretext for coming together to gratify compelling needs for the acceptance and acknowledgment which they cannot possibly get elsewhere. George, the night
watchman for the One Mile House, generalized the import of this
phenomenon beyond the unique structure of the bottlegang group to
the entire setting of the Bowery. "The men are here [on the Bow-
ery]," George said pensively, "because, though they can drink almost
anywhere else in the city, here they get companionship. I know all the
people here at the One Mile House and I love the familiarity. We come
here for acceptance and not only here because I've been to other skid
rows and it's the same there as anywhere. . . . [Looking around.] It's
the whole context that's attractive."

George reminds us that the bottlegang is but one form in which the
men organize their social scene and engage in their ritual bonding.
Indeed, it is the "whole context" which, in a compelling way, completes the process—interrelating all its viable parts. Alcohol is the
initiation into the Bowery subculture and, once past the threshold, it is
the symbol which perpetuates the men's social contract. Yet drinking
resides within the overall "program" of affiliation, which exerts its own
patterning of conduct and degrees of social stability, whether within
paired alliances, groups, or the more diffuse arrangements of general
relationship on the Bowery.

I had the pleasure of meeting Jack and Jerry in the first bottlegang
group that I accidently stumbled into. They were with another man at
the time, drinking from the holy bottle, stopping cars for money,
singing show songs, dancing, locking arms in a dwindling chorus, and
whispering conspiracies. Jack and Jerry were extolling each other's
friendship, patting backs and squeezing necks. Jerry gestured toward
Jack, "This guy will cut his head off for me, he really will!" I thought to
myself that this was quite a leap from offering the shirt off one's back.
The turning of this phrase implied the ending of one life for the survival
of another and unwittingly commented on the significance of self-
preservation within Bowery subculture. Jerry revealed that he was a
former New York City cop and, prior to that, a high school teacher.

Jack used to work as a lifeguard at Jones Beach and as a sanitation man for the city. But they waved their hands over their pasts, signaling that it was neither here nor there. After some of the excitement diminished, Jerry pulled me aside, his hands and stomach shaking nervously. "Guys that go about alone," he warned, "do so at the risk of their own lives; guys down here that keep to themselves are dead before long." He went on to tell of incidents in which men were jackrolled and beaten.

Jerry's concerns were well founded. Bowery men have often been the quarry of gangs or muggers. This is often exacerbated during the first week of each month, when some of the men receive some type of marginal annuity from the city, state, or federal government. In more severe cases, reported not only by the men but also by city newspapers covering the scene, some men have been doused with gasoline and set aflame. The exigencies of the Bowery man's ecological setting (and the activities which prey upon his dehumanized state) demand that the men coalesce in times of high fear and anxiety. In doing so, they find strength and protection, which provide them with a feeling of control over their lives and security within the community.

Sometimes fear emanates from within, fear of other Bowery men. This is usually limited to petty thievery among strangers, though it may also occur among acquaintances and friends. A captain in the Salvation Army along the Bowery commented that this was rare because of the men's implicit "code of honor": "Unless they're really desperate," the captain reiterated, "they don't rob from each other."

The "code of honor" among the men is their impressionistic blueprint for governing the rules of behavior, ensuring safety and reducing the degree to which the men "rip each other off." If someone should conspicuously breach the code, he may suffer undesirable sanctions imposed by his preferred network of friends. Hewey informed me of one case in which this occurred:

> I've been down here a long time, seventeen years. A while ago I was friends with Tom Cagney, the brother of Jimmy Cagney, the famous actor. Yah, Tom used to hang out down here quite a bit. Once, when we were drinking at the Old Dover, a friend of mine got jackrolled by some guys out on the street. He got beaten up real bad. His face looked real bad. I thought he was dead, but turned out he wasn't. He was just beaten a lot. . . . Well, Tom knew what was happening. He saw my friend get rolled but he didn't say nothin' to nobody. He kept quiet. When we heard that

Tom had been a witness and did or said nothin' about it we cut him off from the Old Dover, completely cut him off.

Tom Cagney was ostracized by Hewey and others in the Old Dover Bar because he failed to be a "watchful eye" on the streets, because he failed to exert his share of social responsibility and insure the safety and well-being of a member of his particular network of friends. This is all behavior which the code of honor desperately requires of the men. For this mistake, considered the exception rather than the rule, he was punished, and he was punished precisely for exercising those social qualities which the proponents of disaffiliation advance as "characteristic" of Bowery men (that is, "anomic," "inert," and "non-responsible" conduct).

Affiliation in the Bowery, with its collective endurance of burdens, enmeshes the men into a dense web of cooperation, mutual collaboration, and support, rare delicacies in their present lives. The men attempt to reconstruct each other's unattended and deteriorated affective domains, to lift one another up emotionally from the cold pavement. Living in a state of chronic deprivation, the men are in need of sustenance, and they are all that is left open to themselves; their last hope issues from reliance upon one another, from those who share their present reality. These friendships, like most other friendships, are sculpted to allow for the cathartic expression of personal concerns, for nurturance, for the promotion of self-esteem, and for security when one is again threatened with the anxiety of loss and loneliness. The men also assert certain subcultural imperatives consistent with their "program" that reach beyond the dimension of survival and into the constructs which complete a distinct way of life.

Jerry turned my attention closer toward this regnant meaning of affiliation in the Bowery when I met him on the street one day. We were standing in the entrance to the Prince Hotel, a flophouse, in refuge from the rain. Jerry was shaking and asked if I wanted to hear about his latest "caper." He lit a cigarette. Jerry told me that he had sobered up for one day so that he could tend bar at the One Mile House. The cigarette was jumping up and down between his fingers. He told me that all his friends had seen him pouring behind the bar and requested favors—free drinks. Jerry refused because he didn't want the owner to "go bankrupt." The situation grew tense: pressures from his friends, his role reversal behind the bar, and his abstention from alcohol culminated in Jerry walking off the job (with a handful of cash from the register). He merely picked up his coat, dipped his hand in the till, and moved briskly out into the rain. It was then that we passed on the street.

Jerry leaned forward and asked if I would do him a favor. He qualified, emphasizing that he did not need money. Instead, he asked if I would go into the One Mile House and ask Jack, his close friend, to meet him at the Prince. I walked into the bar and took Jack aside. He directly left the group he was with, along with a full glass of wine at his vacated seat, and accompanied me back to the hotel. I left the two of them there and continued my walk, finding temporary shelter a few blocks farther down under the portico of a bank. Ten minutes later I saw both Jack and Jerry pass by together on the sidewalk in front of the bank. We exchanged hellos and they remarked that they were heading for another bar. Jerry inserted, "For a change of scenery."

What struck me about this event—Jerry's upended experience as bartender—was Jack's availability in a time of crisis. When I had forwarded Jerry's message to him in the bar Jack did not hesitate, go into detailed explanations with the men in his company, or finish his drink. He simply led me out the door and into the rain. Jack was there for Jerry in a period of concentrated need when all was seemingly collapsing for him. When I ran into Jerry several days later he reflected on the bartending incident and with a heave said, "I really needed to talk over a drink." At the same time he heartily acknowledged Jack as a good friend.

Before long, Jerry was back drinking at the One Mile House. (The name of the bar derives from the fact that it is precisely one mile from the Tombs, New York City's notorious prison, thus demonstrating that Bowery men and Bowery entrepreneurs have a rather uncanny sense of their own mythic destiny.) Evidently, no one seemed to hold a grudge. Now Jerry was suffering from a different form of distress, a conflict over some news he had discovered about his wife. Jack, Jerry, and I were at a table. Jerry was very distraught. He vacillated from rage to helplessness when revealing that his wife had left him to stay with her father in Ireland. "My back's up against the wall," he repeated. "But I don't hold anything against her; she's fed up with my alcoholic tendencies." When Jerry spoke of his father-in-law he could barely remain seated in his chair: "I'll kill that son of a bitch." All the while, beneath the dialogue between Jerry and myself, Jack was offering animated subtitles, carefully choosing grossly exaggerated gestures to signify anger, compassion, disappointment, conviction, and the like as each became appropriate in fitting Jerry's articulated mood

and attitude. Jerry admitted that when he originally found his wife's
note he was scared. When asked why, Jerry replied, "Of losing my
baby." But he apparently managed to compose himself long enough to
hurriedly notify Jack, and together they had considered alternatives to
a resolution of the problem. They graphically illustrated to me a glori-
ous fable they had created in which, through a well-developed five-
step plan, they would both fly to Ireland and rescue Jerry's wife. Jerry
declared Jack's role: "He'll stay in the back seat and give me support."
They spelled it all out for me, each step, from obtaining the necessary
funds to the enraged demands at the father-in-law's pub in Ireland and
then the heroic flight home. They assured me that they would fly
there so as not to squander any time; and naturally they would appear
on the plane clean-shaven and wrapped in new tweed suits, "like the
gentlemen we are," Jerry interjected. They were reading an amazing
tale into the smoke of the bar. I read along, too, compelled by the
sheer elegance of the plan, and pictured them on earthen roads rolling
through sunless green Irish countryside. I imagined them dining in fine
taverns, toasting in pubs, and making loquacious inquiries along the
way as to the whereabouts of the red-headed woman. I could hear the
rhythmic sound of their gnarled shillelaghs pounding the cobbles and
the fragments of their playful vaudevillian banter as they inched closer
and closer toward the great wall of gray fog, Dublin.

Both story and happening (the performative nature of its telling) are
intriguing because of the interrelated levels which reveal more than
appears at face value. What was interesting to me about Jack's dramatic pantomime was its underlying self-reflective quality, which thick-
ened the meaning of the conversation. The enhanced dimension added
by Jack worked, in a fashion, to good-naturedly burlesque the overriding text of Jerry's commentary while, at the same time, focusing my
attention on the implicit yet driving subtext of affiliation and its patterning of ritual bonding. In offering his mock-heroic subcommentary,
Jack placed the thematic emphases of Jerry's intense reactions within a
much larger framework. Together, text and subtext enriched the expressive form, for although they indicated that marriage, estrangement, separation, rescue, and reunion were, indeed, the apparent
subject matter of the story, they also gave voice to the fact that the
entire household rested rather unsettledly on the deep structure of
affiliation between the two men. In a sense, story became an effective
medium for reinforcing the subcultural "program" of affiliation, with its
attendant qualities of trust, support, empathy, stability, and collabora-

tive effort. Recall that Jack played an integral role in devising and relating the story, thus making him an active partner in both the design and anticipated execution of the plan.

Yet this assertion of "program" through the integration of text and subtext points to a more central conflict or fundamental contradiction: given the choice, should one complete his self in society through a formal and legal alliance with culture or through the radically altered subcultural code and way of life? In attempting to reconcile this conflict (and the related one over primary and secondary kinship ties), Jerry incorporated Jack into the texture of the story and, in doing so (given Jack's representativity for subculture), effectively invited the Bowery into his living room. In taking Jack with him as he mentally projected himself out of the Bowery, Jerry attested to the strength of the Bowery's program of affiliation in reshaping his identity and role and the structure of his life-style. It was impossible for Jerry to make a clean break precisely because of his enrollment in Bowery subculture—the whole context. In manifesting this conflict over rival forms of affiliation and social control, Jerry realized that a pure coexistence between culture and subculture was unrealizable. Completing himself within the mental projection of culture, Jerry still desired a strong link to subculture, an active degree of continuity. I asked Jerry what would happen to his friendship with Jack, providing the plan was successful and led to him living with his wife again. He said that nothing would alter, that Jack was welcome into his home at any time. Jerry added, "It's all written. I want to tell you something. [Leaning back in his chair.] Jack and I are really close friends." Jack nodded his head in energetic affirmation. Though the reconciliation of culture and subculture is unrealistic in the "real world," the exercise worked to momentarily appease that troublesome contradiction basic to Bowery subculture. In giving the conflict symbolic form, Jerry and Jack, in a spontaneous and unconscious manner, provided an incisive commentary on their experience living-in-subculture. The "meta-social commentary" (as Geertz refers to it) given here lends further credence to the complexity of Bowery expression and the ability of the men to interpret their subcultural experience in an alternative and representational way and thereby gain knowledge and meaning into the totality of their condition.

That night, when Jerry's and Jack's richly textured story was completed, a long pause filled the bar. Jerry scanned the faces in the room: "Quite a nefarious bunch of guys, eh?" His elbow hung on my ribs. Willy, another friend, shuffled into the One Mile House and sat down at our table. Tears had gathered on his cheeks. Jerry turned to me and said, "He looks sick." Jack reached over to Willy and warmly squeezed his shoulders while passing his glass of wine over to him. Willy gave Jack a frail hug in return. Jack excused himself and began whispering to Willy. Soon Willy perked up and started speaking of various things, most notably his boxing prowess. He claimed to have fought both Muhammed Ali and his brother during their pre-Olympic days. The men began to banter back and forth. Willy looked into Jerry, "I could beat you, man." Jerry calmly laid back in his chair as if leisurely stretched out against the ropes and, with a hand supporting his chin, teased: "Ah, go on, you couldn't even beat your meat, Willy." In characteristic style, Jack followed Jerry's cue, "Yah, he can't even get the proper grip on it!" Sufficiently challenged, Willy peered into the long alley of his empty glass and briskly stood up. "Watch this," he boasted. He then walked with his glass over to another table in the bar and received a refill from a man sporting a heavy bottle of white port. Willy returned to our table gloating in definitive exclamation, "Now that's friendship!" With that, and to the delight of us all, Willy had won the immediate round.

Friendship it is, and many men are captivated by the obvious rewards and social comforts it radiates. Bowery men stand in critical relationship to one another, regarding the affiliation they have constructed as a serious undertaking. The more they invest themselves in each other the more fervently they come to embrace the purpose of friendship in the Bowery and replicate its kind. Their affiliations proceed by way of a generalized reciprocity, a sort of gift giving which implies joint obligations and favors among the men. This is the process of exchange by which affiliation is communicated, reinforced, and perpetuated, ensuring a sense of stability and cohesion to the social organization of subculture. Alliance networks, both formal and informal, are formed in this manner, primarily due to an implicit understanding that, sooner or later, one good turn deserves another. So when one man helps another either tangibly or intangibly (be it liquor, food, affection, shelter, protection, or the like), he is wittingly or unwittingly articulating this language of exchange. In effect, the giver is drafting an invisible but binding contract that he will, in return, be guaranteed assistance at some perhaps unforeseen later date.

Reciprocal obligations yoke the men whether they are closely or distantly related, whether they are novice or habitual faces, whether they are in the Bowery for one day or a lifetime. Even if someone vehemently dislikes a man because of racial heritage, ethnic background, or personality, he will still come through with a favor, if in a position to grant one, in a time of need. This is a general knowledge that they have, an undercurrent of their lives, an implicit and, at times, explicit code of the road.

Nicky Star forcefully expressed this pragmatic philosophy one night as we were talking. We were interrupted now and then by red traffic lights, when Nicky would turn abruptly around and melt the metal of a car with his hard, penetrating stare: "Can ya help a guy out, man?" The wind pulled back Nicky's great ragged overcoat and sent him staggering. The wind was always a bit delerious when Nicky was around; everything was intensified by his presence. As Nicky's tongue searched his mouth for more words, harsh lumps of gravel mined from the base of his throat, a young man approached us and asked for a nickel to help him buy a bottle of white port. Nicky methodically picked around in his palm and selected a nickel. "Here ya go, Red." The man thanked Nicky and left.

When I asked Nicky if he knew the man he said, "No, I never saw him before."

"But you called him Red," I responded.

"That's because he's a lighter shade of black," Nicky said, "and I call all of them who look like that Red. Hey, let me tell you something; now you listen good and hard. I don't drink with niggers."

My face twisted in puzzlement: "Then why did you give him a nickel?"

Nicky drew back a few steps, his arms outstretched as if to delineate the configuration of a world before me: "You see, maybe I never met that guy before, maybe I did—I don't know. I could have walked up to him one night and asked him for a nickel. Now, listen here, he might of pulled his knife out on me or he may have called me a white-ass-mother-fucker, I don't know. So, I give him a nickel cause maybe one day he gave me one; or maybe in the future I'll need one from him. Ya see, one hand washes the other down here, that's how we live."

These shared assumptions about the nature and process of affiliation in the Bowery attest to the powerful impact and endurance of subcultural "program." As witnessed previously, reciprocity in the Bowery was not confined to exchanges of money or immediately self-gratifying commodities. It extended far beyond that into the more profound layers of personality and self-image. It is as if every man stepped inside a mirror, for, in this relationship between culture-making process and personality, each man reflects back to the consciousness of self in society. There is no escape from this for some men even after they have managed to transcend the Bowery. Nicky Star, who had been on and off the Bowery for some years, told me about the visits he would pay his old neighborhood while he was away: "You know, once in a while I used to come down here when I lived uptown. I'd walk around and look at these guys. And, you know, every time I looked at one of them it was like looking into a mirror; I saw myself. I had to buy them a bottle and make sure they were all right." The ritual patterning of affiliation in the Bowery, with its driving mechanism of generalized reciprocity, functions to solidify and maintain subculture. As Mary Douglas reminds us, "rituals enact the form of social relations and in giving these relations visible expression they enable people to know their own society."[11] And, as Nicky Star demonstrates, with ritual comes the lasting effect of survival, compassion, and deep understanding of self and other, other and self—an iteration of meaning. Or, to shift to the vernacular of subculture, perhaps what Nicky had responded to was this fact: "You can't spell bum without *u* in it." That ubiquitous *u* was too near to the dignity of his own experience.

My encounters on the Bowery, of which the aforementioned are representative, have made me realize the valuable function of affiliation as an attempt to restore a degree of order, acceptance, and communality to the lives of Bowery men. The social controls which the Bowery enforces and the forms of interaction which it offers demand a level of communication and personal integration that keeps its participants in a sort of declensional holding pattern. The Bowery homeless are dancing above the abyss, and they owe this precariously balanced posture to their assimilation of an ethos and world view exacted by the subculture they have settled into. Of course, this assimilation brings the contradictory values of culture and subculture into contention and expression. The transition to total acceptance of the Bowery is premised upon complete rejection of the world at large. The resultant life-style is thus an extreme departure from the dominant forms of American society; it represents a type of social antistructure in which not only particular behaviors like failure, alcoholism, and drug abuse become socialized, but so do one's entire frame of reference and point of view. Perhaps I should defer to one Bowery man who, from his corner on the world, so adequately summarized both process and position: "I love the Bowery, but I hate the human race!"

This statement is an expression of conviction, a voice that heralds the transformation of process into condition. "Identification," Kenneth

Burke argues, "is not in itself abnormal; nor can it be 'scientifically' eradicated. One's participation in a collective, social role cannot be obtained in any other way. In fact, 'identification' is hardly other than a name for the function of sociality."[12] In facilitating this sense of identification, affiliation within the Bowery subculture shaped the vagaries of descent into something meaningful, something tangible. The ritual process, engendered by the separation from structure, defines a mode of being characterized by descent and submergence. Yet the liminality of the descent is both culturally and subculturally codified by virtue of one's being there; that is, within the Bowery's context, its symbolic systems of value. Affiliation works to take away the ambiguities of the stranger and remake him into the image of subculture—the bum. Yet the fatal key to this rite is the fact that it is one of degradation rather than elevation. The Bowery man's emergence in subculture paves the way for the continuity of his being—submergence. This is the irony he must learn to live with, for once the cycle is set in motion the refinement of his new identity necessitates a quickening of descent, an allegiance to form, and a complete symbolic merger with the primary qualities of the Bowery—structural inferiority, social death, and the pathetic condition of tragedy replete with its disturbing wails of finality. If affiliation is compensatory, it is also complete, steeping one further and further in the depths of urban entrapment. This deepening sense of entrapment, with its correlative adaptive strategies such as mistrust, conniving for personal gain, disillusionment, and self-deception, also works in some instances to militate against the purely cohesive and functional qualities of affiliation; it is in some ways akin to Oedipus' condemnation of condition without realization of the process which led him there.

The descent from culture, which gives the process its momentum, flattens into a condition which seeks the perfection of its kind. The symbolic system that ensues and captivates is one whose valence is peculiarly altered to fit the recontextualization of being. In a state of antistructure (structural inferiority), contentment takes on renewed meaning. As Frank put it: "I'm not really happy unless I am as *dirty* as I can be and as *broke* as I can be. I've reached the point where I wouldn't even use a napkin if it were handed to me." Desolation with a purpose, one might say. Statements such as this one adequately summarize the blend of poverty, antistructure, and subculture as they have worked their way into a man's heart.

An incident I recall with Jimmy lends a more dramatic rendering of the antistructural attitude and its frame of acceptance in the Bowery.

Jimmy was behind the bar in the One Mile House one afternoon, tending and drinking. He was also working with Pete, who seemed agitated and worried while pouring drinks and ringing up the sales on the register. Jimmy appeared friendlier than the last time we met. He said that the previous night he had called his "old lady," who lived in the Bronx. Ten minutes after he hung up the phone with her, Jimmy's sister from New Jersey called and urged him to visit for a few days. Jimmy, cynically marveling at the direct and expedient communications line between girlfriend and sister, said that he should have realized that his call would initiate their combined efforts at rescue and rehabilitation. He refused to go to his sister's home and said he felt somewhat like a stranger in her family and often forgot names and familial relations. This familial distance seemed difficult for Jimmy because, as he put it, he "loves her much"; he also spoke of a fondness for his retarded nephew. "But I can't stay there," he repeated. "I get too nervous and jumpy after just one day."

While Jimmy was bartending he was required to exercise his authority several times to control some of the overzealous drinkers; he even had to bounce a couple of people out of the bar. He moved with facility from one role to another and joked about the truly gentle nature of his character. He complained of all the responsibilities he had to attend to as bartender, duties which he was flagrantly neglecting at the time, much to his co-worker's distress. Jimmy, as if physically illuminating his conflict, eventually moved to the patron's side of the bar and seated himself on a stool next to mine. Peter was very distraught at the sight of Jimmy on the recipient side of the bar and reiterated vile oaths never to work with him again: "I no work with you again! You drink too much!"

Jimmy turned to me, knowingly, sardonically: "I guess this is why I'll never go into business." He looked over the great playing field of the bar. "I'd rather be dangling drunk from one of those chairs with nothin' in my pocket than be behind this bar. . . . Let me tell ya, money is never a problem with me."

This theme was a recurrent one for Jimmy, and it speaks of when he felt his best—in a state of total dispossession, complete relief and freedom from anxiety. Money was never a problem with Jimmy, not because he had any or wanted more, but because he wanted less, drastically less, commensurate with his longing for an accustomed state of antistructure. In this particular instance, the accretions of girlfriend, sister, and the role of bartender all conspired in an overwhelming semblance of structure and normalcy. To be consistent and

true to both setting and style, Jimmy had to fight back. He had no
other choice.

Being on the inside of all this for so long, the nether side of structure, I understood how the feeling Jimmy played out could be so
contagious. It had swept over me at times when I had given myself
over to the ambience of the One Mile House, withdrawn from urban
concerns, removed from the sunlight that seemed to hesitate like a
diffident stranger at the doorway. In scanning the human debris around
me and in hearing the drone of broken lives reassembling, I too felt
completely transformed into this tradition of relief and sadness—of
reaching the finality, of being there in that place you have feared all
your life, that devastated state of self-abandonment where over the
jukebox plays the delicate and sordid mixture of irony and pity.

There is a tragic irony in the fact that the Bowery men's search for
solidarity further entrenches them in the dark side of subculture. They
land on the Bowery and seek out others similar to them in order to
assuage the trauma of alienation. These affiliations in turn root them
into the bedrock of the Bowery. The result is that the men feel their
immense isolation from culture even more convincingly. For a while
they do not exactly know where they are going, but they realize that,
wherever it is, they are going together. This offers some solace. Yet
one day the men awake and feel it—the irrevocable transformation.
They seek, they search; they slide deeper into the underworld of the
Bowery. Round and round and round; down and down and down. They
have finally found out where they are, where they were going all
along, and now they settle disconsolately into its bed.

The consequences are layered in the depth of the men's stare; it is a
look of disbelief and disillusionment, a look that betrays their recurrent
thought that they are the endless butt of some insidious form of
sorcery and now they must live out the cursed spell. The cast of the
spell is excruciatingly painful to break, and with each successive day
the likelihood of this occurring becomes even more complicated, more
arduous, and as probable as Sisyphus quitting his burden and merely
walking down the other side of the mountain. In the end, it all seems
just to have happened. And it all leads to the laggard realization that
the men have inevitably claimed a home that they may never return
from; or, as Peter clearly put it: "No one gets out of this place alive."

The homeless men are left with no other choice than to accept the
Bowery as their new home. (However paradoxical this might seem,
we must remember that the men are, in their own words, a "bundle of
paradoxes.") And if they meditate on finding another home, or even if

they are successful in leaving the physical dimension of the Bowery, they will often be drawn back daily into its spiritual geography. The damage has been done. Richie once told me that he was considering relocating to Jersey City. But he was quick to stipulate that, if he did make the move, he would commute daily into the Bowery.

Undoubtedly, the condition the men find themselves in is extreme, for, to reiterate, "no one gets out of this place alive." This grim though realistic phrase speaks not only for the accelerated movement toward physical death but for the utter transformation of self which occurs when reaggregation back into culture is blocked or forestalled. The resulting perspective fixes on the slope of black humor, often scatalogical but always accommodating to condition. Witness Donny's casually yet definitively delivered dictum: "Do you know what we all have in common down here? Optical mitosis—the nerve from the eye to the asshole. That's what gives us such a shitty outlook on life." Anatomically speaking, Donny's words reveal the link between world view and societal location: the men have positioned themselves in the bowels of social structure amidst its waste. The tragic pattern of disillusionment and despair, a pattern both activated by and suffused with the consciousness of death as the only way out of the Bowery, is operative here in fostering a lasting state of structural inferiority.

Yet despite the desperation of their condition, the dialectic between culture and subculture is still formative for the men, even more generative, one could argue, given the intensification of struggle and hardship. The symbolic expressions which result from the conflict between the two social modalities are not diminished but rather "enriched," keeping the culture-making process actively "alive." As such, culture is treated as "real"; it is not put into question, as Crane and Dreiser would have it, but instead placed in contention. Though down, the men are not out, and so they continue dancing above the abyss until that last moment when their legs atrophy and give way. Culture, in fact, remains such an intimate part of the men's lives as to be astonishing. One might think that, by this time, they would have given up the ghost for good. But culture is so woven into the daily fabric of their lives that they cannot escape it. Often the reverse is the case, whereby the men become preoccupied with it, as when Harry, at the abrupt conclusion of a protracted argument with another man in the bar, threw up his arms and exclaimed in both anger and justification: "I'm a bum. . . . That's right; and I have nothin' to live for. And now I'm going out to talk to the public." By "going out to talk to the public," Harry alluded to begging. But he also meant much more than that accustomed means of subsistence, for he sought to meet culture and engage it in a moment of articulation, to declare something to some other and thereby know himself through sheer encounter with the opposition. At the time, the clarity of this remark and action (Harry bolting out the door and into the street) struck me as both comical and wondrous. Harry distilled the essence of this cyclical perspective rather forcefully, making a taut, looping connection among designation (defeated bum on the Bowery), activity (the encounter with culture), and result (the ensuing confirmation of his inferior social position). Yet Harry had swiftly betrayed the pity of the designation of "bum" ("I have nothing to live for") by his penchant for praxis. The public is what in fact fed Harry's sense of aliveness, for he could more resolutely frame both identity and condition precisely because of this symbiotic relationship. He obviously could not gain affirmation from the fellow Bowery man he was arguing with. Strange as it might appear, the clarity given in the script between culture and subculture had a way of winning out and quenching the confused rage mounting within. The reflexivity which underlies the inherent conflict between culture and subculture grants its own unique form of compensation, a perhaps bitter yet assured sense of completion.

As Harry attests, symbolic action propels the steps to the dance. But whereas Harry kept the definition of bum and consequent mode of being contained within, internalized, if you will, Nicky Star projected both label and context outward as if in defiant response to the position of inferiority. "Hey, let me tell you something. Now you listen good and hard. The only difference between a bum and anybody else is that they wear a white shirt and a tie, go to an office, and have their secretaries do all of the work for them. They're bums. The only difference is that they maintain a living." Nicky was eager to dissolve the distance between culture and subculture, albeit in a metaphoric way. Yet the import here, more ardently and eloquently asserted in the following passage, is the notion that the Bowery's meaning is transcendent and, as such, projected outward into culture as a pervasive existential condition of man. One need not be physically positioned on the Bowery in order to experience some of its qualities; the conceptual transport of subculture to culture is a way of redirecting both the pain and responsibility associated with the condition of structural inferiority. On the street, Nicky Star enacted this redirection to culture, but only after he had appropriately merged himself with the context of subculture, as if to lend to the transcendent meaning the litany of experiential strength—a certified voice of the street.

See that gutter, man, I laid in it; see those stairs, I laid on them;
see that railing, I laid against it; see that curb, that step, that
sewer, that grating, I laid on them all. I've been in every gutter on
the Bowery. . . . Hey, let me tell you something now, hey, hey,
listen here, the Bowery's at 43rd and 8th; the Bowery's at 30th
and Lex; the Bowery's at 14th and 5th. Uptown! The Bowery's in
their fuckin' room—in their apartment. Hey, let me tell you
something. Now you listen good and hard—the Bowery can be
everywhere.

Nicky Star's exteriorized statement about the Bowery as a metaphoric haunt was complemented by Joey's incorporation and expiation
of guilt in a little ritual drama, the tragic amplification of social being in
consciousness. In the One Mile House, Joey spontaneously staged a
mock trial. At first, in an act of displacement, he put another Bowery
man in the prisoner's box; appointed the bartender, a paternal and
authoritarian figure, as judge; and regarded the habitués as jurors and
himself as prosecutor. Joey approached the bar, now transformed into
the bench, and commenced his argument, a tangled assortment of offenses and crimes against the state. The Bowery man in the imaginary
prisoner's box looked on with a growing sense of awareness as the
makeshift proceedings gained momentum. Yet, even before the closing summation and deliberation, Joey sought to mete out justice on his
own accord, putting an abrupt halt to the formal analogy to judicial
mediation and due process. Suspecting some foul play, the "defendant" spoke out in warning: "I can get emotionally upset." Joey countered in a manner of one-upmanship, "I can get emotionally upset too,
you know." With a terse grin pasted on his face, Joey fastened his hand
to the "defendant's" shoulder and hurled him to the floor. Moe, the
"defendant," fell backwards amidst broken glasses and bottles, crash-
ing into a table. Moe picked himself up slowly from the floor and
moved to the other end of the bar. The bartender sent out some men
to clean up the mess and, within minutes, things were back to their
normal routine. Joey shuffled down to where Moe was sitting and, in
seeming reparation, apologized to him with a kiss on the cheek while
ordering another drink for him to make up for the one spilled in the fall.
Then Joey returned and this time placed himself directly in the prisoner's box. The bartender leaned forward and inquired, "How do you
plead?" With a resonant voice, Joey proclaimed, "Guilty as charged!"
Joey leaned forward and pleaded with the bartender his extenuating
circumstances. Then he retreated and grew silent for a moment, as if

he accepted the judgment and was waiting in anticipation for the subsequent sentence. A calm had settled over the bar. After awhile, Joey turned to me, as a perceived outsider to the Bowery, and began imploring, "I want to talk to you, please. I want to talk to you, please. I want to talk to you, please." He was overcome with emotion and his eyes became watery. He began fervently to advise me, "Go to school . . . so you can help somebody . . . help yourself . . . then [looking up toward the ceiling of the bar] go tell God to fuck himself."

Joey's mock trials, both the displaced one and the personalized one, and his closing statement dramatically enacted the pathos of the Bowery men's tragic vision. "Tragedy," Kenneth Burke writes, "is a complex kind of trial by jury in which the author symbolically charges himself or his characters with transgressions not necessarily considered transgressions in law, and metes out condemnation and penance."[13] The Bowery man's transgression is, of course, his loss of structure and slide into antistructure. The sense of guilt associated with this tragic pattern, the reversal from culture and the descent into subculture, is often, as in the case of Joey, placed into a framework of ill-fated resignation in the face of entrapment. If he could break out, Joey would send fate ("God") on its heels and assert his dominance, the dominance of man over a hostile and menacing universe. Joey's reformulation of culture into the universe of classical tragedy, whose forces mess around with human designs and render human beings helpless, becomes the transferred target of his animosity and defeat. His sense of failure, and the guilt which issues from this, is thus given a tragic cast, for the justification of guilt and condition, which pivots on reversal, ends in cathartic recognition and the arousal of pity.

In contrast to Joey's drama, Sugar Hart's way of symbolically envisioning the condition of inferiority brings us back into the vivid social plane of culture and subculture. Less tragic in scope, Sugar Hart's response reasserts the incongruity and disruption between the cultural framework of meaning and the patterning of subcultural reality. The unintended result is the defamiliarization of the cultural code as well as the pathos that surfaces in the opposition between his genuine espousal of the code and his disfigured condition. Once, on the street, Sugar Hart shuffled a bit and assumed the well-balanced stance of a boxer. He rumbled, "Hey man, you ever heard of Emille Griffith? He was a five-time welterweight and middleweight champ." Sugar Hart then pointed to his chest and said rather proudly, "I fought him. That's right. I went the distance with him—fifteen rounds. . . . Hey, listen here, I'm a boxer, not a chump." Sugar Hart paused from his boxing

scenario as if he had heard the clang of a bell in his ear. He looked up
from his position in the world. "Hey, man, don't ever be on the bottom; don't ever let anyone be above you. Always fight to be on top."

I wondered for whom this advice was meant. The effect of Sugar
Hart's message was to accentuate aspects of the cultural code which
emphasized competitive struggle, power, status in the social hierarchy, and success. Of course, boxing, as the form in which to manifest these values, is particularly appropriate. It is a skill that can afford
the concrete sense of accomplishment; it brings money and high status; it demands discipline; it calls for the display of prowess, force, and
action—of fighting a foe before an audience of onlookers and of coming
out on top. Yet all of this was either spoken or implied by Sugar Hart,
who was about as far as one could get from acting upon his words.
Nevertheless, those words were spoken with true conviction as if
remnants of another soul were still resident within. The resulting
disfigurement extended in both directions—to cultural code as well as
to subcultural embodiment. One could say a simultaneous knockout
was registered at that moment, for the effect was to flatten the zeal-
ous posturing of the code on the one hand and to deflate the distorted
conviction of its proponent on the other. Yet after the mandatory
count, after the reviews, when they return to the ring for the re-
match, one has to look on in astonishment at both the jabbing impact of
culture and the unfailing resilience of subculture in this seemingly
unending bout. Both entangled entities of the dialectic make the contest more than worth the price of admission. The Bowery men know
this only too well and what a dear price they have paid.

As I relate these culture-making events and processes of the men
on the Bowery, I do so with the knowledge that I have made these
accounts my final chapter. Yet another sense of completion is at work
here as well, one of historical finality, for the modern evolution of
homelessness has rendered the Bowery obsolete. As I have previously mentioned, since the early 1980s when I completed my extended sojourn among its inhabitants, the Bowery has indeed become
homeless, and this fact presents an irony which militates against the
formation and reinforcement of subculture. The consequences of this
new, uprooted form of homelessness are grave indeed, for the dissolution of a cohesive subcultural base (complete with a well-defined ecological infrastructure) puts the generative culture-making process of a
distinct homeless subculture into question. This is particularly evident
among the prevalent deinstitutionalized mentally ill population of
modern-day homelessness, which according to the literature ranges

from 20 percent to 90 percent.[14] Being homeless is likely to have a qualitative impact on the already preexistent condition of mental illness. The complete loss of all structural affiliations and any semblance of containment, the lack of involvement in any identifiable subculture, and the physical and emotional hardships of living *in extremis* can only further the deterioration of one's psychic equipment to the point where the damage becomes irreparable. This is true as well for those who arrive at the condition of homelessness without any prior pathological history, for existence outside both culture and subculture—marginality in a dual sense—creates daily pressures which are extremely disorienting and overwhelming. Without the checks and balances of subculture, one's mental capabilities undergo rapid deterioration. One wonders about the possible implications of the present situation. Does the removal of the modern homeless both from culture and from the support system of subculture adumbrate a condition where the culture-making process itself has deteriorated? If so, would not the very nature of man in this extreme social state and the moral legitimacy of the broader host culture both be rendered suspect from an anthropological as well as a humanistic perspective? Perhaps Crane and Dreiser were correct, not in the implicit sociocultural theory which they imposed on the experience of the Bowery, but for their fidelity to seeing the social depths of condition as harbinger—what might come to pass in historical actualization when the symbiotic relationship between culture and subculture has been dissolved.

Yet popular opinion, as voiced by advocates for the modern homeless, still clings to the upended notion that the condition and process of subculture, and the identity which ensues from both, are still intact, despite the decentralized phenomenon. In a public hearing before the Subcommittee on Housing and Community Development, Ellen Baxter and Kim Hopper have argued: "The received wisdom of the postwar commentators who predicted the imminent demise of skid row has, in the course of the past decade, been proven flatly wrong. Skid row—as a way of life, not a distinct place, is flourishing in a manner not seen in this country for fifty years."[15]

What Baxter and Hopper fail to realize, however, is precisely that requisite link between a "distinct place" and a "way of life," an intimate connection which the modern, dispersed condition of homelessness has not been able to construct. Bowery subculture could not have flourished as it did for more than one hundred years if it were not for the evocative sense of place which defined condition and character, delimited a collectivity, and determined the generative nature of sym-

bolic action and the ensuing depth of completion. All these factors
contributed to the heightened tension between culture and subculture,
a dialectic which served as the primary catalyst for the former's ideological position of social distance and mystification and for the latter's
culture-making processes. Though Baxter and Hopper are highly
aware of the altered condition of modern homelessness, they do not
seem to grasp the consequences for the nature of the dialectic and the
possibility that it too has been rendered homeless.

> Life on the streets isn't what it used to be. In the first place, skid
> row is no longer contained by well demarcated "tenderloin" sec-
> tions in the inner city, nor is it confined to the religious missions
> and public refuges. . . . The subways, train and bus depots, the
> doorways and abandoned buildings, public parks, and loading
> docks, the alleys or sidewalks of an entire city, these are home to
> thousands of New Yorkers every evening. It is not only the Bow-
> ery any more.[16]

In light of this diffused situation, subculture has lost its integrity, its
coherent sense of "program." Undoubtedly, modern homelessness "is
not the Bowery any more." And if one were to go in search of the
present-day Bowery—of the men in their context which have filled
these pages—one would return as if from an abyss, without the discovery of subculture or the sense of a viable place which could breed
it. The Bowery, as it existed, cannot be tracked down; only the whorling traces of the patterned dance remain, as if the troupe had simply
vanished into the seams of its historical moment.

Yet the Bowery, as it endured from the late nineteenth century to
the early 1980s, stands as a reminder to our poor cultural memory,
which tends to view the modern condition of homelessness as an
epiphenomenon of the 1980s. It is true that the social character of
contemporary homelessness is quite different in terms of its composition, territoriality, and lack of subcultural integrity. No longer contained by the Bowery or conveniently identified by the label of bum,
homelessness has transcended both its geographical and categorical
boundaries. It is a social phenomenon unique in nature and extent, and
one which has recently given rise to a great flurry of ambiguity, investigation, expenditure, and argument. The new homeless, varying anywhere from a quarter million to upwards of three million nationwide,
include women, young minorities, children, whole families, deinstitutionalized mentally ill patients, the economically disadvantaged, the
aged, substance abusers, and the fallout from the chronically poor of

the social system at large. Today we do not refer to a subculture of homelessness but, rather, to discrete subgroups related to such factors as deinstitutionalization, lack of low-income housing, unemployment (primarily among minority members), and social policy decisions relative to cuts in government expenditure.

This new and dispersed condition of homelessness has caused a deep sense of disturbance in the cultural domain. The intensified activity among municipal officials, health practitioners, advocates, government representatives, and private citizens has signaled a searching reorientation to a new and challenging problem of homelessness evident in all major American cities. Yet in this flurry of debate and deed we have unwittingly persisted in viewing homelessness through a cultural perspective shaped by the past; that is, by the symbolic systems of mystification and critical realism. In effect, our present-mindedness has led us to ignore just how we are using the past in order to confront the situation at hand. This simultaneous assimilation and concealment of the past thus serves to affirm the present, and in the public arena the present, that moment of ephemeral motion, is all. The practical consequences of this paradox lead to a disjointed view of the homeless and an uncoordinated approach to alleviating their condition. So, while advocates focus rather one-sidedly on systemic variables and on the need for shelter, health practitioners narrow in on treating the results of mental illness and substance abuse; and while city government officials scramble to implement efficient programs, state administrators, still recovering from the fiasco of deinstitutionalization, react in exasperation; and while social policy and urban-planning experts look to the development of community support structures to relieve the burden from already overcrowded health facilities, citizens respond in strident protest to the perceived devaluation of property. At least one can say that the present situation does not lack for activity.

To the extent that this heightened specialization continues to take command, we will approach the symptoms of contemporary homelessness from somewhat isolated and disconnected perspectives, thus establishing its modern reification. The shift in perspective to a deep consideration of the underlying causes and processes of the visible condition of contemporary homelessness would require an intensive effort at coordination among social practitioners, planners, and administrators. But, on a more fundamental level, it would also entail a candid confrontation with the persistent meaning of homelessness to American society. For the notion of victimage as an inherent principle of social order, a rather unpalatable proposition to a civilized and democratically organized society, points to both condition and historical process, and the process necessarily hooks culture back into that formative dialectic with the social phenomenon of homelessness. In zooming in on the specter of homelessness, we have ultimately lost sight of the whole vision and thus of ourselves as members of culture and as principal actors engaged in a seemingly endless series of social dramas.

It is a curious dialectic, this interplay between mystification and critical realism, for although the content of the various social dramas changes to accommodate a particular historical era, the underlying and contradictory form retains its constancy throughout. In this sense, then, the dialectic can be seen to be both diachronic and synchronic. The symbolic systems of mystification and critical realism, so important to the early discovery of poverty among the homeless, have therefore donned new costumes in our own time; and though the language is contemporary, the total effect of both sight and sound is a familiar enactment of an essential dramatic structure. Perhaps it would be best if we, with our spotlight directed for the moment on the mystifying side of the stage, let the players themselves exemplify the unwitting continuity between past and present for this portion of the dialectic. So, from Rev. T. DeWitt Talmage, pastor of the Brooklyn Tabernacle Church during the late nineteenth century, to Mr. Harvey Vieth, the head of a federal task force on contemporary homelessness, we can bear witness to a lineage of over one hundred years in which the mystification of homelessness has retained its tenacious quality. In keeping with the social perception of mystification endemic to the dominant culture, Vieth, like Talmage, also believes in "unroll[ing] the scrolls of new revelations." Recently, Vieth, countering a suggestion that defense spending be cut in order to divert funds for social spending, replied that defense dollars provide "freedom for our homeless people."[17] History refines itself in curious ways.

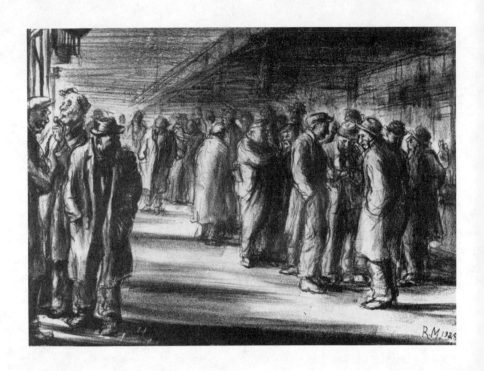

The Bowery, 1928, *lithograph by Reginald Marsh. Yale University Art Gallery.*

Tattoo-Shave-Haircut, *1932 etching by Reginald Marsh, restruck in 1969.
From the portfolio* 30 Etchings and Engravings. *Collection of the Whitney
Museum of American Art, New York City. Original plate donated by William
Benton.*

The Bowery, ca. 1935, by Reginald Marsh. Museum of the City of New York.

From The Bowery, *1975, by Michael Zettler. Courtesy of Michael Zettler.*

From The Bowery, *1975, by Michael Zettler. Courtesy of Michael Zettler.*

From The Bowery, *1975, by Michael Zettler. Courtesy of Michael Zettler.*

From The Bowery, *1975, by Michael Zettler. Courtesy of Michael Zettler.*

APPENDIX

Ethnography, a Retrospective

I n undertaking a firsthand study of the contemporary Bowery, I left a particular social and cultural terrain for another stretch of urban land in order to observe, engage, and record the life world of what I came to understand as a distinct subculture of homeless men. These men were residing within the skid row section of New York City; that is, a one-mile stretch of Bowery from Chatham Square on the southern end to Cooper Union and St. Mark's Place on the northern boundary. The fieldwork naturally spilled over to the vicinity immediately east and west of the Bowery: parts of the Lower East Side, Little Italy, Chinatown, and the East Village also comprised the general context and ecological base in which the Bowery homeless maneuvered, subsisted, and situated themselves.

On the Bowery proper, the fieldwork was conducted among that vivid and well-established institutionalized network of the skid row underclass: amidst a conglomerate of street corners, median strips, bars and taverns, liquor stores, pawn shops, flophouses, lodging houses, missions and social service agencies, cafeterias, used clothing stores, abandoned buildings, and fire rings. Since I was concerned with Bowery men in their natural context, both the men and their intricate relationship to this setting were explored.

The fieldwork was conducted from the fall of 1977 to the fall of 1980. Throughout the first year, the project was supervised by Professors Chaya Piotrkowski and Rayna Rapp, who were on the Graduate Faculty of the New School for Social Research. Professor Rapp continued to be involved during the second year as a resource to the project's continued development. After the first year of fieldwork and upon completion of my graduate program, I maintained an affiliation with the New School for the remaining two-year span in which the fieldwork ranged.

The fieldwork moved along by way of regular sojourns into the Bowery. For two years this amounted to an average of two field visits per week for a period of two or three hours per visit. The fieldwork was conducted at various times of the day and night and throughout all seasons of the year. During the third year of the project the research was conducted on a more intermittent basis in order to extend personal relationships, meet new men, and gain a long-range perspective on the study of Bowery subculture. The encounters with Bowery men were documented in field notes. These notes provided the basis for further analysis and discussion, future direction, and representation of the Bowery in ethnographic accounts and various forms of discourse.

The fieldwork quickly demonstrated that, as a skid row, the Bowery was predominantly an all-male community and subculture. This accounts for my reference to Bowery men as the central focus of ethnographic encounter. There is a historical precedent for this phenomenon. During the late nineteenth and early twentieth centuries skid row reflected the domination of the labor force by men and acted as a barometer of their ebb and flow in times of economic prosperity and depression. For a time, the fluctuations of seasonal employment and casual labor demands contributed to the male-oriented nature of skid row and its role as a reservoir of cheap labor. The men's shelter, or Municipal Lodging House (MUNY Building), located on 3rd Street and Bowery, may have also helped to shape this condition well on into the 1970s and early 1980s. During the fieldwork, only one homeless woman was seen regularly and two others sporadically. In a conversation with a clerk at one of the flophouses, he revealed that women on the Bowery were extremely rare; there were no sleeping accommodations for women on the Bowery except for one resident lodging house, supported by the city and state, several blocks off the main artery. Though skid row was not a viable place for homeless Bowery women, it did, along Bowery and Delancey Street, provide a niche for female prostitutes. This intersection of two distinct social phenomena, however, worked to reinforce the male-dominated character of the area.

Initially, the Bowery men were encountered by virtue of accident and exigency. Repeated encounters with the same men worked to develop collaborative relationships characterized by a growing sense of trust and rapport. These relationships engendered further contacts with related networks of friends and associates so that by the end of three months in the field we (Mr. Jeffrey Grunberg, a fieldwork partner, and myself) had engaged about 40 men. (From 1977 to 1979, Mr. Grunberg was an indispensable research collaborator. He currently directs a treatment program for the mentally ill homeless at Columbia Medical Center, serves on the teaching faculty of Columbia University, and consults on program development and evaluation for various New York City public and private agencies addressing the problems of homelessness.) By the end of the first year, we had made contact with

over 80 men, and by the end of the second year with over 150. At the
end of three years this snowball effect resulted in an overall sample
size of well over 200 men. Of these men, 20 became centrally involved
throughout the course of the study; and 6 of these men, who grew to
be close friends and fieldwork associates, formed the very core of the
project. Although the racial characteristics of the Bowery men were
primarily Caucasian, they also included blacks, American Indians, and
Hispanics. The ethnicity of the men varied widely. Their ages spanned
the range from twenty-six to seventy-two.

Participant observation was the mode of encounter through which
we engaged the men. We incorporated a method of inquiry and encounter, shaped and refined by interactions with the men, which facilitated our purpose of gradually gaining access into the deep structure
of Bowery life to discover its essential meanings, patterns, and relationships. Because of this interest in exploring the Bowery's internal
condition and perspective, we did not use questionnaires, surveys,
and structured interviews. Instead, we sought an unmediated involvement with the men, an involvement that would, in adapting to the
unique qualities of the setting, move us into the sanctuary of subculture.

This movement into Bowery subculture was accompanied by the
rhythm of descent and discovery, a process premised upon joint inquiry between the men and ourselves. To aid the process and reduce
research bias, we held our hypotheses in abeyance and entered the
scene with no prestructured framework to guide our inquiry. In addition, we moved along by a process of bracketing; that is, we held in
check or self-consciously examined our own personal and cultural preconceptions, biases, and stereotypes in order to explore without being
ideologically organized or prejudiced. As Mr. Grunberg aptly put it in
summarizing our initial entry into the Bowery, "we wanted to experience the sensations that only the ignorant could." This strategy of
bracketing was cleansing and helped us to reconstitute the possibility
of subculture by enabling the structure, categories, and themes to
emanate from within rather than being imposed from without.

In establishing our presence with the men, we met them on their
level and on their terms. Our general purpose in coming down to the
Bowery was explained in order to clarify our identity and intention.
They accepted this purpose and generally appreciated our interest in
understanding the world of the Bowery and the life-style of those who
lived there. Most of the men were indeed flattered by our genuine
interest in getting to know them and in establishing relationships. As

more time was spent on the Bowery, we developed a history of shared experiences with the men characterized by lively interactions and dynamic encounters. This commingling of lives and incidents, a natural extension of the participant observation method, proved invaluable in distinguishing ourselves from others who had encountered the men on the Bowery only to reaffirm social distance between culture and subculture.

At first the men were somewhat skeptical of our presence and, even though our role was explicit, they associated us with journalists, photographers, undercover policemen, social scientists, and social workers. It was through sheer persistence and authentic encounter that we were able to disassociate ourselves from these precursors. After several months in the field we were able to legitimize our dual role as participants and observers and enjoy credibility with the men. They responded to our continued presence by involving us more intimately in their lives and community. Soon we participated quite naturally with them in their daily rounds: we drank socially with them, joined in their bottlegang groups, ate with them, accompanied them as they begged from cars and passersby, reminisced and prophesied together, listened to their stories, exchanged fantasies and dreams, witnessed their little ritual dramas, spun metaphors, strolled, joked, laughed, cheered, sang, mourned, supported, embraced, reveled, probed, and discussed. Through our participation in Bowery subculture we witnessed the fully embodied tragic, comic, and ironic dimensions of the men's lives as they were made manifest in the quotidian. To the extent that our role permitted, we were fully present in our encounters with the men and shared on many levels—as researchers, as friends, as urban dwellers, as fans of the same baseball team, as fellow travelers, as citizens of the republic; in short, we came together as people meeting in the human condition in which that condition happened to be a radical descent from the structure of American society.

Because of this balance between our research role and the intersubjectivity shared between the men and ourselves, we were granted further access into the structure of feeling resident in the Bowery. This involvement produced an intensification of experience which characterized our encounters with the men. The men were, after all, one of us; as William put it, "Remember, you can't spell bum without *u* in it." As one of us, existing deep within the domestic fold of American society, the Bowery men both challenged and invited. They challenged us to breach that formidable social distance between culture and sub-

culture and, by evoking our sense of empathy and identification, invited us to bear witness to the depths of condition indigenous to
American society. In this case, ethnography on native grounds re-
figured that disjunctive "us/them" dichotomy into an intimate whole,
that of "we."

By being present and involved in ways that transcended a strict
definition of our research role, we were increasingly drawn from the
margins of Bowery subculture and eventually placed within its center.
Our approach and style of encounter not only enhanced our intellectual
quest but stimulated personal journeys as well. Evidently, the Bowery
had been working on us and we responded by taking it all in without
being rigidly compartmentalized. We let the Bowery seek its own level
inside us and drew on this self-awareness to broaden the scope of the
project and deepen its personal as well as social value.

The effect of our relationships in the Bowery was a two-way street.
Over time, our interactions with the men influenced them in ways that
we could not have anticipated or solicited. Jack, for instance, spoke of
us to his eighty-one-year-old mother, to whom he paid weekly visits.
Jerry prevented us from dropping coins into the jukebox at the Old
Dover Tavern. "Stop, let someone else play it," he exhorted. "You
guys don't have the money—your tuition is skyrocketing." In their
occasional excursions out of the Bowery, Pee Wee and George sought
us out near the New School and New York University. We were introduced to Billy's associates as if esteemed Bowery fellows who "come
down here to visit friends." Jimmy would screw himself out of his
barstool at the One Mile House as we passed down the street and,
with a screeching whistle, call us back toward him. Frank stood incredulous as he discovered we were not out on a mission of rescue and
rehabilitation. "I can't figure you guys out," he would repeat in a half-
mocking, half-serious tone. "I just don't know; I can't figure you guys
out. You guys are somethin' else." Peter confirmed that we had
reached the men on a certain level: "You guys bring good feelings
down here." We were bought drinks, invited to Thanksgiving dinners,
given a bus ticket to visit Camp LaGuardia (an upstate facility for
homeless men), and used as go-betweens for the men in crisis situations. All of this attests to the intensely interpersonal dimension of our
encounters with the men and to the humanistic qualities which
emerged from them. We welcomed and enjoyed the men's company
and we believed that, for the most part, they welcomed and enjoyed
ours. After all, the Bowery is a very friendly place, especially to those
who seek its meaning and value.

By acknowledging and accepting the integrity of the men's lives within the realm of Bowery subculture, we were, in turn, accepted by the men as insiders to their setting. Over time, our method evolved to the point whereby, in simply showing up and being present, events took off and were rendered spontaneously. The urgency with which we questioned and probed diminished significantly as we gradually blended into the scene which the study encompassed. This more unobtrusive style worked to enhance the immediacy of the moment and to attenuate the psychological processes of censorship operative among the men during the early phase of the research, when our approach was at times confused with the distancing techniques of outsiders. This transition gratified our keen interest in unmediated and unguarded encounter and served as a catalyst for further minimizing whatever distance remained between ourselves as members of culture and Bowery men as an embodiment of subculture.

So, while on the Bowery, we observed, we participated, and we engaged the men; and we came away from the encounter with detailed descriptions and analyses of settings, events, interactions, conversations, movements, and gestures that dealt with the fundamental dimensions inherent in the men's life-style within the subculture. In recording our experiences, we did not employ any sophisticated techniques, such as tape recorders or cameras, nor could we feel genuine in the context by taking notes during our encounters with the men. Given the precedent set by outsiders on the Bowery, the use of sophisticated techniques or on-the-spot note taking would have registered distance between the men and ourselves and thus prevented us from gaining access into subculture.

Our strategy of unmediated encounter necessitated a reliance upon field notes as the method of documentation. After each field visit, while walking out of the Bowery, we would carefully restructure the nature of our encounter (or series of encounters) and sketch out on a pocket-sized notepad the flow of events, the players involved, along with the specific events, key phrases, luminous details, and descriptive features which constituted our interactions. In one sense, this process served as a mnemonic device by involving us in the organization and retelling of our experience. Yet by laying out the whole experience and keynoting form and content, this process also served to stimulate dialogue between the research partners concerning the import of events, emergent themes and patterns, and methodological considerations. By grounding our discussions in the concrete referents of events and activities, this dialogue worked to surface even more detail, thus fleshing out both the general form of encounter as well as its particularistic and constituting features. This preliminary process of documentation proved critical to the further retention of descriptive detail when the field notes were later written in their fully developed form. Obviously, two fieldworkers helped tremendously here in the reconstruction and documentation process of the project. Most of the time, we formed one extensive field note by merging our accounts; occasionally, we generated two separate field notes and let them exist side by side. This collaborative process of producing Bowery field notes characterized by analytical description was the primary mode of documentation that ran throughout the first year and a half of the study.

In addition to the construction of field notes, the partnership between Mr. Grunberg and myself proved methodologically invaluable to gaining access into Bowery life and attaining a close involvement with subculture. Because this fieldwork partnership manifested our involvement in affiliation, we reflected the Bowery men's primary program and adaptive strategy. The men could thus relate to us with much greater ease, for, as two rather than one, our presence signaled the safety and familiarity associated with commonality and served to reinforce the men's subcultural pattern of affiliation as displayed in friendships and surrogate primary groups. In fact, to many men the fieldwork partners became an inseparable unit. Whenever one of the partners was down on the Bowery alone (which happened on occasion), invariably he would be queried as to the whereabouts of the other. Partnership signified cohesion to the men, a cohesion that reflected back to the men their own mutual bonding by which they were held together in the body of subculture.

Aside from disrupting the social distance between the men and ourselves and representing their motif of affiliation, this partnership also helped tactically to complement and fully develop our interactions with the men. It allowed for smooth transitions between the two modes of encounter, participation and observation, and enabled each of the partners, while in the observer mode, to rehearse the emerging flow of events and conversations while still being present in the moment. In this manner, the immediate organization of the data occurred simultaneously with their very unfolding. This latitude to freely stand back at times and observe the fieldwork process in action while registering its content enhanced the spongelike absorption and retention of events; it also facilitated the reflexive quality of the project as each of the partners could, in turn, view the fieldwork in its totality; that is, from a vantage point which included the interaction between the form of encounter (method) and the content which issued from this involvement (results).

Our inquiry and involvement in Bowery life led to an overall focus on the subcultural paradigm which defined the men's interactions, ethos, and world view. Throughout the first year and a half of the study, we concentrated on the men's relationship to their environment both in terms of their internal integration into subculture and their external adaptation to culture. The physical, social, and symbolic boundaries between culture and subculture were explored as well as the critical and complementary processes of disaffiliation and affiliation which accompanied their descent into the Bowery. Affiliation within subculture was demonstrated and understood to be a compensatory and culture-making process which emerged from beneath the broader social condition of alienation. Moreover, it became apparent that affiliation constituted the deep structure or subcultural "program" of the Bowery's way of life. Affiliation within the Bowery, therefore, occupied our central interest and led to an investigation of its social processes of descent and enculturation, adaptive strategies, subcultural forms, functions, and values. As the chief organizing principle of human activity and relationship on the Bowery, affiliation was also pursued as the mediation between the worlds of culture and subculture that worked to formulate, communicate, and manifest the symbolic code of the latter.

Related to this concern with affiliation, our fieldwork also led to discovering the nature of reality and truth within the Bowery and to the men's corresponding conceptions of time and space. The Bowery men's ethos and world view were revealed, then, by living on the streets *in extremis*. This form of existence and social life became the cherished source of experience, knowledge, and wisdom in which conceptions of life, strategies for living, and reorientations to time and place were tested out and refined. Identity and truth (who we are and how we know the world) were bolstered by the men's rejection of culture and by their inevitable acceptance of subculture. This dual process ultimately invigorated their project; that is, the contravention of a dominant cultural system of value and order.

The men's condition of structural inferiority and their presence within the subcultural realm of antistructure deepened our understanding of the men's struggle for definition, integration, and completion. Although apparent during the first half of the fieldwork, our awareness of this dimension became foregrounded during the latter

half. As an embodiment of inferiority and antistructure, the men gave
expressive form and commentary to their evocation of the cultural
notions of pollution and taboo as well as to their own inherent system
of meaning and value resident within subculture. The generative dialectic between culture and subculture was forcefully present as we
turned our attention to the symbolic processes which articulated this
dimension and relationship.

During the second half of the fieldwork, this focus on the dialectic
between culture and subculture and on the competing systems of
meaning which inhere in both was also accompanied by a submergence
into the existential realities of Bowery life. Perhaps Peter's sincere
comment, "You're studying our death," signaled the turning point
during the second year of fieldwork, for soon after, in seeking the
depths of condition, we began following more intensely the tragic
slope of the men's lives. The themes and conditions of death (both
physical and social), disillusionment, despair, and entrapment loomed
before us as we continued our involvement with the men. To increase
our sensitivity to these impending Bowery truths and the emotionally
complex manner in which they emerged, we reflected them in our
more personalized field notes and in other forms in which the structure of feeling strove to express itself. Since our experience within the
aesthetic-existential realm of Bowery life deepened our own subjective
sense of involvement with the men, we experimented with different
forms, such as journals, sketches, prose poems, dream analysis, and
short fiction, so as to reflect this level of encounter. These forms
played off the more objective, analytical accounts and confirmed the
general struggle for representation we experienced in trying to adequately encompass the full range of Bowery life.

Perhaps the distillation of any fieldwork into a specific genre will
carry with it certain trade-offs. All these words given in this retrospec-
tive, all the words used to account for the Bowery in field notes and
various forms of expression, all the words contained in this present
study do not and cannot exhaust the resonant structure of feeling
experienced on the Bowery. This structure of feeling carries with it its
own universe of discourse, generative and degenerative as the case
may be. Now eleven years after the fact, the experience is still alive
for me. In moments of spontaneous recovery, I recall images and
movements, forms and settings, words and phrases that become figural and captivating. They still my present and work to remind me of
what I must carry with me so as to re-engage the moment as a force
for life and literature. In the absence of re-experience we must re-

count; and what a story these men did tell, continue to unfold. It is nothing less than a continuous struggle for completion. Now as before, the Bowery confronts me like this, attesting to its potent value as an experience that, though perhaps encompassed, can never be exhausted.

NOTES

1. BACKGROUND CIRCUMFERENCE

1. See Harlow, *Old Bowery Days*, p. 24. Though short on interpretation, Harlow's descriptive study is the best and most comprehensive historical treatment of the Bowery yet to appear. Completed in the 1930s, it will most likely remain the definitive work on the subject as seen from a perspective of social history.

2. For a more detailed account of these transactions and developments within the Bayard and De Lancey estates, see "The Bowery," in *Valentine's Manual of the Corporation of the City of New York* (1866), pp. 573–589, esp. pp. 582, 584–585. The Grim Plan of 1742–1744 and the Ratzer Map of 1767 can be viewed in *Valentine's Manual of the Corporation of the City of New York* (1854), pp. 246, xii, respectively.

3. An account of the Rutgers lineage in America, including the concentration and squandering of property over four generations, appears in Mott, "The Road to the Bouwerij," pp. 487–495, esp. p. 493.

4. The Bridges's Map of 1811, an engraved plan based on the Randel Survey of 1807, can be seen in Stokes, *Iconography*, vol. 3, pl. 80.

5. As quoted in ibid., p. 482.

6. Ibid., p. 478.

7. See Harlow, *Old Bowery Days*, p. 50.

8. Ibid., p. 153.

9. See Rikeman, *Evolution of Stuyvesant Village*, p. 73. Rikeman's felicitous characterization of Bowery Village (also known as Stuyvesant Village) during the 1830s is corroborated by the diary of Michael Floy, Jr., a young resident. The most recurrent activities recorded by Floy include singing parties, prayer meetings, love feasts, church attendance, Bible class, neighborly visitations, horticulture, and bucolic ruminations on romance, mortality, and mathematical quandaries. See Brooks, ed., *Diary of Michael Floy, Jr.* Incidentally, Bowery Village was, at one time or another, a refuge for William Cullen Bryant, H. C. Bunner, and Brander Matthews.

10. Quoted in Schlesinger, *Rise of the City*, p. 84.

11. Walt Whitman, "The Old Bowery," in Stovall, ed., *Collected Writings of Walt Whitman*, 2: 595.

12. See Grimsted, *Melodrama Unveiled*, p. 56.

13. "The Bowery boy was very proud and full of an affectation of rough airs that he considered exquisite. He dyed his mustache jetblack, oiled his hair profusely, and was much given to loud perfume. He wore a lustrous silk hat, a flannel shirt with a huge black-silk scarf under its collar, trousers that were very tight and needed no suspenders, a coat that he usually

carried on his arm, well-polished boots . . . , and carried a cigar tilted heavenward above his nose, and spread his elbows apart so that nobody could pass him on a narrow pavement without jostling him. . . .

"It is said that Thackeray much enjoyed meeting a Bowery boy. The great novelist desired to go to Houston street. He was not certain whether he was right in pursuing the directions he had taken, so he stepped up to one of these East-Side Adonises and said: 'Sir, can I go to Houston street this way?' 'Yes, I guess yer kin, sonny,' said the boy—'if yer behave yerself.'" Quoted from Ralph, "The Bowery," p. 228. For the presence of the Bowery Gal and the social value of women on the antebellum Bowery, see Stansell, *City of Women*, pp. 89–101.

14. One of Ned Buntline's creations, "Mose, the Bowery B'hoy," was officially unveiled to the American public in 1849 at the old Olympic Theater. The play starred Frank Chanfrau in the leading role. See Asbury, "The Old-Time Gangs," pp. 478–486. The character of Mose lent itself to many variations. One successful rendition, "New York as It Is," again featuring Chanfrau, virtually announced its claim to mimesis for an urban populace eager to see a more self-conscious representation of its life and surroundings.

15. For a detailed account of the riot between the Dead Rabbits and the Bowery Boys, see Harlow, *Old Bowery Days*, pp. 296ff.

16. Ibid., pp. 218–219. Contained herein is George Foster's tabulation of oyster houses, taverns, and trades, as well as a more elaborate listing of business concerns along the Bowery at this time.

17. Browne, *The Great Metropolis*, p. 129.

18. See Weber, *Growth of Cities*, p. 442. For a more developed treatment of urbanization and its dynamic offices of differentiation, specialization, and segregation (as well as their consequences for the physical, social, and economic structure of the city), see Robert E. Park, "The City: Suggestions for the Investigation of Human Behavior in the Urban Environment," in Park and Burgess, eds., *The City*, pp. 1–46; and Wirth, "Urbanism as a Way of Life," pp. 1–24.

19. See Weber, *Growth of Cities*, p. 22, Table II. The growth of great cities, with populations over 100,000, gives further testimony to the powerful social and economic changes that had accompanied the nineteenth century. From nine great cities in 1800, with a fledgling urban populace of just under 210,000, the nation had expanded to twenty-eight such centers by 1890, containing over 9,500,000 seasoned metropolitan residents (see Table II, column 4).

20. Ibid., p. 21.

21. For a comparison of the distribution of wealth between rural and urban environments during the 1880s and 1890s, see Spahr, *An Essay*, pp. 46–49. The average wealth of urban families also exceeded that of rural families by a ratio of 2 to 1. One qualification, however, is in order: though

the wealth of cities was far greater than that of their counterpart, it tended
toward a much narrower concentration into a select upper class as opposed to the more widely distributed and proportionately held wealth in
small towns and farming districts (see pp. 53–64).

Also, for a corroboration of the shift in wealth from rural to urban areas
from 1860 to 1900, see Robert E. Gallman, "Trends in the Size of Distribution of Wealth in the Nineteenth Century: Some Speculations," in *Six
Papers on the Size Distribution of Wealth and Income*, Studies in Income
and Wealth, vol. 33 (New York and London: National Bureau of Economic
Research, 1969), pp. 1–30, esp. pp. 10–11.

22. The various authors of this eponymous series are, respectively, Mark
    Twain and Charles Dudley Warner, Ray Ginger, Lewis Mumford, Vernon
    Louis Parrington, Thomas Beer, and Alan Trachtenberg.
23. Trachtenberg, *Incorporation of America*, pp. 3–4.
24. For a comparison of industrial consolidation during the 1870s to 1890s
    with that of 1898 to 1904, see Cochran and Miller, *Age of Enterprise*, pp.
    190–192; see also pp. 140–143.
25. From 1840 to 1865, prices and wages were positively correlated in an
    increasingly upward direction. This correlation was disrupted, however,
    during the Gilded Age, when prices rapidly declined while wages remained
    relatively fixed. Thus, "by 1892 labor's living standard in terms of income
    and price levels was higher than it had ever been, or was to be prior to the
    end of the First World War." See the chart, "Wages and Prices Prevailing
    in the United States, 1840–1890," in Coman, *Industrial History*, p. 306.
    Figures which document the increase in national and per capita wealth
    during this period may be found on p. 292 (whereas the nation's wealth had
    doubled in the twenty years from 1860 to 1880, per capita income had
    doubled in the thirty-year span from 1860 to 1890). For corroborations and
    qualifications of the relationship between prices and wages in the Gilded
    Age, see Cochran and Miller, *Age of Enterprise*, pp. 139, 234, 261; Leon
    S. Marshall, "The English and American Industrial City of the Nineteenth
    Century," in Callow, ed., *American Urban History*, p. 152; and Spahr, *An
    Essay*, pp. 109–113. While Cochran and Miller underscore the qualifica-
    tion that a higher standard of living was countered by poor housing and
    working conditions, and while Marshall points to the forceful undercurrent
    of economic insecurity which undermined this standard, Spahr isolates the
    economic consequences of trade cycles and falling prices as the very inter-
    nal disruptions to the more improved situation. Both economic depression
    and industrial overproduction had resulted in reoccurring periods of wide-
    spread unemployment and substantial wage reductions which continually
    threatened to upset the tenuously propped standard of the age.
26. See Holmes's estimated wealth distribution for American families in 1890
    in Jeffrey G. Williamson and Peter H. Lindert, *American Inequality: A
    Macroeconomic History* (New York, London, Toronto, Sydney, and San

Francisco: Academic Press, 1980), pp. 47–48. Holmes's estimates for 1890 are confirmed by Gallman, "Trends," in Soltow, ed., *Six Papers*, esp. p. 11.

27. Trachtenberg, *Incorporation*, p. 90.

28. Spahr, *An Essay*, pp. 57, 67; see also pp. 55–70 for full context of discussion and data base. The situation in New York City was only marginally improved in other metropolitan clusters. Spahr reports that in American cities above 100,000 only 23 percent of the residents owned their own homes. This compares with 66 percent home ownership (of farms) in the rural areas (see Holmes' tables, pp. 53–54).

29. See Howe, *The City*, p. 194.

30. Between the years 1881 and 1905, Trachtenberg estimates close to 37,000 strikes involving as many as 7 million workers. See Trachtenberg, *Incorporation*, pp. 79–80. Severe economic contractions during the period 1870 to 1900 occurred in the following years: 1873 to 1878, 1883, and 1893 to 1898—the worst depression to date in American history.

31. The estimate of 45,000 tramps is given in J. J. McCook's 1893 survey, "A Tramp Census and Its Revelations," pp. 753–766, esp. p. 760. Eighty-three percent of this tramp sample took to the road because of economic circumstances, such as unemployment or enforced occupational transiency. The latter estimate of 100,000 tramps and hoboes appears in E. Lamar Bailey's descriptive sketch of an insider's experience as a tramp, "Tramps and Hoboes," pp. 217–221, esp. p. 220. Bailey also offers definitions which distinguish the categories of tramp, hobo, and vagrant.

32. See Park, "The City," p. 40.

33. Quoted from Cochran and Miller, *Enterprise*, p. 124.

34. Jacob Riis's study of tenement conditions revealed that in 1890 1,250,000 people (out of a total city population of 1,513,501) lived in 37,316 tenement buildings. See Riis, *The Other Half*, pp. 201–205. Although the extent of the populace that lived in tenements was outstanding, this should not be taken as a reliable index of poverty within the city. In 1867 the Metropolitan Board of Health established the Tenement House Law, which defined the tenement as such: "A tenement house . . . shall be taken to mean and include every house, building, or portion thereof which is rented, leased, let or hired out to be occupied as the home or residence of more than 3 families living independently of another, and doing their cooking upon the premises, or by more than 2 families on a floor, so living and cooking, but have a common right in the halls, stairways, water closets or privies, or some of them." Quoted from Lubove, *Progressives and the Slums*, pp. 25–26. Such an innocuous law helped to obscure the conditions of tenements, which varied widely depending upon their location and degree of density, overcrowding, and sanitation. Since not all tenements were situated within urban slums, it would be hasty to assume that five-sixths of the population lived in penury. The above description of

the tenement indicates an all too inclusive definition of terms as well as a vague regulatory effort to control poor housing conditions. Though the definition of slum varies greatly in the literature, it may be helpful to provide one condensed illustration based on several unifying physical factors: *"The slum is a residential area . . . in which the housing is so deteriorated . . . , so substandard . . . , or so unwholesome . . . as to be a menace to the health, safety, morality, or welfare of the occupants."* I might add to this that urban slums are also characterized by a cultural dimension, a defining ethos and world view that summarize their inhabitants' way of life. For the above definition of slums, see James Ford, *Slums and Housing,* 2 vols. (Cambridge, Mass.: Harvard University Press, 1936), 1: 13.

35. See Lubove, *Progressives,* pp. 261–263.
36. See Weber, *Growth of Cities,* pp. 415–416.
37. Ibid., pp. 258–260.
38. The description of this luminous tenement block is taken from Veiller, *Tenement House Reform,* pp. 42–43. The Tenement House Exhibition of 1900 was arranged by the Tenement House Committee of the Charity Organization Society. For many years Veiller, an effective reformer and municipal official, was the secretary and director of this committee. The exhibition was held in New York City for a two-week period and was viewed by over ten thousand people. It was taken on tour to other American cities and appeared at the Paris Exposition of 1900. Conferences were held during the display to offer a forum for debate and discussion on the tenement house problem. For more background on Veiller's contribution to urban reform, see Lubove, *Progressives,* chaps. 5 and 6.
39. Ibid., p. 45. The oversized Poverty and Disease Maps were provided to me courtesy of the New-York Historical Society. Meticulously constructed, these maps showed the extent of poverty and disease in ten tenement districts of the city. Each block within a district was schematically charted, indicating which buildings were tenements, commercial establishments, or vacant structures. The street number of each building was given along with its height in stories, extent of land covered, design of construction, and degree of land available for light and air. The maps also showed the density for each block, the number of families seeking charitable aid, and the incidence of four major diseases: tuberculosis, scarlet fever, diphtheria, and typhoid. The Bowery tenement districts comprise maps numbers 4, 6, and 10.
40. Cochran and Miller, *Enterprise,* p. 264.
41. Lubove, *Progressives,* p. 131.
42. See the "Population of the 'Lower East Side,' Manhattan, by Countries of Birth,—1855, 1905, 1910, 1920 and 1930," in Walter Laidlaw, ed. and comp., *Population of the City of New York, 1890–1930,* p. 243. The foreign-born population for 1910 is more than twice that of native Ameri-

cans within the Lower East Side. The table also indicates the dramatic shift in immigration over the years from northwestern to southeastern Europe, a general phenomenon which made for the more conspicuous presence of new immigrants due to racial, national, and religious heritage. By 1890 in greater New York, fully 80 percent of the metropolitan populace was either foreign-born or of foreign parentage. See John M. Blum et al., eds., *The National Experience: A History of the United States* (New York: Harcourt, Brace and World, 1963), p. 467.

43. For a discussion of this paradox of physical proximity and social distance, see Park, *City*, pp. 40–45, and Wirth, "Urbanism," pp. 10–16.

44. Hewitt and Hewitt, "The Bowery," pp. 405–406.

45. An account of the Red House and its harlequin sales pitch can be found in Lloyd Morris, *Incredible New York: High Life and Low Life of the Last Hundred Years* (New York: Random House, 1951), p. 36.

46. See Harlow, *Old Bowery Days*, pp. 447–448 for a description of the live model's attire and studied movements.

47. Ralph, "The Bowery," pp. 233–235. The World League against Alcohol reports an even higher number of barrooms for the earlier year of 1886: ninety-seven bars facing the Bowery and over two hundred saloons on all of the square Bowery blocks. See Robert E. Corradini, comp., *The Bowery, New York City: A Survey of that Notorious District Comparing Present Conditions with those of Pre-Prohibition Days*, p. 4. The Excise Law of 1896 had reduced the number of licensed Bowery bars by 54 percent over three decades (from 1886 to 1916). Increasing enforcement of the Volstead Act further diminished the number of official bars to six by 1923. Of course, this dry period was compensated for by the growing number of illicit speakeasies along the Bowery. In the 1920s, one nightwalker had estimated two bars for every fronting Bowery block.

48. See Riis, *The Other Half*, p. 61.

49. For the many social functions of the saloon, see Stelzle, *A Son of the Bowery*, pp. 47–48. As a source of sustenance for the homeless, Harlow notes: "In the saloon the homeless man for a nickel could get not only shelter from the storm, not only the 'Largest Glass of Beer in the City' . . . but a free lunch of meats, salt and pickled fish, kraut, cheeses, pickles, rye bread, and what not, sufficient to sustain him for the day; likewise a choice of newspapers which he could not afford to buy, and an hour or so in a warm, jovial atmosphere." See Harlow, *Old Bowery Days*, p. 404.

50. Quoted from Royale, "The Vaudeville Theatre," p. 488.

51. Ibid., p. 495.

52. Crane, "The Men in the Storm," in Stallman and Hagemann, eds., *The New York City Sketches of Stephen Crane*, p. 92.

53. See Campbell, Knox, and Byrnes, *Darkness and Daylight*, p. 230; and Riis, *The Other Half*, p. 60.

54. See King, ed., *King's Handbook*, 1: 237; and Riis, *The Other Half*, pp. 60–61.
55. This sample is contained in Alexander Irvine's autobiography, *From the Bottom Up*, pp. 101–102.
56. See Riis, *The Other Half*, pp. 163–164. The ordering of nationalities among street beggars, from greater to less, is given as follows: Irish, Americans, Germans, and Italians. McCook's survey of tramp nativity has Americans heading the list with 56 percent of the recruits, followed by the Irish and English, respectively. See McCook, "A Tramp Census," p. 756.
57. This improved condition should not obscure the fact, however, that by 1932 8,000 tenements were still extant on the Lower East Side as well as 431 rear tenement houses with a population alone of 10,000, one-fifth of the 1905 rear house figure of 50,000. Large estates owned more than 10 percent of these rear houses and, in general, "real estate ownership on the Bowery today [1929] would read like a page from the Social Register." On the Bowery, 24 estates owned 20 percent of the land. In addition, the Bowery vicinity was plagued by the neglect associated with absentee landlordism and trusteeship. These facts suggest that, while poverty had indeed diminished in this quarter, the conditions of its lingering presence had not been eradicated. See Joseph Platzker's series of articles on the community problems of the Lower East Side: "Who Owns the Lower East Side," repr. from the *East Side Chamber News* (New York City), July 31, 1929; "A Survey of Lower East Side's Rear Houses," *East Side Chamber of Commerce* (New York City), February 17, 1930; and "Land and Management," *East Side Chamber of Commerce* (New York City), February 23, 1932. These articles, as well as others in the series, can be found in the Municipal Reference Library of the City of New York, 31 Chambers St., Room #112, under author.
58. A photograph of "the Bowery with the lid off" can be seen in the collection of Whitehouse, *New York: Sunshine and Shadow*, pl. 342.
59. Quoted from Robert M. Coates, "The Street that Died Young," *New York Times Magazine*, September 14, 1924.
60. Nascher, *Wretches of Povertyville*, p. 24.
61. This study appears in Stelzle, *A Son of the Bowery*, p. 232.
62. See Anderson, *Report on the Municipal Lodging House*, 1: xiv.
63. The volunteer is Michael Harrington and his observation, made during the early 1950s, is given in his seminal work, *The Other America*, p. 92.
64. For this steady decline in the Bowery's skid row population, see Bahr, "The Gradual Disappearance of Skid Row," pp. 41–45.
65. This estimate of 36,000 homeless men and women in New York City was made popular by Ellen Baxter's and Kim Hopper's study, *Private Lives/ Public Spaces*, pp. 8–10. This estimate given in 1981, has been revised upwards to 60,000 to reflect the growing incidence of homelessness in New York City throughout the 1980s.

1. For a discussion of this individualistic interpretation of poverty, including its development during the nineteenth century, see Bremner, *From the Depths*, pp. 16–30. Bremner argues that the liberation from orthodox puritanical theology significantly altered the explanation of poverty from God-given to manmade. Accordingly, with the transition to more democratic religious creeds, which emphasized salvation and regeneration, an attitude toward poverty arose that rallied against the individual evils of intemperance and immorality. These vices were seen as personal obstacles to a state of redemption. "The individualistic interpretation of poverty began as a hopeful and essentially radical doctrine. Well before the end of the century, however, it had been converted into a formidable bulwark of that strange brand of conservatism espoused by the dominant business classes. Like the other principles of laissez-faire economics, the individualistic interpretation was given a supposedly scientific basis by the teachings of Herbert Spencer and his American disciples, and also by the early application of Darwinian biology to social thought" (pp. 18–19).

2. Parrington, *Main Currents in American Thought*, 3: xix. In this last, unfinished volume of Parrington's trilogy, *The Beginnings of Critical Realism in America, 1860–1920*, he traces the rise of "critical realism" to three primary factors: "the stratifying of economics under the pressure of centralization; the rise of a mechanistic science; and the emergence of a spirit of skepticism" (p. xix).

3. In 1890, newspapers and periodicals were the second leading industry in New York City, while book publishing was sixth. See Weber, *Growth of Cities*, p. 207.

4. See Douglas's provocative study of popular culture during the nineteenth century, *Feminization of American Culture*, particularly p. 72. Douglas's definition of sentimentalism, "the political sense obfuscated or gone rancid," applies as well to the notion of mystification. Both sentimentalism and mystification are anti-intellectual in design, thoroughly domesticated in nature, and ostensibly idealized in expression. And both offer the diversion of publicity in lieu of self-examination and social evaluation, a situation which results in the complacent state of cultural narcissism. For a focused discussion on sentimentalism and its consequences, see especially p. 307.

5. Nationwide, the number of dailies nearly doubled from 1880 to 1890 while their cumulative circulation almost tripled. Cochran and Miller note the extension of corporate organization to the newspaper business during the Gilded Age: "The trend from individual to collective enterprise that marked American business after the Civil War was as apparent in journalism as in oil, steel, or railroads. . . . By the 1890s city papers came to be published by large corporations for the financial benefit of stockholders and directors. They became primarily profit-making enterprises rather

than vehicles of private opinion. And their advertising revenue by 1890 was their most important source of income. Thus journalism took its place in the ranks of Big Business. Soon it was marked by trade associations, combinations, and overcapitalized mergers, and just as control of capital and credit came to be concentrated in the hands of a few city bankers, so influence over opinion came to be concentrated in the hands of a few city journalists." See Cochran and Miller, *Enterprise*, pp. 269–270.

6. Trachtenberg, *Incorporation*, p. 125. Trachtenberg's essential position is that metropolitan life in general was steeped in mystification and "failed to comprehend the city as a social force whose fusion of factory, marketplace, and home in a process of incorporation reshaped the entire society and its culture. That process altered relations, defied inherited values, transformed instruments of perception and communication, even as it transformed the perceptible social world" (p. 112).

7. "The Modern Editor and His Boss," by J. Opper, *Puck*, January 1, 1890, back page.

8. As revealed in Burgess's article, "The Newspaper as Charity Worker," pp. 249–268. Burgess informs us that during this time the *World* contributed $43,000 toward its free bread fund, the *Herald* $35,000 to the maintenance of a free clothing fund, and the *Tribune* $21,536 toward a combined free coal and food fund.

9. See "Walking through the Bowery," *Outlook*, 48 (December 1893): 1001.

10. Some of the apportioned spatial and social slices include Broadway, Chatham Street, the Bowery, the Tombs, gambling houses, literary soirées, pawnbrokers, mock auctions, the volunteer firemen companies, and eating houses. See also Foster's *New York Naked*.

11. In their respective order: Matthew Hale Smith, *Sunshine and Shadow in New York*; Helen Campbell, Col. Thomas W. Knox, and Supt. Thomas Byrnes, *Darkness and Daylight; or Lights and Shadows of New York Life*; Edward Winslow Martin, *The Secrets of The Great City: A Work Descriptive of the Virtues and the Vices, The Mysteries, Miseries and Crime of New York City*; Edward Crapsey, *The Nether Side of New York; or The Vice, Crime and Poverty of the Great Metropolis*; Charles Loring Brace, *The Dangerous Classes of New York and Twenty Years' Work Among Them*; J. W. Buel, *Metropolitan Life Unveiled; or The Mysteries and Miseries of America's Great Cities*; T. DeWitt Talmage, D.D., *The Masque Torn Off*; and Commissioner and Mrs. Ballington Booth, *New York's Inferno Explored*.

12. See the inner flap of Booth's *Inferno*. Incidentally, the commissioner's book appeared one year after his very successful and highly popular account, *In Darkest England and the Way Out*.

13. Talmage, *Masque*, p. 83.

14. Buel, *Metropolitan Life*, p. 1 of prologue.

15. Respectively, "Our Homeless Poor"; or, "How the Other Half of the World

Lives," March 2, 1872, p. 390; Buel, *Metropolitan Life*, p. 51; Smith, *Sunshine and Shadow*, p. 366; and Rev. Fred Bell, *Midnight Scenes in the Slums of New York; or Lights and Shadows*, p. 81.

16. Smith, ed., *Wonders of a Great City*, p. 410. The wholesale condemnation of an entire section of New York City is given in George G. Foster's scathing account of Five Points during the mid-nineteenth century. The supposedly immanent qualities of corruption and contamination turn Five Points into the very monster of civilized life that is "the Great central ulcer of wretchedness—the very rotting Skeleton of Civilization, whence emanates an inexhaustible pestilence that spreads its poisonous influence through every vein and artery of the whole social system, and supplies every heart-throb of metropolitan life with a pulse of despair." See Foster, *Slices*, pp. 22–25.

17. Smith, ed., *Wonders*, from the publisher's preface.

18. Third Annual Report, 1882–1883, p. 14. The annual reports of the Bowery Mission and Young Men's Home, New York, nos. 1–10, range from 1880, when the mission concluded its first year, to 1890. Opened in 1879, the mission was originally located at 36 Bowery, "in the centre of one of Satan's most noted strongholds." From its inception, the purpose of the mission has been twofold, that of evangelistic work for the homeless combined with suitable facilities and activities for sound Christian housing and conduct. In 1894, the Bowery Mission was incorporated by some well-known philanthropists. Among them were Rev. T. DeWitt Talmage, D.D., Rev. Josia Strong, D.D., Mrs. Sarah J. Bird, known as the "mother of the Bowery" and an assistant to Henry Ward Beecher, and Dr. Louis Klopsch, proprietor of the *Christian Herald*. The mission became known for its midnight breadlines, timed so as "to ensure that the guests [were] really out for the night." On an average annual basis, the mission provided some 200,000 meals to the hungry and 8,000 to 10,000 lodgings for the homeless. Put into perspective, 200,000 meals annually comes to a daily average of 568 meals or less than 200 people at each meal; the lodging comes to a daily average of 28 a night—all in a city of 3 million. Today the Bowery Mission is located at 227 Bowery. It is still a Christian Herald Ministry and remains devoted to the religious goals of salvation and regeneration outlined more than a century ago. For further information regarding the early workings and successes of the mission, see *A Plea for the Homeless Men and Boys of the Bowery; An Intensely Interesting Illustrated Story of the Work Done in the Greatest Rescue Mission in the World.*

19. First Annual Report, 1880–1881, pp. 12–13. This testimonial was presented in the form of a written letter addressed to the mission.

20. Bell, *Midnight Scenes*, p. 82.

21. Ibid., p. 81.

22. As pastor of the Brooklyn Tabernacle Church, Talmage was earning a salary of $12,000 per year, an income that was supplemented by his

lecture tour, which brought in $100 to $200 per night. Talmage presided over a wealthy and fashionable congregation of New York Society, placing him in a select circle of influence and social control. This privileged relationship attests to the strong association between Christian ministry and upper-class culture, a situation which would have profound effects upon the perception and attitude toward subculture. For the high salaries of such ministers, see Buel, *Metropolitan Life*, p. 38.

23. Talmage, *Masque*, pp. 86–87.
24. Ibid., pp. 90, 92.
25. See Crapsey, *Nether Side*, p. 110.
26. The series of articles on the conditions of the homeless in New York City appear in the following editions: March 2, 9, 16, and 23, 1872. The representatives of the weekly newspaper consisted of an editor and an artist; they were accompanied by a party of humanitarian reformers and public officials.
27. "Our Homeless Poor," March 23, 1872, p. 6.
28. Ibid.
29. Talmage, *Masque*, p. 95.
30. Ibid., pp. 95–96.
31. See Grimsted, *Melodrama Unveiled*, p. 196.
32. For the original version of the play, along with its penciled-in adaptation, see Robert Nelson Stephens, *On the Bowery*, unpublished typescript, in the Billy Rose Theater Collection, New York Public Library, Lincoln Center Branch.
33. See Theodore Kremer, *The Bowery after Dark*, unpublished typescript, in the Billy Rose Theater Collection, New York Public Library, Lincoln Center Branch. The relationship between mystification and form, though somewhat attenuated by the debunking quality of humorous or burlesque depictions, can also be seen in American farce comedies, which played off immigrant and tough native stereotypes. See, for instance, John T. McIntyre's *The Bowery Night-School: A Vaudeville Sketch*; Charles H. Hoyt's *A Trip to Chinatown*, in Hunt, ed., *America's Lost Plays*; and E. J. Kahn's *The Merry Partners: The Age and Stage of Harrigan and Hart*. The infamous popular song, "The Bowery," which cemented the district's declining reputation during the 1890s, is contained in Hoyt's *A Trip to Chinatown*. Though innocuous to us now, the song's chorus raised havoc among proprietors and denizens alike in its claim for deterrence. The chorus ran: "The Bow'ry, the Bow'ry! / They say such things, and they do strange things / On the Bow'ry! The Bow'ry! / I'll never go there anymore!"
34. See Bernard R. Bowron, Jr.'s discussion of Bret Harte in "Realism in America," pp. 273–274. Bowron also notes that local color writers, such as Stowe, Eggleston, Kirkland, Cable, Freeman, and Jewett, "with all due allowance for romantic and sentimental excrescences," were beginning to feature region and environment as active and dynamic forces in shaping

lives and communities. For the relationship of local color to realism, see his discussion on pp. 274ff.

35. See Ziff, *The American 1890s*, p. 14 (see also pp. 15–23).

36. Quoted from Warfel and Orions, eds., *Local-Color*, p. x.

37. Ibid., p. xi.

38. Quoted in Stallman, *Stephen Crane*, p. 73. Crane's damning phrase was also meant for the moralistic tracts of the day.

39. See Brander Matthews's dedication to Theodore Roosevelt in which this comparison is made in *Vignettes of Manhattan*.

40. The form had also made its influence felt in the related industry of book publishing, as over one hundred volumes of local color stories were published between 1887 and 1900. See Warfel and Orions, eds., *Local-Color*, p. xxii.

41. Bunner, "The Bowery and Bohemia," in *Jersey Street*, pp. 86–87.

42. Ibid., p. 90.

43. Bunner, "Jersey and Mulberry," in *Jersey Street*, p. 17.

44. Bunner, "The Bowery and Bohemia," in *Jersey Street*, pp. 91–92.

45. Ibid.

46. In Matthews's collection, *Vignettes*, pp. 59–71.

47. A professional attribute given in a related vignette in which Rupert De Ruyter appears as a dinner guest. See Matthews, "A Candle in the Plate," in *Vignettes*, p. 326.

48. Matthews, "In Search of Local Color," in *Vignettes*, pp. 62–63.

49. Ibid., p. 64.

50. Ibid., p. 71.

51. Matthews, *Vignettes*, pp. 241–262. For further evidence of Matthews's mystification of social process and discovery, see his related vignettes: "Before the Break of Day," "In the Midst of Life," and "A Candle in the Plate."

52. In Davis *Van Bibber and Others*, pp. 47–53, esp. p. 48.

53. Ibid., pp. 101–130, esp. p. 107.

54. Ibid., p. 112.

55. Ibid., pp. 115, 117.

56. Ibid., pp. 126, 129, italics in original.

57. Ralph, *People We Pass*, pp. 4, 138, 88–89.

58. Sullivan, "Not Yet: The Day-Dreams of Ivan Grigorovitch," in *Tenement Tales of New York*, p. 180.

59. Ibid., pp. 176, 177.

60. Ibid., p. 194.

61. Influenced by the pervasive picturesque treatment and, indeed, limited by Victorian cultural standards, Sullivan, in stories such as "Minnie Kelsey's Wedding" and "Cohen's Figure," resorts to the feminine ideal as a mechanism for freedom or escape from industrial bondage. In the first story, a beleaguered factory girl is rescued from her hard contract by her marriage

to a gentleman. In the second story mentioned, the female character, in warding off her employer's crude advances, finally leaps from an upper-story window of the sweatshop where she modeled clothes. In preferring death over degradation, Sullivan upholds the feminine mystique. "Not Yet" is by far the best of Sullivan's short tales, and with it he marked a departure from the predominant attitude of his time as well as from his own typical work.

62. For a comprehensive discussion of this broad intellectual conflict between idealism and critical realism, religion and science, and the transitional phase of realism, see Robert P. Falk, "The Rise of Realism, 1871–1891," in Clark, ed., *Transitions*, esp. pp. 383–396; Parrington, *Main Currents*, 3: xii–xxvi, 4: 189–191, 239; and Bowron, "Realism in America," pp. 268–285. Falk summarizes the essence of the era's intellectual tension in these words: "The critical discussions of realism, and the literature which practiced its principles, were the literary aspects of a broader intellectual conflict between science and religion, idealism and materialism, teleology and natural selection. As a moment of intellectual history, realism may be regarded as part of the clash between the bright promise of democratic individualism and the darker shadows of a deterministic outlook. Between these polar extremes American thought moved hesitantly away from its earlier romantic and idealistic basis, taking color and shape from the grotesque fantasy of Gilded Age politics and business materialism" (p. 383).

63. Riis, *Making of an American*, pp. 152–153.

64. Ibid., p. xi.

65. Turner, *Significance of the Frontier*, p. 57.

66. The book went through eleven editions in a matter of five years. Its success can in part be attributed to Riis's documentation of his own personalized experiences on the streets as well as to the powerful impact of his photographs, which were reproduced and included in the book. The timing of Riis's publication also helped to promote its popularity. It was issued originally in 1890, the same year that Commissioner Booth's *In Darkest England and the Way Out* and Ward McAllister's *Society As I Have Found It* appeared. Taken together, the three books reflected one of the major tensions of the age, the social contrasts of poverty and affluence. See also Riis's sequel, *A Ten Years' War: An Account of the Battle with the Slums in New York*.

67. See, for instance, the preface to Arthur Pember's *The Mysteries and Miseries of the Great Metropolis with Some Adventures in the Country: Being the Disguises and Surprises of a New-York Journalist*. Here Pember states: "More than one class of persons, I am inclined to think, will be apt to consider that an ordinary sense of propriety should lead me to apologize for publishing, for the benefit of one-half the world, some of my varied experiences while investigating how the other half lives." See also the

series of articles released in 1872, "Our Homeless Poor"; or, "How the Other Half of the World Lives."

68. Riis first began his experimentation with photography while a police reporter for the *Tribune*. He was originally accompanied by a party of amateur police photographers, but later he hired a professional to make the photos. Disappointed by his partner's shady business dealings, Riis got hold of a camera himself and thus commenced his amateur career as documentary photographer. Riis's ultimate interest in the camera was its usefulness in providing tangible evidence to his fervent moral appeal regarding "the other half." His clumsy and untutored handling of the flash-lit camera led to frequent overexposures, graininess, shadows, compositional intrusions, awkward framing, and inadequate control over contrast. Ironically, these amateurish mistakes often enhanced Riis's photos and inadvertently accommodated form to the grotesque finish of his subject matter. Riis's first photo was an overexposed shot of an open trench in Potter's Field. Rather than detract from the end result, the overexposure lent the photo its symbolic tonal effect. "The very blackness of my picture," Riis remarked, "proved later on, when I came to use it with a magic lantern, the taking feature of it. It added a gloom to the show more realistic than any the utmost art of professional skill might have attained." See Riis, *Making of an American*, p. 174. For high quality reproduction of Riis's photographs, see Alland, Sr., *Jacob A. Riis*, pp. 50–213.

69. Riis, *The Other Half*, p. 162.

70. Ibid., pp. 92, 101. Riis's role as a transitional figure in the perception of poverty and his abiding moral fervor ultimately precluded his embrace of this new and more inclusive interpretation of poverty. By the turn of the century, this new perspective, championed by progressives such as Robert Hunter, considered poverty in relation to economic, social, and political developments, thus countering the formerly held notion of poverty as an isolated phenomenon. Rather than adhere to an amorphous construct of want, the economic view defined poverty in terms of an objectified standard of living that was inadequate to support a household. Impersonal factors such as low wages, dangerous work settings, unemployment, poor health, risk and extent of industrial accidents, substandard housing, and child labor were all incorporated in describing the conditions of poverty. In addition, the poverty line was established so as to measure the extent of the problem in relation to a minimum level of annual income. These objective approaches to poverty externalized its condition and facilitated the collection of research data to support legislative improvements. For a thorough discussion of this new view of poverty, see Bremner, *From the Depths*, pp. 68–69, 83, 85, 123–125, 131, 135, 138, 152–153.

71. Ibid., pp. 32–33. Other similar examples of this merger between touristic motif and tonal emphasis can be found on pp. 23ff., 30ff., 82ff.

72. Ibid., pp. 54–55 and pl. 13.

73. Quoted in Szasz and Bogardus, "The Camera and the American Social Conscience," p. 431.

74. Riis admits that he prefers the thief to the tramp: "The older I get, the more patience I have with the sinner and the less with the lazy good-for-nothing who is at the bottom of more than half the share of the world's troubles. Give me the thief if need be, but take the tramp away and lock him up at hard labor until he is willing to fall in line and take up his end." See Riis, *Making of an American*, p. 163.

    Riis's derision of immigrant groups became more strident the further they diverged from the Judeo-Christian tradition. His hatred of the Chinese, and their purely alien ways, led him to describe their cultural heritage and religion as "ages of senseless idolatry, mere grub-worship." He saw no useful purpose to their presence in America and, infected by the "yellow peril," advised the following: "The severest official scrutiny, the harshest repressive measures are justifiable in Chinatown. . . . To the peril that threatens there all the senses are alert, whereas the poison that proceeds from Mott Street puts mind and body to sleep, to work out its deadly purpose in the corruption of the soul." See Riis, *The Other Half*, pp. 63, 69. Riis also had harsh words for the stale-beer dives and black-and-tan cellar saloons, which mixed races and genders. See ibid., pp. 50–54.

75. Ibid., pp. 166–167.

76. Ibid., p. 176. "Philanthropy and five percent" was the motto and practical program voiced by Alfred T. White, a builder and model tenement developer, and his followers. This type of voluntaristic tenement reform, self-regulated by a reasonable and not usurious interest rate, was viewed by Riis as the "gospel of justice, the solution that must be sought as the one alternative to the man with the knife." For Riis, the program was the material counterpart to the spiritual efforts raised by Protestant clergymen, who convened on the problem of urban poverty at Chickering Hall in 1888. Incidentally, Riis felt that the Chickering Hall convention on the religious dimension of poverty completely missed the crucial message contained by White's tenement reform appeal. Riis was, in fact, admonished by one minister for being too preoccupied with the material side of the problem. Riis's response to the minister who leveled the charge of ignoring the "inner man" attests to his transitional status: "You cannot expect to find an inner man to appeal to in the worst tenement house surroundings. You must first put the man where he can respect himself. To reverse the argument of the apple: you cannot expect to find a sound core in a rotten fruit" (p. 176).

77. See Cady, ed., *W. D. Howells as Critic*, p. 83.

78. Ibid., pp. 114–115. The views of the opposing position are adequately

summarized by Charles Dudley Warner, who asserts that "art requires an idealization of nature." For an elaboration of his position regarding the role of the novel, see Warner, *Relation of Literature to Life*, pp. 135–151.

79. Ibid., p. 94. Incidentally, the "more smiling aspects" passage was contained in a *Harper's Monthly* editorial column written in September 1886. The quote is not entirely representative of Howells's later period that followed the events of the Haymarket Riot, in which the author took a more serious and critical view of American society.

In regard to Howells's conception of the universe as an expression of divine purpose, he writes: "In life [the realist] finds nothing insignificant; all tells for destiny and character; nothing that God has made is contemptible. . . . He feels in every nerve the quality of things and the unity of men; his soul is exalted, not by vain shows and shadows and ideals, but by realities, in which alone the truth lives" (p. 83).

80. Howells's social vision was influenced simultaneously by the Haymarket Riot and his reading of Tolstoy. Both event and writer brought Howells to an awareness of the larger social values and responsibilities in the relationship of man to society. For the influence of Tolstoy upon Howells, see Altha Leah Bass, "The Social Consciousness of William Dean Howells," *New Republic*, April 13, 1921, pp. 192–194.

The influence of the Haymarket Riot is evident in a letter Howells wrote to Henry James in 1888, two years after its occurrence: "I should hardly like to trust pen and ink with all the audacity of my social ideas; but after fifty years of optimistic contact with 'civilization' and its ability to come out all right in the end, I now abhor it, and feel that it is coming out all wrong in the end, unless it bases itself anew on a real equality." Quoted from Van Wyck Brooks, *New England: Indian Summer, 1865–1915* (New York: E. P. Dutton and Company, 1940), p. 382, footnote.

Howells's transition to Christian socialism was entered by way of older Christian values and contemporary readings of American reformers and utopian authors. He was led to a middle-class understanding of socialism, not by Marx or Lasalle, but by Edward Bellamy's novels and Fabian Clubs, Lawrence Gronlund's utopias, Henry George's land reform schemes, and, of course, the teachings of Moses and Jesus. Howells's fusion of the old moralism with a new social program for justice was accomplished by a fundamental adherence to Christian values and the republican creed of divine individualism. The method for social change was evolutionary, along the lines of Darwinian thought. For an account which typifies this brand of socialism, see Irvine's discussion, *Bottom Up*, pp. 285–291.

81. Parrington, *Main Currents*, pp. 237, 242.

82. Ibid., pp. 252–253.

83. Howells, "Tribulations of a Cheerful Giver," in *Impressions and Experiences*, p. 163.

84. Ibid. The events of this encounter are contained in Howells's chapter.

85. Ibid., p. 183.
86. In Howells, "The Midnight Platoon," in *Literature and Life*, pp. 154–160, esp. p. 159.
87. Ibid., p. 160.
88. Howells, "New York Streets," in *Impressions and Experiences*, pp. 251–252.
89. Ibid., pp. 252–253.
90. Howells, *A Hazard of New Fortunes*, p. 56.
91. Ibid., pp. 159–160.
92. Parrington, *Main Currents*, 3: 252.

3. DESCENT AND DISCOVERY

1. Crane, "The Open Boat," in Stallman, ed., *Stories and Tales*, p. 236.
2. Quoted from Katz, ed., *The Complete Poems*, p. 125.
3. Crane, "The Open Boat," p. 233.
4. Katz, ed., *The Complete Poems*, p. 52.
5. Parrington, *Main Currents*, 3: 325.
6. Kazin, *On Native Grounds*, p. 15.
7. See Stallman and Gilkes, eds., *Letters*, pp. 159–160.
8. For a fuller discussion on the permutations of classical Aristotelian textual elements (scene-agent-agency-purpose-act-attitude), see Kenneth Burke's analysis of the hexadic structure, which illuminates the significance of its various dramatistic ratios. Contained in "Dramatism," pp. 445–452, and in *A Grammar of Motives*, esp. part 1, chap. 1, "Container and Things Contained."
9. Pizer, *Realism and Naturalism*, p. 31, italics mine.
10. Ibid., p. 14.
11. Quoted from Moers, *Two Dreisers*, p. xvi.
12. Proponents of this liberal movement in the 1890s, such as Howells, Edward Bellamy, Henry George, Robert La Follette, and Thorstein Veblen, were linked by their refutation of an "individualistic, Spencerian doctrine." They were thus drawn to a more collectivistic approach to American society. Concerning Crane's aesthetic relationship to this movement, Russel B. Nye distinguishes between the author's dual vision of nature and society: "He [Crane] did not let a naturalistic view of the universe lead him into an amoral social philosophy of survival of the fittest, of life as a state of war on the social level. . . . The cleavage in Crane's philosophy seemingly is explained thus: the forces of destiny are blind and impersonal and cannot be conquered, as we see in 'The Open Boat'; but the forces of society, those which lead to the social evil seen in *Maggie* and other stories, are man-made forces, and can be controlled by man, who set them in motion. The world of nature we can only face with stoicism; the

world of society, however, can be reshaped—progress is possible on the human and social level. The individual, then, Crane feels, must adjust himself to two spheres of life." See Nye's article, "Stephen Crane as Social Critic," in Gullason, ed., *Crane's Career*, pp. 221–227, esp. pp. 224–225.

13. See Pinkus, ed., *Conversations with Lukács*, pp. 117–118.

14. Ibid., p. 42.

15. Stallman and Gilkes recount the publishing venture: "Published in mustard-yellow covers, this page-bound *Maggie*, priced at 50 cents, sold not at all. In 1930, however, this first edition was described as 'the rarest in modern literature,' an inscribed copy then fetching $3,700. Having given away about a hundred copies to friends (out of the 1,110 copies printed in 1893), and having used the remainder to kindle his boardinghouse stove, Crane himself possessed only one copy in 1896. The number of extant copies known to collectors was reported in 1937 to be fewer than thirty. . . . But most of these copies were chipped, torn, or stained. They had been stored in a wagon-house for twenty years and mice had nibbled them." Thus went the birth of modern American literature, consumed by fire and eroded by those delectably discriminating rodents. See Stallman and Gilkes, eds., *Letters*, pp. 12–13.

16. Beer, *Stephen Crane*, pp. 96–97.

17. Ibid.

18. Between 1892 and 1896, Crane had published *Maggie, George's Mother, The Red Badge of Courage, The Black Riders*, and most of his "Midnight Sketches." Crane had thought highly of his short sketches and considered them to be among his "best work." In a letter written to his brother William, just prior to sailing off on the *Commodore*, Crane reveals the significance of these sketches. The letter is actually a fragment of Crane's will constructed before his shipwrecked misadventure, retold in "The Open Boat." Though an early draft of the will was lost, this letter attests to its existence. Crane instructs his brother: "[The collecting of my stories] will make considerable work, but there are some of them which I would hate to see lost. Some of my best work is contained in short things which I have written for various publications, principally the New York Press in 1893 [1894] or thereabouts. There are some 15 or 20 short sketches of New York street life and so on which I intended to have published under the title of 'Midnight Sketches.' That should be your first care." Quoted from Stallman and Gilkes, eds., *Letters*, p. 135.

19. Berryman, *Stephen Crane*, p. 288.

20. Crane's pronouncement regarding "the eternal mystery of social conditions" is contained in his sketch, "An Experiment in Luxury," in Stallman and Hagemann, eds., *New York City Sketches*, pp. 46–47.

21. Crane's study of a Bowery breadline was originally prompted by Hamlin Garland. As Garland was feeding the hungry artist one evening, he sug-

gested to Crane: "Why don't you go down and do a study of this midnight bread distribution which the papers are making so much of? Mr. Howells suggested it to me, but it isn't my field. It is yours. You could do it beyond anybody." Garland's mention of the papers may be a reference to the relief activities of the New York *Herald*, *World*, and *Tribune* during the depression years 1893 and 1894. Each newspaper provided sensational coverage of its own charitable practices (see chap. 2, p. 38) or it might simply be an allusion to Fleischmann's midnight breadline on the corner of Broadway and 9th Street. In any case, Garland's intuition of Crane's talents in working up such material proved accurate. See Stallman and Gilkes, eds., *Letters*, pp. 302–303.

22. For the original 1894 publication of the sketch which includes this opening frame, see Stallman and Hagemann, eds., *New York City Sketches*, pp. 33–34.
23. Ibid., p. 34. The opening and closing frames of the sketch were deleted from its reprint in an 1898 collection, as well as from all subsequent republications. Crane's purpose in dropping the envelope structure was, as Alan Trachtenberg rightfully puts it, "to intensify attention on the experience itself, and to indicate that the social drama of displacing one's normal perspective already is internalized in the action." In the sketch's revision, the purpose of the youth's experiment is simply stated without the expository intrusion of the opening frame: "He was going forth to eat as the wanderer may eat, and sleep as the homeless sleep." There are other changes in the sketch's republication which suggest Crane's interest in integrating a more forceful pattern of imagery in order to specify and reinforce a sense of misery. For instance, the revised presentation of the elevated railroad in the introductory pages is more forcefully depicted and its interrelationship with the latter image of grinding wheels becomes a more clarified cross-reference than in the original. As Trachtenberg writes: "These revisions and others suggest an intention more fully realized: the creation of physical equivalents to the inner experience of a 'moral region' of misery." See Trachtenberg's informative article, "Experiments in Another Country," pp. 265–285, quoted from pp. 280–281.
24. Stallman, ed., *Stephen Crane*, p. 27. Unless otherwise noted, the following quotations from the revised sketch which appear in the first section of this chapter are taken from the above edition, pp. 27–38.
25. Victor Turner, "Betwixt and Between: The Liminal Period in Rites de Passage," in William A. Lessa and Evon Z. Vogt, eds., *Reader in Comparative Religion: An Anthropological Approach* (New York: Harper and Row, 1979), p. 241. Turner also notes that "during the liminal period, neophytes are alternately forced and encouraged to think about their society, their cosmos, and the powers that generate and sustain them. Liminality may be partly described as a stage of reflection" (p. 240). For a more complete discussion of social antistructure and the liminal stage of

the *rite de passage,* see Turner's *The Ritual Process* and *Dramas, Fields, and Metaphors.*

26. This closing frame to the originally published edition of the sketch is quoted from Stallman and Hagemann, eds., *New York City Sketches,* p. 43. A contradiction presents itself here in the correspondence between text and autobiographical material. In a response to a Miss Catherine Harris, a seemingly missionary type, Crane wrote in 1896, two years after the publication of his "Experiment" and in the overall context of *Maggie* and missions: "I do not think that much can be done with the Bowery as long as the [word blurred] are in their present state of conceit. A person who thinks himself superior to the rest of us because he has no job and no pride and no clean clothes is as badly conceited as Lillian Russell. In a story of mine called 'An Experiment in Misery,' I tried to make plain that the root of Bowery life is a sort of cowardice. Perhaps I mean a lack of ambition or to willingly be knocked flat and accept the licking." Quoted from Stallman and Gilkes, eds., *Letters,* p. 133.

Perhaps Crane had tailored his letter to suit the particular prejudices of his reader, Miss Harris. Or, perhaps the mixed chemistry of the ironist had caught him in a critical mood of cool detachment, leading him to discount a formerly held position. But assuming that Crane meant what he wrote to Miss Harris, what can we make of this radical discounting of the disparity between text and authorial comment? A close reading of the ideology inscribed in the sketch makes it plain that Crane did not reduce Bowery life to a root sense of cowardice. Conceit, superiority, false pride, and heroism are clearly alien constructs in summarizing Crane's treatment of the Bowery subculture. A virulent critic could not have distorted the social meaning of an "Experiment" any better than Crane had done with his own confusing admission. It is as if he had rewritten the synopsis of the sketch, as many of those modern jacket descriptions provided by publishing firms do which bear no relationship whatsoever to the contents of the text. Clearly, the attitude expressed in the sketch bears an incongruous relationship to its author's later opinions. If Crane's mood in writing to Miss Harris was indeed an enduring ideological trait, we can only conclude that his own "considerable alteration" in perspective brought about by virtue of the "Experiment" was short-lived. Perhaps fame and a measure of fortune (by the time of his letter Crane's *Red Badge,* a bestseller in 1895, had made him a successful author both in America and England) had reestablished and hardened the social distance between culture and sub-culture which he had so artfully taken to task in a previous period of his career.

His struggling New York period, one of hunger, invisibility, pain, and liminality, most likely prepared Crane for his empathic treatment of sub-culture, drawing him to its side. If his later opinions were true in their overriding discount of the insights gleaned from this period, a problem for biographers to disentangle, then Crane had slipped back into the domain of culture, donning its perceptual template of social conditions. Yet the ironist is never pure. In his later life, while living at Brede Place in England, Crane was accused by one faction of emulating the aristocracy and by another for parodying it. Such is the fate of the ironist. Yet the picture of Crane dwarfed by the bulkhead of his desk in the Brede Place study is hardly the same portrait of the writer crapped-out in a Bowery lodging house. Perhaps the lesson learned from Howells's self-admonishment will illuminate the distance: "The whole spectacle of poverty . . . is incredible. As soon as you cease to have it before your eyes,—even when you have it before your eyes,—you can hardly believe it. . . . When I get back into my own comfortable room, among my papers and books, I remember it as I remember something at the theatre. It seems to be turned off, as Niagara does, when you come away" (see chap. 2, p. 77). Howells's culture had finally claimed Crane as one of its own, despite his equivocation. The ultimate lesson through all of this, however, is to trust the immanent features of the text, features which do not equivocate or dissemble in their representation of social purpose and ideological form.

27. In Stallman and Hagemann, eds., *New York City Sketches*, p. 51. Unless otherwise noted, the following quotations from "An Experiment in Luxury" which appear in the first section of this chapter are taken from the above edition, pp. 43–51.

28. Turner, *Dramas, Fields, and Metaphors*, pp. 46–47.

29. Ibid., p. 47. Though beyond the scope of this essay, this dialectic between structure and antistructure speaks to one of the dominant conflicts of the Gilded Age; that is, to the tension between an increasingly differentiated social hierarchy, what Trachtenberg refers to as an "ethos of incorporation," and its corrective antithesis expressed, for instance, by Bellamy's "religion of solidarity," an attitude referred to again by Trachtenberg as an "ethos of mutuality." See Trachtenberg, *Incorporation*, pp. 93–100, 110, 112.

This division in thought, social allegiance, and political action was repeatedly manifested in the growing collectivist movement of the 1880s and 1890s. The challenge to the integrated pattern of industrial capitalism (structure) can be witnessed by the activities of such countercultures as the Knights of Labor, the Nationalist Clubs, the Farmer's Alliance or Populist movement, the Social Gospel efforts, Christian socialism, and the general attempt at the unionization of labor. In their voices of dissent, all represented a type of normative *communitas* which sought to replace the principle of competition (the moving force of inequality) with that of cooperation (the mode of equality, an organic unity of the people).

This contention between structure and antistructure was actualized in both a historic and a critical sense, promoting efforts at social change and a redirection in social theory. The division is again embodied in the age—in

Veblen's distinction between the "invidious" forms of the leisure class, negativized in terms of predatory motivation and pecuniary emulation, and the positive qualities of the "non-invidious," represented by the industrial workmanlike values of peaceful cooperation and collective productivity; in Bellamy's utopian vision, which asserted the law of solidarity over Carnegie's opposing law of accumulation of wealth; among the Christian socialists' (Bliss, Herron, Rauschenbusch, Bellamy, Gronlund, etc.) attempt to fuse a transfigured Marxian socialism, devoid of the class struggle, with a divine Darwinian evolution, assuming Spencer's organic interpretation of society while dropping his individualistic position in order to arrive at the "Kingdom of God"; and in Henry Adams's taut symbolic opposition between the Virgin and the dynamo, respectively, the very difference between aesthetic unity and industrial multiplicity. The list can be expanded upon, but the gist of the dialectic suggests itself here. Perhaps no other era in American history, including the depression years of the 1930s and the counterculture movement of the 1960s, summarizes so succinctly and in so many related spheres of activity the generative interaction between the domains of structure and antistructure as the Gilded Age, a period of unprecedented incorporation and refutation.

30. It appears to me that social differentiation (present in the ordering of human affairs) naturally breeds conflict and discord. Thus the class distinctions given in a social system are by nature factional, one class pitted against the other, as opposed to the universal virtues aimed at by religion—harmony. We may conclude that, whereas the upper, middle, and lower classes are caught in a social net of conflict, the Bowery as an underclass, as a tension beneath the tension, may signify an almost religious quality by its implicit moral criticism of an inequitable social system. The cultural significance of the Bowery can be revealed through an evocation of its visibility. Seen from this perspective, the Bowery homeless might then connote the stripping away of the discrete categorization of urban civilization. The counterpose is that of essential man hovering in community, an act of primitive solidarity, far beneath the precipice. For Crane, this may very well account for the resonant meaning of the Bowery as an imaginative construct (symbolically charged and fortified by blizzard imagery).

31. For interpretive and documentary accounts of Stieglitz's photographs, including *Winter on Fifth Avenue*, see Frank et al., eds., *America and Alfred Stieglitz*; Norman, *Alfred Stieglitz*; and Rosenfeld's tribute, "Alfred Stieglitz," in his *Port of New York*, pp. 237–279. Though a fine reproduction of *Winter on Fifth Avenue* is contained in the Norman text, the reader is advised to view the excellent reproduction of the photograph, the closest approximation to the original gravure extant, in Greenough and Hamilton, *Alfred Stieglitz*.

In Stieglitz's own account of his seminal photograph, he writes: "I have

always loved snow, mist, fog, rain, deserted streets. All seemed attuned
to my feelings about life in the early 1890s." Regarding his studies of the
Lower East Side, he notes: "I felt that the people near by, in spite of their
poverty, were better off than I was. . . . There was a reality about them
lacking in the artificial world." Both statements suggest an affinity for the
atmospherics and conditions of antistructure and *communitas*, a feeling for
that forcible presence of reality "lacking in the artificial world"; that is, the
world of formalized social structure. Stieglitz's accounts are quoted from
Norman, *An American Seer*, pp. 36, 39, respectively.
32. As described by Trachtenberg, "Experiments," p. 275.
33. Stallman, ed., *Stories and Tales*, p. 19. Unless otherwise noted, the fol-
    lowing quotations from "The Men in the Storm" which appear in the
    second section of this chapter are taken from the above edition, pp. 19-26.
34. For a discussion of the influence of these two precedents upon Dreiser,
    see Ellen Moers's critical study, *Two Dreisers*, pp. 10–14, 38, 61–69.
    Regarding the general significance of blizzard imagery during the 1890s,
    Moers writes: "Because of Stieglitz and the artists who followed him,
    because of Crane and the literary journalists, perhaps because of Howells'
    perception that New York was not entirely unlike Tolstoy's wintery
    Moscow, and finally because of *Sister Carrie*, the blizzard came to mean to
    New York what fog had long meant to London—the city's unique sign, its
    hard challenge to the eye and to the spirit. Blizzard was the first contribu-
    tion of the nineties to the iconography of a city which, until that decade,
    had had virtually no literature and no art of its own" (p. 13).
         Concerning the impact of Crane's sketch, "The Men in the Storm,"
    upon Dreiser's own Bowery realism, Moers notes: "It is evident . . . that
    Dreiser studied Crane's treatment of this subject—his mannered, highly
    colored, essentially painterly use of words in the service of realism" (p.
    38). Dreiser may not have noticed the original 1894 publication of Crane's
    sketch in the *Arena*, but there is no doubt that he was made sharply aware
    of the sketch's 1897 reprint in the *Philistine*, for George C. Jenks had run
    a review of it in Dreiser's magazine, *Ev'ry Month*. Dreiser's own treat-
    ment of the Bowery homeless waiting before the closed doors of a lodging
    house first appeared in *Demorest's Family Magazine* in November 1899
    under the title, "Curious Shifts of the Poor," pp. 22–26. Sections of the
    piece, which describes four scenes of mass begging in New York City,
    were reworked into the ending of *Sister Carrie*, charting Hurstwood's final
    decline (fragments of the article appear in chaps. 45 and 47 of the 1900
    Doubleday, Page and Company first edition and in chaps. 48 and 50 of the
    1981 University of Pennsylvania restored edition). In the Doubleday, Page
    and Company publication, "Curious Shifts of the Poor" also appears as a
    chapter title for number 45. The lodging house scene, which concludes
    the novel in the restored edition, is the one which closely resembles
    Crane's sketch. Over the years, in the various reprintings of Dreiser's

"Curious Shifts of the Poor," he eventually dropped the heading and adopted "The Men in the Storm." As Moers suggests, Dreiser's title revision reveals an implicit indebtedness to Crane's sketch. In Dreiser's 1923 collection of urban sketches, *The Color of a Great City*, the heading "The Men in the Storm" appears in lieu of "Curious Shifts." Equally significant in this edition of the sketch is the sense of narrative restriction, for instead of four scenes of collective poverty, Dreiser presents only one—the lodging house line. Both designation and content are thus mutually arranged in alignment with Crane's literary study.

35. Theodore Dreiser, "The Camera Club of New York," pp. 328–329; cf. Dreiser, "A Master of Photography," p. 471.

36. The phrase is William Kennedy's from his novel *Ironweed* (New York: Penguin Books, 1983), p. 16. Though Kennedy's phrase appears in a different context, I am adapting the essence of it, the erasure of human traces, to suit the pattern of Hurstwood's descent.

37. Theodore Dreiser, "A Wayplace of the Fallen," in *The Color of a Great City*, p. 181.

38. Theodore Dreiser, *Sister Carrie* (New York: Penguin Books, 1981), p. 45. Unless otherwise noted, the following quotations from the novel which appear in this chapter are taken from the above restored edition.

The text of the above edition is a photo-offset reproduction of the Pennsylvania edition of *Sister Carrie*, Neda M. Westlake, general editor (Philadelphia: University of Pennsylvania Press, 1981). The text presented in both editions is authoritative and restores Dreiser's original manuscript, which ends with Hurstwood's suicide rather than with the nebulous philosophical abstractions of Carrie's romantic dissatisfaction. Taken in its entirety, the restored edition of *Sister Carrie* presents the reader with an entirely new text, one that compels critical reevaluation. My preference for the Penguin edition was solely determined by its portability and by the fact that I could claim ownership to it for a reasonable $3.95 plus tax. I have consulted the Historical Commentary section of the Pennsylvania edition and urge the reader to do the same. It is an invaluable contribution to modern Dreiser scholarship, presenting a thorough treatment of both historical and textual materials. For the significance of the restored edition, particularly concerning the reinstatement of Dreiser's originally intended ending, which fulfills the tragic design of the novel, I defer to the editors: "The manuscript of the novel preserves Dreiser's text in an uncorrupted state—before Arthur Henry, Jug [Dreiser's first wife], the typists, the publishers, and the printers began adding layers of censoring, cutting, editing, and error. The Pennsylvania edition . . . presents a text of *Sister Carrie* which is very close to what Dreiser first conceived and wrote. The Pennsylvania edition also restores Dreiser's original ending for the novel, the ending that his initial instinct told him was right. . . . It is in fact a new work of art, heretofore unknown,

which must be approached freshly and interpreted anew. The Pennsylvania *Sister Carrie* differs from the Doubleday, Page *Sister Carrie* most
markedly in characterization, philosophy, and theme. In its expanded
form, *Sister Carrie* is infinitely richer, more complex, and more tragic than
it was before" (p. 532). For an account of the most significant revision of
all, the alteration of the novel's original ending, see pp. 514–519.

39. I am indebted to Moers's study, *Two Dreisers*, pp. 6–7, for bringing this to
my attention.

40. Quoted from ibid., pp. 55–56.

41. Dreiser's imagery of men "melted inward, like logs floating," then disap-
pearing, is an analogue to Crane's more perfervid description of the men
as a "thick stream" and "turbulent water."

In this passage, Dreiser seems to have directly transfigured one of
Crane's sentences, displacing its position within the sequence of events.
Dreiser: "It was just six o'clock and there was supper in every hurrying
pedestrian's face." Crane: "There was an absolute expression of hot dinners in the pace of the people." Dreiser follows the sentence with "and yet
no supper was provided here—nothing but beds." Crane follows his sentence, several lines down, with "there was a collection of men to whom
these things were as if they were not." Crane provides the precedent and
Dreiser follows. The excerpts from both writers reveal a rhythm of statement and counter-statement, the presence of culture contrasted to that of
subculture. While Dreiser is more mundane in his style, Crane strikes a
poetic sensibility. Yet in this example, Dreiser not only appropriates the
sense of Crane's technique but comes close to taking him at his very
word.

42. According to Aristotle, acts are compulsory "when the cause is in the
external circumstances and the agent contributes nothing. . . . The compulsory, then, seems to be that whose moving principle is outside, the
person compelled contributing nothing," thus, the fatalistic exclamation "I
have no choice!" as in the tragic phrase of Agamemnon prefacing the
sacrifice of his daughter, Iphigenia. Similarly, Hurstwood's own statement
of finitude at the end of the novel: "What's the use." Though the immense
difference between classic and modern tragedy is obvious (the paradig-
matic shift from religion to science), the sense of fatality, of constricted
limits, is structurally homologous. It could be argued whether or not
Hurstwood, as agent or character, contributed to his own demise—the
character of his act. But, overall, he does seem to be a tragic antihero, an
agent acting *in* ignorance and not through the pretext of ignorance. Aristotle writes: "Everything that is done by reason of ignorance is *not* voluntary: it is only what produces pain and regret that is *in*voluntary." An
involuntary agent (in a scene-agent ratio) depends upon "ignorance of
particulars, that is, of the circumstances of the action and the objects with
which it is concerned. For it is on these that both pity and pardon depend,

since the person who is ignorant of any of these acts involuntarily." Thus, in retrospect, one's life appears fated, turning upon an act, such as the stolen money, of which the consequences are unforeseen. The tragic reversal is activated by this pivotal turning of events. An agent-scene ratio would reformulate the pattern as such: "Since that which is done under compulsion or by reason of ignorance is involuntary, the voluntary would seem to be that of which the moving principle is in the agent himself, he being aware of the particular circumstances of the action." *The Nichomachean Ethics of Aristotle, 1110a–1111b1*, trans. Sir David Ross (London: Oxford University Press, 1963), quoted from pp. 49–50, 51, 52.

4. BOWERY TALES

1. Bennett, *Formalism and Marxism*, p. 20. See Bennett for a full discussion of the concept and formalist technique, especially in the context of Grotesque Realism and the medieval ritual of Carnival.
2. For a reprint of this earlier edition, which includes the full title, see Katz, ed., *Portable Stephen Crane*, pp. 3–74. The above edition is a reprint of Crane's self-published manuscript issued originally in 1893. At the time of its first edition, *Maggie* had already undergone four revisions.
3. Quoted from *Maggie: A Girl of the Streets*, in Stallman, ed., *Stephen Crane*, p. 102. Unless otherwise noted, the following quotations from the latest revised edition which appear in this chapter are taken from the above collection. There are several drafts and revised editions of *Maggie*, but the one contained in Stallman is considered the authoritative and final revision of the novella.
4. Brennan, "Ironic and Symbolic Structure," in Gullason, ed., *Crane's Career*, p. 326. Except for the quoted statement, Brennan's article is an otherwise flawless examination of Crane's highly crafted literary style and technique.
5. Solomon, *Stephen Crane*, p. 32. Though I take issue with Solomon's evaluation concerning Crane's motivation in writing *Maggie*, I find his thesis (the progression of Crane's literary art from parody to realism) to be a fresh and compelling framework in which to appreciate the author's artistic career.
6. Knight, *Critical Period*, p. 112.
7. Donald Pizer, "Stephen Crane's *Maggie* and American Naturalism," in Gullason, ed., *Crane's Career*, p. 339.
8. Frye, *Anatomy*, p. 47.
9. Riis, *The Other Half*, p. 106.
10. Frye, *Anatomy*, p. 48.
11. Pizer, *"Maggie,"* in Gullason, ed., *Crane's Career*, p. 340.
12. The rhythm of sound which Crane employs to evoke the gruesome

claustrophobia of tenement conditions is eloquently expressed in the following passage. In the passage, the sounds within the tenement flat weave
together with the sounds of the building and street, composing a rever-
beration which unites in a crescendo of activity. "Above the muffled roar of
conversation, the dismal wailings of babies at night, the thumping of feet in
unseen corridors and rooms, and the sound of varied hoarse shoutings in
the street and the rattling of wheels over cobbles, they heard the screams
of the child and the roars of the mother die away to a feeble moaning and a
subdued bass muttering." *Maggie*, in Stallman, ed., *Stories and Tales*, pp.
46–47.

13. Knight, *Critical Period*, p. 112.
14. Crane's depiction of the Bowery theater and related forms of entertainment implicitly asserts their dependence upon a normative standard for
the consumption of leisure. Focusing on the top layer of wealth and reputation, Thorstein Veblen, in *The Theory of the Leisure Class*, revealed how
the divisive issues of class and status are unified through the consumer-
oriented mechanisms of social purchase, imitation, "pecuniary emulation,"
and display: "The leisure class stands at the head of the social structure.
. . . The result is that the members of each stratum accept as their ideal of
decency the scheme of life in vogue in the next higher stratum, and bend
their energies to live up to that ideal" (p. 70).

For the Bowery, the next highest stratum might be embodied in Carrie
Madenda and her appearance within the Broadway theater. Dreiser
makes explicit Crane's indirection, completing in detail the cultural frame
of reference which overdetermines Bowery leisure. Dreiser's Carrie lends
palpable form to the guiding paradigm of leisure. The qualities of its
"showy parade" are visibly apparent both indoors and out, whether dining
at Sherry's or promenading up Broadway. Regarding the former, Dreiser
writes, "in every direction were mirrors—tall, brilliant, bevel-edged mirrors, re-reflecting and reflecting forms, faces and candelabra a score and a
hundred times." Carrie fades into the general condition of American urban
society during the 1890s, a society intent more on the collective consumption of goods and leisure than upon their production. In response to this
condition of affluence and the narcissism that it fosters, Dreiser philoso-
phizes: men are "more mirrors than engines." See Dreiser's *Sister Carrie*,
pp. 332, 78, respectively.

Crane's own direct criticism of American society's transition from a
production-oriented to a consumer-minded culture is stated succinctly
within his scathing report on the parade of the Junior Order of United
American Mechanics at Asbury Park. "Asbury Park creates nothing,"
Crane writes. "It does not make; it merely amuses." These lines are
perhaps the most benevolent ones in the entire piece, but the theme is of
interest here. *Maggie* reiterates subtly this same concern—the cultural
neglect of America's productive capacity and the supplanting infatuation

with leisure. As Maggie reaches the end of her suicide walk, she stands in the midst of black factories in the "gloomy districts near the river." The glitter and leisure of urban culture is far removed from this "fringe" of alienation, a comment on the descent of both character and social value. For Crane, it is not so much industrial exploitation that prompts Maggie's death as it is the false moral code of a commercial culture driven by its own self-generating ethos and marketplace values. The result is a regimented view of the masses with that "metropolitan seal upon their faces," the unmistakable stamp of urban indifference. See Crane, "On the New Jersey Coast," in Stallman, ed., *Stories and Tales*, p. 167; and *Maggie*, in Stallman, ed., *Stories and Tales*, pp. 98, 96.

15. For a reprint of Crane's interview with Howells, see "Howells Fears Realists Must Wait," in Stallman, ed., *Stories and Tales*, pp. 163–166, esp. p. 166.

16. Solomon, *Parody to Realism*, p. 57.

17. Quoted from *George's Mother*, in Stallman, ed., *Stories and Tales*, p. 105. Unless otherwise noted, the following quotations from this edition of the novella which appear in this chapter are taken from the above collection.

18. For the full context of his use of the phrase "absent cause," see Jameson, *Political Unconscious*, pp. 35–36.

CONCLUSION

1. Geertz, *Interpretation of Cultures*, p. 49.
2. Ibid., p. 89.
3. Kenneth Burke, "Over-All View," a paper presented by Burke to the Graduate Institute of Liberal Arts during a symposium held in his honor, 1983.
4. Geertz, *Interpretation*, p. 216.
5. Ibid., p. 453.
6. See Caplow et al., "Homelessness," p. 494.
7. Ibid., p. 495. For further discussions on the construct of disaffiliation and the homeless, see Bahr and Caplow, "Homelessness, Affiliation, and Occupational Mobility," pp. 28–33; Bahr, *Skid Row*; and Bogue, *Skid Row in American Cities*.
8. Main, "The Homeless of New York," p. 18.
9. For two recent articles that address the complexity and breadth of contemporary homelessness in terms of composition, characteristics, and interpretation, see Marin, "Helping and Hating the Homeless," pp. 39–49; and Rossi et al., "The Urban Homeless," pp. 1336–1341.
10. See, for instance, Jackson and Conner, "The Skid Row Alcoholic," pp. 468–486; Rooney, "Group Processes among Skid Row Winos," pp. 444–460; Wallace, *Skid Row as a Way of Life* and "The Road to Skid Row," pp.

92–105; and Spradley, *You Owe Yourself a Drunk.* In addressing the importance of nonalcoholic behavior on Seattle's Skid Row, Spradley ascertained over one hundred discrete semantic categories the men employ to designate various sleeping accommodations in their environment, thus attesting to the complexity of their conceptual framework for both adaptive and communicative purposes.

11. See Douglas, *Purity and Danger,* p. 128.
12. Burke, *Attitudes toward History,* p. 144.
13. Burke, *Permanence and Change,* p. 195.
14. See Rossi et al., "Urban Homeless," p. 1336.
15. Contained in *Homelessness in America,* p. 34.
16. Ibid., p. 23.
17. Contained in Mark Pazniokas's article "Federal Official Advises Mayors to Seek State Money for Homeless," in the Hartford *Courant,* January 18, 1985.

SELECTED BIBLIOGRAPHY

CULTURE STUDIES: CRITICAL THEORY AND METHODS

Benjamin, Walter. *Reflections*. Trans. Edmund Jephcott. New York: Harcourt Brace Jovanovich, 1978.

Bennett, Tony. *Formalism and Marxism*. London: Methuen and Company, 1979.

Burke, Kenneth. *Attitudes toward History*. Boston: Beacon Press, 1937.

————. "Dramatism." *International Encyclopedia of the Social Sciences*, vol. 7, 1968, pp. 445–452.

————. *A Grammar of Motives*. New York: Prentice-Hall, 1952.

————. *Language as Symbolic Action: Essays on Life, Literature, and Method*. Berkeley and Los Angeles: University of California Press, 1966.

————. "Literature as Equipment for Living." In Hazard Adams, ed., *Critical Theory since Plato*, New York: Harcourt Brace Jovanovich, 1971, pp. 942–947.

————. *Permanence and Change: An Anatomy of Purpose*. Los Altos, Calif.: Hermes Publications, 1954.

————. *Philosophy of Literary Form: Studies in Symbolic Action*. Baton Rouge: Louisiana State University Press, 1941.

Douglas, Ann. *The Feminization of American Culture*. New York: Avon Books, 1977.

Douglas, Mary. *Purity and Danger: An Analysis of the Concepts of Pollution and Taboo*. London: Routledge and Kegan Paul, 1966.

————. *The World of Goods: Toward an Anthropology of Consumption*. New York: W. W. Norton and Company, 1979.

Frye, Northrop. *Anatomy of Criticism*. Princeton, N.J.: Princeton University Press, 1957.

Geertz, Clifford. *The Interpretation of Cultures*. New York: Basic Books, 1973.

Grimsted, David. *Melodrama Unveiled: American Theater and Culture, 1800–1850*. Chicago: University of Chicago Press, 1968.

Jameson, Fredric R. *Marxism and Form*. Princeton, N.J.: Princeton University Press, 1971.

————. *The Political Unconscious: Narrative as a Socially Symbolic Act*. Ithaca, N.Y.: Cornell University Press, 1981.

————. *The Prison-House of Language*. Princeton, N.J.: Princeton University Press, 1972.

Kuklick, Bruce. "Myth and Symbol in American Studies." *American Quarterly* 24 (October 1972): 435–450.

Liebow, Elliot. *Tally's Corner: A Study of Negro Streetcorner Men.* Boston
and Toronto: Little, Brown and Company, 1967.

Lukács, Georg. *History and Class Consciousness: Studies in Marxist
Dialectics.* Trans. Rodney Livingstone. Cambridge, Mass.: MIT Press,
1968.

———. *Realism in Our Time: Literature and the Class Struggle.* Trans.
John and Necke Mander. New York: Harper and Row, 1964.

Marcus, George E., and Fischer, Michael M. J. *Anthropology as Cultural
Critique: An Experimental Moment in the Human Sciences.* Chicago and
London: University of Chicago Press, 1986.

McCall, George J., and Simmons, J. L., eds. *Issues in Participant
Observation.* Reading, Mass.: Addison-Wesley Publishing Company, 1969.

Percy, Walker. *The Message in the Bottle.* New York: Farrar, Straus and
Giroux, 1975.

Pinkus, Theo, ed. *Conversations with Lukács.* Cambridge, Mass.: MIT
Press, 1967.

Sontag, Susan. *On Photography.* New York: Dell Publishing Company,
1977.

Spradley, James P. *You Owe Yourself a Drunk: An Ethnography of Urban
Nomads.* Boston: Little, Brown and Company, 1970.

Stack, Carol B. *All Our Kin: Strategies for Survival in a Black Community.*
New York, Evanston, San Francisco, and London: Harper and Row,
1974.

Trachtenberg, Alan. *The Incorporation of America: Culture and Society in
the Gilded Age.* New York: Hill and Wang, 1982.

Turner, Victor. *Dramas, Fields, and Metaphors: Symbolic Action in Human
Society.* Ithaca, N.Y.: Cornell University Press, 1974.

———. *The Ritual Process: Structure and Anti-Structure.* Chicago: Aldine,
1969.

Wallace, Samuel. *Skid Row as a Way of Life.* Totawa, N.J.: Bedminster
Press, 1965.

White, Hayden, and Brose, Margaret, eds. *Representing Kenneth Burke.*
Baltimore: Johns Hopkins University Press, 1982.

Wise, Gene. "'Paradigm Dramas' in American Studies: A Cultural and
Institutional History of the Movement." *American Quarterly* 31
(Bibliography Issue, 1979): 293–337.

BACKGROUND CIRCUMFERENCE

Abbott, Bernice. *New York in the Thirties* [formerly titled: *Changing New
York*]. New York: E. P. Dutton and Company, 1939; repr. New York:
Dover Publications, 1973.

Adams, Henry. *The Education of Henry Adams: An Autobiography.* Boston: Houghton Mifflin Company, 1961.

Addams, Jane. "A Function of the Social Settlement." *Annals of the American Academy of Political and Social Sciences* 13 (May 1899): 323–345.

Anderson, Nels. *The Hobo: The Sociology of the Homeless Man.* Chicago: University of Chicago Press, 1923.

————. *Report on the Municipal Lodging House of New York City.* Vol. 1. New York: Welfare Council of New York City, Research Bureau, 1932.

Asbury, Herbert. "Old Time Gangs of New York." *American Mercury* 11 (1927): 478–486.

Bahr, Howard M. "The Gradual Disappearance of Skid Row." *Social Problems* (1967): 41–45.

————. *Skid Row: An Introduction to Disaffiliation.* New York: Oxford University Press, 1973.

Bahr, Howard M., and Caplow, Theodore. "Homelessness, Affiliation, and Occupational Mobility." *Social Forces* 47 (September 1968): 28–33.

Bailey, E. Lamar. "Tramps and Hoboes." *Forum* 26 (October 1898): 217–221.

Baxter, Ellen, and Hopper, Kim. *Private Lives/Public Spaces: Homeless Adults on the Streets of New York City.* New York: Community Service Society, 1981.

Beer, Thomas. *The Mauve Decade.* New York: Garden City Publishing Company, 1926.

Bell, Daniel. *Marxian Socialism in the United States.* Princeton, N.J.: Princeton University Press, 1967.

Bendiner, Elmer. *The Bowery Man.* New York: Thomas Nelson and Sons, 1961.

Bogue, Donald. *Skid Row in American Cities.* Chicago: University of Chicago Press, 1963.

"The Bowery." *Manual of the Corporation of the City of New York* [a.k.a. *Valentine's Manual of Old New York*]. New York: Edmund Jones and Company, Publishers, 1866, pp. 573–589.

Brandt, Nat. "The Great Blizzard of '88." *American Heritage* 28 (February 1977): 32–41.

Bremner, Robert H. *From the Depths: The Discovery of Poverty in the United States.* New York: New York University Press, 1956.

Brooks, Richard A. E., ed. *The Diary of Michael Floy, Jr., Bowery Village, 1833–1837.* New Haven: Yale University Press, 1941.

Browne, Junius Henri. *The Great Metropolis: A Mirror of New York.* Hartford, Conn.: American Publishing Company, 1868.

Burgess, Charles O. "The Newspaper as Charity Worker: Poor Relief in New York City, 1893–1894." *New York History* 43 (July 1962): 249–268.

Callow, Alexander B., Jr., ed. *American Urban History*. New York: Oxford University Press, 1969.

Caplow, Theodore, et al. "Homelessness." *International Encyclopedia of the Social Sciences*, vol. 6, 1968, pp. 494–500.

Cochran, Thomas C., and Miller, William. *The Age of Enterprise: A Social History of Industrial America*. New York: Macmillan Company, 1942.

Coman, Katharine. *The Industrial History of the United States*. New York: Macmillan Company, 1905.

Erenberg, Lewis A. *Steppin' Out: New York Night Life and the Transformation of American Culture, 1890–1930*. Westport, Conn.: Greenwood Press, 1981.

Ginger, Ray. *Age of Excess: The United States from 1877 to 1914*. New York and Toronto: Macmillan Company, 1965.

Grunberg, Jeffrey. "Homelessness as a Lifestyle." In C. L. M. Caton, ed., *People without Homes: Homelessness in American Society*. New York: Oxford University Press, forthcoming.

Harlow, Alvin F. *Old Bowery Days*. New York: D. Appleton and Company, 1931.

Harrington, Michael. *The Other America: Poverty in the United States*. New York: Penguin Books, 1962.

Harris, Neil, ed. *The Land of Contrasts, 1880–1901*. New York: George Braziller, 1970.

Herron, Stella Wynne. *Bowery Parade and Other Poems of Protest*. New York: Delphic Studios, 1936.

Hofstadter, Richard. *Social Darwinism in American Thought*. Boston: Beacon Press, 1955.

Homelessness in America. Hearing before the Subcommittee on Housing and Community Development, of the Committee on Banking, Finance and Urban Affairs, House of Representatives, 97th Congress, December 15, 1982. Washington, D.C.: U.S. Government Printing Office, 1983.

Howe, Frederick C. *The City: The Hope of Democracy*. New York: Charles Scribner's Sons, 1905.

Irvine, Alexander. *From the Bottom Up*. New York: Doubleday, Page and Company, 1910.

Jackson, Joan K., and Conner, Ralph. "The Skid Road Alcoholic." *Quarterly Journal of Studies on Alcohol* 14 (September 1953): 468–486.

James, Edmund, Jr. "The Growth of Great Cities." *Annals of the American Academy of Political and Social Sciences* 13 (January 1899): 1–30.

Kahn, E. J. *The Merry Partners: The Age and Stage of Harrigan and Hart*. New York: Random House, 1955.

King, Moses, ed. *King's Handbook of New York City*. Boston: Moses King, 1893; reissued in 2 vols., New York: Benjamin Blom, 1972.

Laidlaw, Walter, ed. *Population of the City of New York, 1890–1930*. New York: Cities Census Committee, 1932.

Levitt, Morris. *We Strike, and On the Bowery: Two One-Act Plays.* New York: October Br., IWO, 1931.

London, Jack. *The People of the Abyss.* New York and London: Macmillan Company, 1904.

Lubove, Roy. *The Progressives and the Slums: Tenement House Reform in New York City, 1890–1917.* Pittsburgh: University of Pittsburgh Press, 1962.

Main, Thomas J. "The Homeless of New York." *Public Interest* 72 (Summer 1983): 3–29.

Marin, Peter. "Helping and Hating the Homeless." *Harper's* 274 (January 1987): 39–49.

McCook, J. J. "A Tramp Census and Its Revelations." *Forum* 15 (August 1893): 753–766.

McMurry, Donald L. *Coxey's Army: A Study of the Industrial Army Movement of 1894.* Seattle: University of Washington Press, 1929.

Mott, Harper Stryker. "The Hamlet at the Bouwerij." *Americana* 10 (July and August 1915): 2 Parts: Part 1, pp. 660–676; Part 2, pp. 743–763.

———. "The Road to the Bouwerij Historically, Cartographically and Genealogically Considered." *Americana* 8 (June 1913): 483–504.

Mumford, Lewis. *The Brown Decades.* New York: Dover Publications, 1931.

———. *The City in History: Its Origins, Its Transformations, and Its Prospects.* New York: Harcourt, Brace and World, 1961.

Nevins, Allan. *The Emergence of Modern America, 1865–1878.* New York: Macmillan Company, 1927.

———, ed. *The Diary of Philip Hone, 1828–1851.* New York: Dodd, Mead and Company, 1927.

Orwell, George. *Down and Out in Paris and London.* New York: Harcourt Brace Jovanovich, 1961.

Park, Robert E., and Burgess, Ernest W., eds. *The City.* Chicago: University of Chicago Press, 1925.

Patterson, Jerry E., ed. *The City of New York.* New York: Museum of the City of New York, 1978.

Popper, Karl R. *The Open Society and Its Enemies.* Vol. 2. Princeton, N.J.: Princeton University Press, 1966.

Ralph, Julian. "The Bowery." *Century* 43 (December 1891): 227–237.

Rikeman, Ann. *The Evolution of Stuyvesant Village.* Mamaroneck: Press of G. Peck, 1899.

Rooney, James. "Group Process among Skid Row Winos: A Reevaluation of the Undersocialization Hypothesis." *Quarterly Journal of Studies on Alcohol* 22 (September 1961): 444–460.

Rosenfeld, Paul. *Port of New York.* Urbana, Ill.: University of Illinois Press, 1961.

Rossi, Peter H., et al. "The Urban Homeless: Estimating Composition and Size." *Science* 235 (March 1987): 1336–1341.

Royale, E. M. "The Vaudeville Theatre." *Scribner's Magazine* 26 (1899): 485–495.

Sasowsky, Norman. *The Prints of Reginald Marsh*. New York: Clarkson N. Potter, 1976.

Schlesinger, Arthur M. *The Rise of the City, 1878–1898*. New York: Macmillan Company, 1933.

Shulman, Harry M. *Slums of New York*. New York: Albert and Charles Boni, 1938.

Spahr, Charles B. *An Essay on the Present Distribution of Wealth in the United States*. New York: Thomas Y. Crowell and Company, 1896.

St. John, Charles, Jr. *God on the Bowery*. New York: Fleming H. Revell Company, 1940.

Stansell, Christine. *City of Women: Sex and Class in New York, 1789–1860*. New York: Alfred A. Knopf, 1986.

Stelzle, Charles. *A Son of the Bowery: The Life Story of an East Side American*. New York: George H. Doran Company, 1926.

Still, Bayard. *Mirror for Gotham: New York as Seen by Contemporaries from Dutch Days to the Present*. New York: University Press, 1956.

Stokes, I. N. Phelps. *Iconography of Manhattan Island, 1498–1909*. New York: R. H. Dodd, 1915–1928.

Stovall, Floyd, ed. *The Collected Writings of Walt Whitman*. 2 Vols. New York: University Press, 1964.

Tocqueville, Alexis de. *Democracy in America*. Vol. 2. New York: Vintage Books, 1945.

Trachtenberg, Alan, et al., eds. *The City: American Experience*. New York: Oxford University Press, 1971.

Turner, Frederick Jackson. *The Significance of the Frontier in American History*. New York: Frederick Ungar Publishing Company, 1963.

Twain, Mark, and Warner, Charles Dudley. *The Gilded Age: A Tale of To-Day*. 2 Vols. New York and London: Harper and Brothers, 1873.

Veblen, Thorstein. *The Theory of the Leisure Class*. New York: Macmillan Company, 1899; repr. New York and Scarborough, Ontario: Mentor Books, 1953.

Veiller, Lawrence. *Tenement House Reform in New York, 1834–1900*. New York: Evening Post Job Printing House, 1900.

Wald, Lillian D. *The House on Henry Street*. New York: Henry Holt and Company, 1915.

Wallace, Samuel. "The Road to Skid Row." *Social Problems* 16 (Summer 1869): 92–105.

Waring, George E., Jr., comp. *Census Bureau's Social Statistics of Cities, 1880. Part 1: The New England and Middle States*. Washington, D.C.: U.S. Government Printing Office, 1886.

Weber, Adna F. *The Growth of Cities in the Nineteenth Century: A Study in Statistics*. New York: Macmillan Company, 1899.

Weber, Max. *The Protestant Ethic and the Spirit of Capitalism.* New York: Charles Scribner's Sons, 1958.

White, E. B. *Here Is New York.* New York: Harper and Brothers, 1949.

White, Morton G. *Social Thought in America: The Revolt against Formalism.* New York: Viking Press, 1952.

Whitehouse, Roger. *New York: Sunshine and Shadow.* New York: Harper and Row, 1974.

Wiebe, Robert H. *The Search for Order, 1877–1920.* New York: Hill and Wang, 1967.

Willard, J. F. [Josiah Flynt]. *Tramping with Tramps: Studies and Sketches of Vagabond Life.* New York: Century Company, 1901.

Wilson, Douglas L., ed. *The Genteel Tradition: Nine Essays by George Santayana.* Cambridge, Mass.: Harvard University Press, 1967.

Wirth, Louis. "Urbanism as a Way of Life." *American Journal of Sociology* 44 (1938): 1–24.

Zettler, Michael D. *The Bowery.* New York and London: Drake Publishers, 1975.

Ziff, Larzer. *The American 1890s: Life and Times of a Lost Generation.* New York: Viking Press, 1966.

MYSTIFIERS

Bell, Reverend Fred. *Midnight Scenes in the Slums of New York: Or, Lights and Shadows.* Nottingham: John Howitt and Son, 1881.

Booth, Commissioner, and Booth, Mrs. Ballington. *New York's Inferno Explored.* New York: Salvation Army Headquarters, 1891.

Bowery Mission and Young Men's Home, New York. Annual Reports, Nos. 1–10 (1880/1881–1889/1890).

Brace, Charles Loring. *The Dangerous Classes of New York and Twenty Years' Work among Them.* New York: Wynkoop and Hallenbeck, 1872.

Buel, J. W. *Metropolitan Life Unveiled; or The Mysteries and Miseries of America's Great Cities.* St. Louis: Historical Publishing Company, 1882.

Bunner, H. C. *Jersey Street and Jersey Lane: Urban and Suburban Sketches.* New York: Charles Scribner's Sons, 1893.

Campbell, Helen, et al. *Darkness and Daylight; or Lights and Shadows of New York Life.* Hartford: Hartford Publishing Company, 1891.

Corradini, Robert E., comp. *The Bowery, New York City: A Survey of that Notorious District Comparing Present Conditions with Those of Pre-Prohibition Days.* Washington, D.C.: World League against Alcoholism, 1923.

Crapsey, Edward. *The Nether Side of New York; or The Vice, Crime and Poverty of the Great Metropolis.* New York: Sheldon and Company, 1872.

Davis, Richard Harding. *Van Bibber and Others.* New York: Harper and Brothers, 1892.

Foster, George G. *New York Naked.* New York: Robert M. DeWitt, n.d.

———. *New York in Slices.* New York: William H. Graham, 1849.

Hewitt, Edward Ringwood, and Hewitt, Mary Ashley. "The Bowery." In *Half Moon Series*, Vol. 1. New York: G. P. Putnam's Sons, 1897.

Hoyt, Charles H. "Five Plays." In Douglas L. Hunt, ed., *America's Lost Plays*, Vol. 9. Bloomington: Indiana University Press, 1940.

Kremer, Theodore. *The Bowery after Dark.* New York Public Library, Billy Rose Theater Collection, Lincoln Center Branch, n.d.

Marks, Harry H. *Small Change; or, Lights and Shades of New York.* New York: Standard Publishing Company, 1882.

Martin, Edward Winslow. *The Secrets of the Great City: A Work Descriptive of the Virtues and the Vices, The Mysteries, Miseries and Crimes of New York City.* Philadelphia, Cincinnati, Chicago, St. Louis, and Atlanta: Jones, Brothers and Company, 1868.

Matthews, Brander. *Vignettes of Manhattan: Outlines in Local Color.* New York: Charles Scribner's Sons, 1894; repr. 1921.

McCabe, James D., Jr. *Lights and Shadows of New York Life; or, The Sights and Sensations of the Great City.* Philadelphia, Cincinnati, Chicago, and St. Louis: National Publishing Company, 1872.

McIntyre, John T. *The Bowery Night-School: A Vaudeville Sketch.* Philadelphia: Penn Publishing Company, 1906.

Nascher, Ignatz. *The Wretches of Povertyville: A Sociological Study of the Bowery.* New York and Chicago: Jos. J. Lanzit, 1909.

"Our Homeless Poor"; or, "How the Other Half of the World Lives." *Frank Leslie's Illustrated Newspaper*, March 2, 9, 16, 23, 1872.

Pember, Arthur [A. P.]. *The Mysteries and Miseries of the Great Metropolis with Some Adventures in the Country: Being the Disguises and Surprises of a New York Journalist.* New York: D. Appleton and Company, 1874.

A Plea for the Homeless Men and Boys of the Bowery; An Intensely Interesting Illustrated Story of the Work Done in the Greatest Rescue Mission in the World. Pamphlet, Bowery Mission and Young Men's Home, New York, 1905.

Ralph, Julian. *People We Pass: Stories of Life Among the Masses of New York City.* New York: Harper and Brothers, 1895.

Smith, Matthew Hale. *Sunshine and Shadow in New York.* Hartford: J. B. Burr and Company, 1868.

Smith, Matthew Hale, et al., eds. *Wonders of a Great City: or The Sights, Secrets and Sins of New York.* Chicago: People's Publishing Company, 1887.

Stephens, Robert Nelson. *On The Bowery.* New York Public Library, Billy Rose Theater Collection, Lincoln Center Branch, n.d.

Stryker, Reverend Peter. *The Lower Depths of the Great Metropolis: A*

Discourse delivered in the Thirty-Fourth Street Reformed Dutch Church,
New York City, Sabbath Evening, April 29, 1866.

Talmage, T. DeWitt, D.D. *The Masque Torn Off.* Chicago: Fairbanks,
Palmer and Company, 1882.

Warner, Charles D. *The Relation of Literature to Life.* New York and
London: Harper and Brothers, 1896.

BETWIXT AND BETWEEN

Alland, Alexander, Sr. *Jacob Riis: Photographer and Citizen.* Millerton,
N.Y.: Aperture, 1974.

Bowron, Bernard R., Jr. "Realism in America." *Comparative Literature* 3
(Summer 1951): 268–285.

Cady, Edwin H., ed. *W. D. Howells as Critic.* London and Boston:
Routledge and Kegan Paul, 1973.

Clark, Harry Hayden, ed. *Transitions in American Literary History.*
Durham, N.C.: Duke University Press, 1954.

Howells, William Dean. *A Hazard of New Fortunes.* New York: Harper and
Brothers, 1890; repr. New York: New American Library, 1965.

———. *Impressions and Experiences.* Freeport, N.Y.: Harper and
Brothers, 1896; repr. New York: Books for Libraries Press, 1972.

———. *Literature and Life.* New York: Harper and Brothers, 1902.

———. *A Traveller from Altruria.* New York: Harper and Brothers, 1894.

Riis, Jacob A. *How the Other Half Lives.* New York: Scribner's, 1890; repr.
Cambridge, Mass.: Harvard University Press, 1970.

———. *The Making of an American.* New York: Macmillan Company,
1903.

———. *A Ten Years' War: An Account of the Battle with the Slums in New
York.* Boston and New York: Houghton Mifflin Company, 1900.

Stein, Sally. "Making Connections with the Camera: Photography and Social
Mobility in the Career of Jacob Riis." *Afterimage* 10 (May 1983): 9–16.

Sullivan, J. W. *Tenement Tales of New York.* New York: Henry Holt and
Company, 1894.

Szasz, Ferenc M., and Bogardus, Ralph F. "The Camera and the American
Social Conscience: The Documentary Photography of Jacob A. Riis."
New York History 55 (October 1974): 409–436.

Warfel, Harry R., and Orions, Harrison G., eds. *American Local-Color
Stories.* New York: American Book Company, 1941.

CRITICAL REALISTS

Bassan, Maurice, ed. *Stephen Crane: A Collection of Critical Essays.*
Englewood Cliffs, N.J.: Prentice-Hall, 1967.

Beer, Thomas. *Stephen Crane: A Study in American Letters.* New York: Alfred A. Knopf, 1923.

Berryman, John. *Stephen Crane.* New York: William Sloane Associates, 1950.

Bradley, Sculley, et al., eds. *Stephen Crane: The Red Badge of Courage.* New York and London: W. W. Norton and Company, 1976.

Cady, Edwin H., and Wells, Lester G., eds. *Stephen Crane's Love Letters to Nellie Crouse.* Syracuse: Syracuse University Press, 1954.

Dreiser, Theodore. "The Camera Club of New York." *Ainslee's Magazine* (October 1899): 324–335.

———. *The Color of a Great City.* New York: Boni and Liveright, 1923.

———. "Curious Shifts of the Poor." *Demorest's Family Magazine* (November 1899): 22–26.

———. "A Master of Photography: Alfred Steiglitz [*sic*] Has Proven That a Great Photograph is Worth Years of Labor to Make." *Success*, June 10, 1899, p. 471.

———. *Sister Carrie.* New York: Doubleday, Page and Company, 1900.

———. *Sister Carrie.* New York: Penguin Books, 1981.

Frank, Waldo, et al., eds. *America and Alfred Stieglitz: A Collective Portrait.* New York: Doubleday, Doran and Company, 1934.

Garland, Hamlin. *Crumbling Idols.* Chicago and Cambridge: Stone and Kimball, 1894.

———. *Main-Travelled Roads.* New York: Harper and Brothers, 1891.

Greenough, Sarah, and Hamilton, Juan, eds. *Alfred Stieglitz: Photos and Writings.* Washington, D.C.: National Gallery of Art, 1983.

Gullason, Thomas A., ed. *Stephen Crane's Career: Perspectives and Evaluations.* New York: New York University Press, 1972.

Katz, Joseph, ed. *The Complete Poems of Stephen Crane.* Ithaca, N.Y.: Cornell University Press, 1972.

———, ed. *The Portable Stephen Crane.* New York: Penguin Books, 1969.

Kazin, Alfred. *On Native Grounds.* New York and London: Harcourt Brace Jovanovich, 1942.

Knight, Grant C. *The Critical Period in American Literature.* Chapel Hill: University of North Carolina Press, 1951.

Kwiat, Joseph. "The Newspaper Experience: Crane, Norris, and Dreiser." *Nineteenth-Century Fiction* 8 (September 1953): 99–117.

———. "Stephen Crane and Painting." *American Quarterly* 4 (Winter 1952): 331–338.

———. "Stephen Crane, Literary Reporter: Commonplace Experience and Artistic Transcendence." *Journal of Modern Literature* 8 (1980): 129–138.

Moers, Ellen. *Two Dreisers.* New York: Viking Press, 1969.

Nagel, James. *Stephen Crane and Literary Impressionism.* University Park, Penn.: Pennsylvania State University Press, 1980.

Norman, Dorothy. *Alfred Stieglitz: An American Seer.* New York: Random House, 1960.

Parrington, Vernon Louis. *Main Currents in American Thought.* Vol. 3, *The Beginnings of Critical Realism in America, 1860–1920.* New York: Harcourt, Brace and Company, 1927.

Petrey, Sandy. "The Language of Realism, the Language of False Consciousness: A Reading of Sister Carrie." *Novel* 10 (Winter 1977): 101–113.

Pizer, Donald. *Realism and Naturalism in Nineteenth-Century American Literature.* New York: Russell and Russell, 1976.

Sanborn, Alvan Francis. *Moody's Lodging House and Other Tenement Sketches.* Boston: Copeland and Day, 1895.

Solomon, Eric. *Stephen Crane: From Parody to Realism.* Cambridge, Mass.: Harvard University Press, 1966.

Stallman, R. W. *Stephen Crane: A Biography.* New York: George Braziller, 1968.

———, ed. *Stephen Crane: Stories and Tales.* New York: Vintage Books, 1952.

Stallman, R. W., and Gilkes, Lillian, eds. *Stephen Crane: Letters.* New York: New York University Press, 1960.

Stallman, R. W., and Hagemann, E. R., eds. *The New York City Sketches of Stephen Crane.* New York: New York University Press, 1966.

Trachtenberg, Alan. "Experiments in Another Country." *Southern Review* 10 (1974): 265–285.

Westlake, Neda M., general ed. *Sister Carrie.* Philadelphia: University of Pennsylvania Press, Pennsylvania Edition, 1981.

INDEX

Affiliation, in subculture of Bowery homeless, 178–199; and alcohol, 181, 182–183; and antistructure, 191–192, 194–199; and bottlegang groups, 182–184; and reciprocity, 189–191; tragic irony of, 194

Agent-scene, 33, 87–88

Alger, Horatio, myth of, 63, 148, 152, 158

Antistructure: and blizzard imagery, 104, 106–112, 118, 122, 125–126; and *communitas*, 103–104; and descent, 112–114, 115–128; and relationship to Bowery subculture, xvi–xvii, 113, 120–122, 124–126, 172, 191–192, 194–199; and relationship to social structure, 90, 98–100, 102–103, 109–111, 115–117, 121–125, 127–128, 167–170, 241–242n. *See also* Culture and subculture, dialectic of; Descent and discovery, as mode of inquiry; Homelessness, and inferiority

Bandit's Roost, 70–71, 74

Bayard estate, 2, 4

Bell, Rev. Fred, 44

Blizzard, symbolic value of, 104–107, 113, 122–124, 126. *See also* Antistructure; *Communitas*

Bouwerie(s). *See* Bowery

Bouwerij. *See* Bowery

Bowerie(s). *See* Bowery

Bowery: in antebellum era, 6–10; contemporary subculture, 173–199; as designation, 1; as "detached milieu," xiv, 19; as embodiment, xiii, 31; and immigrant enclaves, 18–19; ownership of, 1–4, 227n; as pollution and taboo, 170, 180–181; in prerevolutionary era, 1–4; and social significance, xiv, 113–114, 120–122, 124–128, 129–135, 152, 161–163, 169–170, 172–175; and symbolic merger, 113, 126–128, 172–192; tenement conditions of, 16–18; and transition to skid row, 25–28. *See also* Antistructure, and relationship to Bowery subculture; Culture and subculture, dialectic of; Homelessness; Subculture

The Bowery after Dark, 52

Bowery boy, 8–9, 221–222n. *See also* Mose

Bowery gal, 8, 222n

Bowery Lane, 2, 4, 6

Bowery men: Billy, 215; Donny, 195; Frank, 192, 215; George, 183, 215; Harry, 195–196; Hewey, 184–185; Jack and Jerry, 183–184, 185–189, 215; Jimmy, 192–194, 215; Joey, 197–198; Moe, 197–198; Nicky Star, xviii, 190–191, 196–197; Pee Wee, 215; Peter, 215, 219; Richie, 195; Sugar Hart, 198–199; William, 182, 214; Willy, 188–189

Bowery Mission and Young Men's Home, 43, 230n

Bowery Theater, 7–8, 24

Bowery village. *See* Bowery

Brodie, Steve, 22, 51–52

Buel, J. W., 39, 41, 50

Bunner, H. C., 54–55

Burke, Kenneth, xii–xiii, 90, 173, 175, 191–192, 198